JACQUES VILLON

Jacques Villon (1875-1963) at Bougival, 1950.
Photograph by Francis Steegmuller

Jacques Villon

EDITED BY DANIEL ROBBINS

Fogg Art Museum

Harvard University

Cambridge, Massachusetts

1976

Prepared in conjunction with the exhibition
Jacques Villon, at the Fogg Art Museum
January 17 through February 29, 1976, and
at the Roy R. Neuberger Museum at
Purchase, New York, March 23 through
May 23, 1976. The exhibition and catalogue
were organized with the aid of a grant from
the National Endowment for the Arts in
Washington, D.C., a Federal agency.

Typesetting by Dumar Typesetting, Inc.

Printing by the Meriden Gravure Company

Design by Malcolm Grear Designers, Inc.

LIBRARY OF CONGRESS CATALOGING IN PUBLICATION DATA

Villon, Jacques, 1875-1963.
    Jacques Villon.
    Catalogue of an exhibition held at the Fogg Art
Museum, Jan. 17-Feb. 29, 1976, and at the Roy R. Neu-
berger Museum at Purchase, N.Y., Mar. 23-May 23, 1976.
    Bibliography: p. 208
    1. Villon, Jacques, 1875-1963. I. Robbins, Daniel.
II. Harvard University. Williams Hayes Fogg Art Museum.
III. Neuberger Museum.
ND553.V54R62   760'.092'4   75-43627
ISBN 0-916724-01-8

TABLE OF CONTENTS

In his Foreword to this volume, Daniel Robbins traces the evolution of the present Jacques Villon retrospective exhibition from a graduate seminar more than three years ago into an international endeavor that at last brings to Jacques Villon a long overdue measure of serious scholarly and critical attention.

Throughout these three years, Daniel Robbins has pursued this project with unremitting energy and infectious enthusiasm. He has made certain that his students have been thoroughly involved with the conceptualization as well as the realization of the exhibition and catalogue, in the kind of learning experience that we at the Fogg believe epitomizes a principal part of museum training. My colleagues and I are enormously grateful to him, not only for the exemplary result of these labors, but also for the stimulating process out of which it grew.

Our sincere thanks go, too, to the National Endowment for the Arts for its generous support of the exhibition. Without its grant the extensive borrowing of key works from Europe and the publication of a comprehensive catalogue would not have been financially possible. Air France also provided generous assistance, for which we extend our gratitude.

The invaluable contributions of our many French colleagues have been detailed elsewhere by Mr. Robbins. My special thanks go to Jeffrey Hoffeld, director of the Roy R. Neuberger Museum, whose vivid interest and ready cooperation have made him a most agreeable partner in this joint effort.

S. S.

This exhibition and its catalogue are the result of a seminar focusing on Jacques Villon that I conducted in collaboration with Peter Wick, then curator of Prints and Graphic Arts at the Houghton Library, during the Fall term of 1972. The members of the seminar were so enthusiastic and interested in the subject that, even after the formal work of the course was done, we determined to meet once a week and continue our communal investigation. Already, we had hoped to assemble an exhibition. We knew that only by bringing together a great body of works by Villon could we have the pleasure of demonstrating and sharing our research, testing it, and even rendering it obsolete by comparing our ideas about the artist with many original paintings we had not yet seen, or at any rate not examined in the vivid confrontation of an exhibition.

The hope that the Fogg Art Museum's Villon project might become a reality extends back to a 1970 visit M. Louis Carré made to the United States, and to a dinner in his honor given by his friend and gracious hostess, Mrs. Henry Sharp of Providence, Rhode Island. Remarking on the ironies of public attention, a guest observed how curious it was that Villon, whose appreciative audience in the United States helped to sustain him from the time of the Armory show, had never been given a major retrospective in this country. A small group of Villon enthusiasts determined that the time had come to remedy this situation. Our first debt of gratitude is still to M. Louis Carré, who pledged his cooperation in 1970 and continuously aided the realization of the Villon exhibition, often under difficult circumstances. Our second acknowledgement is to Mrs. Marcel Duchamp, whose encouragement was an essential factor throughout the preparation of the exhibition.

The structure of The Fogg Villon seminar is reflected in the organization of the catalogue. Our method was first to study Villon's earliest efforts, as a print maker. Peter Wick took the lead in this phase, often directing our meetings in the print room of the Boston Museum of Fine Arts. As we became more familiar with Villon's method and witnessed his predilection towards certain subjects, the artist's unusual consistency and thoroughness led us to divide our seminar topics for individual research into thematic groups, rather than chronological periods. Thus, one student was charged with the responsibility of examining portraits and figure compositions, another with the landscapes, still another with Villon's fascination with mathematics and geometry, another with comparing the lives and works of the brothers, another with exploring relationships among the prints and illustrated books with literature. Several reports focused on the transitions to and from abstraction. One of our team, Julianne de Vere, was a member of the Fogg staff deeply involved with the *Color in Art, A Tribute to Arthur Pope* exhibition, then in preparation. Ms. de Vere gave a seminar report on Villon's use of color. Subsequently, she was obliged to withdraw from work on the Villon exhibition, and it is in compensation for her lost contribution to our catalogue entries that I deal at such length with Villon's use of color in my own introduction.

The seminar was also fortunate in being able to involve in its work the participation of experienced and expert scholars long familiar with Villon and his accomplishments. William Lieberman spent a day with us, joined by Riva Castleman in her print room at the Museum of Modern Art. Lucien Goldschmidt and his staff generously placed at our disposal all that they had discovered in recent and productive research into the artist's early years especially, helping us also to trace works which had, as so often and irritatingly happens, unaccountably disappeared. Francis Steegmuller not only spent a day in Cambridge with us, providing the seminar with his exceptional insights into Villon and allowing us access to an important unpublished manuscript of his own; but he also permitted us to keep and study at length the notebooks of his first wife, the late Beatrice Stein, one of Villon's two pupils. Vincent Tovell of Toronto, Villon's other pupil, also kindly furnished us with much useful information.

Cleve Gray, who as a young painter had become Villon's close friend in 1944 and 1945, also spent a day with our group at the Fogg, and shared with us his insights into the artist's personality, method, and especially his use of color. He lent us the copy of Rosenstiehl's *Traité de la Couleur* that Villon had urged him to purchase, with all its rich annotations and marginalia. He also shared with us the extraordinary color charts and color wheel that Julie Beaudeneau had developed from Rosenstiehl's system, and showed us how Villon had instructed

him in their use. Furthermore, he had conserved his correspondence with Julie Beaudeneau, and left this material at the Fogg for the Villon seminar to study.

We received help and encouragement from Anne d'Harnoncourt, whose exhibition of Marcel Duchamp, prepared jointly with Kynaston McShine of the Museum of Modern Art, we had the pleasure of visiting at the Philadlephia Museum of Art. At the Yale University Art Gallery, Alan Shestack made available precious loans, even treating the fragile *In Memoriam* so that it could travel to the French Villon retrospective; he also put at our disposal the information in the (as yet not fully examined or indexed) files of the Société Anonyme. Professor Robert Herbert, too, took an interest in our undertaking and gave valuable advice and encouragement. Professor George H. Hamilton, director of the Sterling and Francine Clark Art Institute in Williamstown and the scholar who has done the most in the United States to advance the study of all the Duchamp brothers, aided the research of our students for their task of preparing seminar reports, and subsequently catalogue entries.

Numerous museum directors and curators, gallery workers, and many private owners of Villon prints, paintings, and illustrated book — not all of them lenders to our exhibition — nevertheless took a special interest in our project as it developed, providing us with photographs and documentation and often sharing with us that special insight into a work which only long familiarity can yield. In this connection we should like to thank Mr. Tracy Atkinson, director of the Milwaukee Art Center; Mr. R. Barclay of Acquavella Galleries; Mr. Robert Buck, director of the Albright-Knox Art Gallery; Charles Buckley, former director of the St. Louis Art Museum; Mr. and Mrs. Alister Cameron of Cincinnati, who visited the Fogg and met with members of the seminar; Mrs. Margit Chanin of New York; Dr. Fred Cummings, director of the Detroit Institute of the Arts; Dr. Kenneth Donahue, director of the Los Angeles County Museum of Art; Mr. William Agee, director of the Houston Museum of Fine Arts; Mrs. Barnet Fain of the staff of the Museum of Art, Rhode Island School of Design; Ms. Sarah C. Faunce of the Brooklyn Museum; Mr. and Mrs. Samuel Glaser of Boston; Mr. and Mrs. Joseph Edinburgh of Boston; Sinclair H. Hitchings, keeper of prints at the Boston Public Library; B. C. Holland of Chicago; Ms. Anahid Iskian of Lucien Goldschmidt, Inc., New York; Mr. and Mrs. Daniel Johnson of New York and Glen Cove, who took an exceptional interest in the Villon research and showed great kindness to one of our students; Stanley R. Johnson of International Gallery, Chicago; Professor Walter Kaiser of Harvard University; Mrs. Frances Kelly of Cambridge; Mr. Frank S. Kent of the Weintraub Gallery, New York; Dr. John Maxon of the Art Institute of Chicago; Mr. and Mrs. Paul Mellon of Upperville, Virginia; Mr. Thomas M. Messer, director of the Solomon R. Guggenheim Museum of Art; Dr. Steven E. Ostrow, director of the Museum of Art, Rhode Island School of Design, who allowed the Fogg to borrow and make laboratory examinations of the important 1914 *Tête de Femme* during the term of our seminar; Mr. Laughlin Phillips, president and director of the Phillips Collection in Washington, D.C.; Miss Eleanor Sayre, curator of prints at the Museum of Fine Arts, Boston, hostess to our group on many occasions; Mr. David Shawan of Columbus, Ohio, who came to the Fogg and visited with members of the seminar; Dr. George Szabo, curator of the Robert Lehman Collection at the Metropolitan Museum of Art, New York; Mr. Eugene V. Thaw, of E. V. Thaw and Co., Inc., New York; Dr. Evan H. Turner, director of the Philadelphia Museum of Art and kind host to our seminar when we visited Philadelphia; Mr. and Mrs. Richard Victor of New York; Mrs. Jane Wade Lombard of New York; Lee Ault of New York; Mr. Emile Wolfe of New York; Mahonri Sharp Young, director of the Columbus Gallery of Fine Arts; Dr. Sherman E. Lee, director of the Cleveland Museum of Art; and Mr. and Mrs. Charles Zadok of Greenwich, Connecticut.

One scholar to whom we owe an inestimable debt is neither art historian nor collector, but a professor of mathematical biology at M.I.T. He is Alan Natapof, who spent a day with us in the art galleries of Boston University (where a Villon print show had been organized by John Arthur), patiently explaining the history and application of theories of proportion as they relate to the Golden Section from a scientific and especially mathematical point of view. His presentation of complex ideas in so lucid and informal a manner led some of us to re-examine the writing of D'Arcy Thompson in a new light, with consequences that are particularly evident in the Introduction to the catalogue. We are grateful that Robert L. Ross possessed a copy of the 1961 edition.

The fact that the Fogg-Neuberger Museum exhibition is a collaboration with the Réunion des Musées Nationaux, in France, with the Musée des Beaux-Arts, Rouen, and the Grand Palais, Paris is due in large measure to Jean-Patrice Marandel, curator at the Art Institute of Chicago. Mr. Marandel, learning of the intentions of Rouen to celebrate the centennial of Villon's birth, informed his French colleagues of the efforts of the Fogg Villon seminar, already far advanced not only in the preparation of a catalogue text derived from seminar topics, but in its effort to secure loans from American and European owners of cardinal works by Jacques Villon. Soon, Mme Olga Popovitch, chief curator of the Musée des Beaux-Arts of Rouen, was in touch, remarking on the parallel nature of our efforts. Soon thereafter, Dora Vallier, who had been doing research in the United States, came to visit us at Harvard. We showed her our catalogue with its integrated series of prints, drawings, and paintings in all the photographic examples we had assembled. Persuaded by our work, Dora Vallier, to whom every student of Villon is vastly indebted, announced her intention of fostering a marriage between the French exhibition effort and our own. Although there were many technical difficulties to overcome, and about a dozen changes were made in the selection of works destined for exhibition, Dora Vallier's intervention led to the present collaboration. Mlle Hélène Lassalle, curator at the Musées de France and visiting scholar in the United States during the fall and winter of 1974, came to work with us, ironing out differences of opinion on which works were to be borrowed, but above all contributing significantly to the body of our knowledge by her careful and critical editing of the second draft of our catalogue text, and by her additions to our bibliography.

With the invitation from the Musées de France to collaborate, we had secured not only a valuable partner certain to strengthen the quality of our exhibition with the contribution of ideas and materials, but we were faced with a deadline: 1975-1976, the centennial of the birth of Jacques Villon. Although the student team welcomed the likelihood of seeing our work realized before they ceased to be students, this sudden stroke of good fortune necessitated a change in plans. The originally-planned American partner for the exhibition had been the National Gallery of Art. The Villon show was intended to be accommodated in its new I. M. Pei addition for modern art, not scheduled for completion within the time period necessary for our new European colleagues. Therefore we reluctantly requested permission to withdraw from our agreement with the National Gallery, permission that was generously given by its director, J. Carter Brown.

Thus, in the summer and fall of 1974, the Fogg, which had already received a welcome grant from the National Endowment for the Arts in support of the Villon show on condition that it be shared with another U.S. museum, needed to find another museum with the desire and capacity to stage the exhibition. With the directorship of the Fogg in transition, and with many museum schedules already filled, budgets strained to the limit, the prospects seemed black. Jeffrey Hoffeld, then acting director of the Roy R. Neuberger Museum, State University of New York at Purchase, in a display of daring initiative and decisive leadership, raised the necessary funds to enable his museum to share the show with the Fogg. He has earned our deep gratitude. In connection with the complex administrative efforts of the Fogg staff to negotiate a new U.S. partner last summer, special thanks are owed also to Agnes Mongan, as ever indefatigable in her service to the museum; and to Seymour Slive, then acting director, for his determination that the Villon show should not founder.

A word on the catalogue entries is in order. The members of the seminar agreed to write entries related to their oral reports. Subsequently, each member of the group read and made editorial suggestions on the essays prepared by fellow students, often writing very candid comments on the text. A second draft of the manuscript, incorporating the collectively suggested comments or following the generally agreed deletions, was submitted to Francis Steegmuller, who read it and contributed extremely useful substantive and editorial advice in the summer of 1974. It was this version which was presented to our colleagues in France. The variations between the French exhibition catalogue and our own result from three causes:

first, faced with severe budgetary restrictions, the Réunion des Musées Nationaux was able to print only a handful of supplementary illustrations, without which much of the reasoning presented in our entries would appear tedious and impossible to follow. Second, the general practice of the Réunion is to follow a fairly strict chronological order, an order the Fogg Villon seminar had rejected for the reason that our approach to Villon had been thematic, cutting across Villon's life's work, as across media variations, the better to grasp the consistency of his personality. Third, there were a number of points on which our colleagues in France disagreed, rejecting our findings as insufficiently documented or as unwarranted speculation. Access to the files of Louis Carré and Co. provided Hélène Lassalle with much new information which she incorporated into her brilliant editing of the French version of the Jacques Villon catalogue. All of this information she shared with us; in some cases, it persuaded members of the seminar to modify their views. We have acknowledged Mlle Lassalle's most important insights in the appropriate catalogue entries, but we should like also to extend to her our admiring thanks for her able, professional, and — above all — intelligent collaboration.

Mlle Lassalle's work, and our own in Europe, was greatly assisted by the help furnished by M. Hubert Landais and Mlle Irène Bizot, both of the Musées Nationaux, Paris; by Jean Adémar of the Cabinet des Estampes, Bibliothèque National; by Mlle de Coster of Paris; by Mme Myriam de Drenzy, Paris; by Mme Diane Foy of Editions Louis Carré, who opened the Villon files for Hélène Lassalle; by Mme C. de Ginestet of Castres, a Villon scholar; by Jahan Jacqueline of Michel Couturier et Cie; by M. Camille Renault, Villon's great friend and admirer; by Mme Françoise Tournie; by Professor R. Vokaer, Brussels; by Eric K. Fernström of Switzerland; by Mme Tabert of the Musée National d'Art Moderne, Paris; by Mr. Haakon Onstad of Sweden; by M. Jan Runnquist of Galerie Bonnier, Geneva; and by M. Livengood of the Galerie Berri Lardy, Paris. All of these good people, not necessarily lenders, furnished the Villon project with information, documentation, essential photographs and good will.

A collaboration between two university museums in the United States and the Musées Nationaux as straightforward and agreeable as ours has been could only have taken place with the assistance of the French cultural services in America. We should like to thank M. Pierre Tabatoni, head of the French Cultural Office in the United States, for coming to Cambridge to read the Villon catalogue in its second draft; we should like to thank M. François Guillot de Rode, head of the Arts department, Ambassade de France, New York, for his valuable help; above all, we should like to thank M. Alain Grenier, Consulat Général de France at Boston for his goodwill and continuing interest since he was first introduced to the Villon seminar by Dora Vallier late in 1973.

All of us also owe a word of thanks to Alvin Martin and David S. Rubin, members of our seminar who assisted in various administrative aspects of the exhibition. Mr. Martin, who spent 1974-1975 in Paris, was able to facilitate communication between the Musées Nationaux and the Fogg. Mr. Rubin spent the summers of 1973 and 1974 as a temporary member of the Fogg staff charged with preparing, from all sources, even beyond the material submitted by each member of the seminar, a complete bibliography and list of exhibitions; he also numbered them — a herculean task. He wrote many letters on our behalf requesting information and photographs, and helped significantly to organize the material of the exhibition, not only for the Fogg publications staff, but for the Fogg registrar's office. Seminar member Jane Hancock helped with final copy editing, especially with French titles. In these connections, we should also like to thank Janet Cox and her able assistants in publications Marylène Altieri and John McClurken for seeing the manuscript through the press, and Malcolm Grear, for his design. We want to express our gratitude to Jane Watts and her staff for arranging complicated loans. We thank Suzannah Doeringer for coordinating the effort with unfailing energy and tact.

A final word about the catalogue and its text. During the winter of 1974-1975, I edited the third draft, and showed it to Cleve Gray who discussed it at length with me. When the results of Hélène Lassalle's editing of our second draft and her original research were sent to us in the spring of 1975, every member of the seminar was offered the opportunity to revise entries. My work as editor and final arbiter for the text had been, from the beginning, to eliminate repetition, insure con-

tinuity, integrate biographical and general information about the period, to judge, weigh, and balance the contributions of six student authors who had assisted in the formulation of a collective attitude toward Villon, but who could not reasonably be expected to forget or forego their individual manners of expression. I hope that Jonathan Fineberg, Susan Grace, Jane Hancock, Alvin Martin, David S. Rubin and Shreve Simpson will still recognize and take pleasure in their texts, even though each page in the fourth and final version has inevitably been diluted by the process of making the whole sober and fairly consistent, if not absolutely so.

The authors of the Villon catalogue are:

Jonathan D. Fineberg	J D F
Susan Grace	S G
Jane Hancock	J H
Alvin Martin	A M
David S. Rubin	D S R
Marianna Shreve Simpson	M S S

DANIEL ROBBINS

LENDERS TO THE EXHIBITION

ANONYMOUS LENDERS

MRS. GEORGE ACHESON

ALBRIGHT-KNOX ART GALLERY, BUFFALO

THE ALSDORF FOUNDATION

THE ART INSTITUTE OF CHICAGO

BENGT NYLEN

BIBLIOTHEQUE DU MUSEE DES ARTS DECORATIFS, PARIS

BIBLIOTHEQUE NATIONALE, PARIS, CABINET DES ESTAMPES

BOSTON PUBLIC LIBRARY, PRINT DEPARTMENT

THE BROOKLYN MUSEUM

MR. AND MRS. ALISTER CAMERON

CENTRE NATIONAL D'ART ET DE CULTURE GEORGES POMPIDOU, MUSEE NATIONAL D'ART MODERNE, PARIS

THE CLEVELAND MUSEUM OF ART

COLUMBUS GALLERY OF FINE ARTS

FOGG ART MUSEUM, HARVARD UNIVERSITY

GALERIE CAMILLE RENAULT

SAMUEL AND DOROTHY GLASER

MR. AND MRS. LUCIEN GOLDSCHMIDT

MARCEL GUIOT

HARVARD COLLEGE LIBRARY, HARVARD UNIVERSITY

MR. AND MRS. DAN R. JOHNSON

MRS. FRANCES W. KELLY

LOS ANGELES COUNTY MUSEUM OF ART

LOUIS CARRE ET CIE., PARIS

LUCIEN GOLDSCHMIDT, INC.

MME ANNE-FRANÇOISE MARE-VENE

THE METROPOLITAN MUSEUM OF ART

MILWAUKEE ART CENTER COLLECTION

MUSEE D'ART MODERNE DE LA VILLE DE PARIS

MUSEE DES BEAUX-ARTS, ROUEN

MUSEUM OF ART, RHODE ISLAND SCHOOL OF DESIGN

MUSEUM OF FINE ARTS, BOSTON

THE MUSEUM OF MODERN ART, NEW YORK

GERSON NORDLINGER, JR.

MICKEY PALLAS

PHILADELPHIA MUSEUM OF ART

THE PHILLIPS COLLECTION

R. S. JOHNSON - INTERNATIONAL GALLERY

MR. AND MRS. SAMUEL SACHS II, '57

THE ST. LOUIS ART MUSEUM

MR. AND MRS. DIMITRI SEVASTOPOULO

SONJA HENIE-NIELS ONSTAD FOUNDATIONS, NORWAY

STEPHEN HAHN GALLERY

UNIVERSITY OF MINNESOTA LIBRARIES

PROFESSOR R. VOKAER

WELLESLEY COLLEGE MUSEUM

YALE UNIVERSITY ART GALLERY

CHARLES ZADOK

GENIA ZADOK

July 31st, 1875
Born: Jacques Villon was born Gaston Duchamp in Damville (Eure), Normandy.

Father: Justin-Isidore Duchamp (also known as Eugène and Eusèbe) began his career as a receiver in a Damville Registry office. He subsequently bought a notary practice in Blainville near Rouen.

Mother: Marie-Caroline-Lucie (Nicolle), talented draughtswoman.

Maternal Grandfather: Emile-Frédéric Nicolle, a shipbroker and engraver who lived in Rouen.

Brothers and Sisters:
Raymond Duchamp-Villon (sculptor) born 1876, died 1918.

Marcel (artist) born 1887, died 1968.

Suzanne (painter) born 1889, married painter Jean Crotti, died 1963.

Yvonne, born 1895.

Magdeleine, born 1898.

1891
Under the guardianship of Émile Nicolle, Gaston Duchamp was a boarding student at Lycée Corneille, Rouen, in classical studies. He learned the rudiments of engraving on Sunday afternoons spent with his grandfather. He also made his first two copper plate engravings: a portrait of his father and a portrait of his grandfather (see cat. nos. 1, 2).

1894
In January, he went to Paris to study at the Faculty of Law of the University of Paris.

He returned to Rouen in July. There he worked from October 1894 to January 1895, and studied art in Rouen at L'École des Beaux-Arts. In a local colorshop, he was taken with the drawings and neo-impressionist work of Toulouse-Lautrec.

He began to send drawings to local illustrated newspapers, *Rouen Artiste* and *L'Étudiant*.

1895
Gaston Duchamp returned to Paris with his father's permission to study art if he also continued his law course. While studying at Atelier Cormon, Boulevard de Clichy, he lived on Rue des Écoles with Raymond Duchamp-Villon, who was studying medicine.

He adopted the name of Jack (then Jacques) Villon. He also did his first lithographs, met Toulouse-Lautrec, and began to contribute to Parisian illustrated newspapers such as *L'Assiette au Beurre, Le Rire, Le Chat Noir, Gil-Blas, L'Étudiant, Cocorico,* and *Frou-Frou*. This was a practice which he continued until 1910. Villon received an allowance of 150 f. a month from his father until 1910, an advance deducted from his inheritance.

1897
Villon served one year with the 24th Infantry Regiment in Paris.

On April 24th, his first drawing was accepted by *Le Rire* for the back cover (the front was done by Toulouse-Lautrec).

On October 3rd, *Le Courrier Français* accepted a drawing and continued to print one each week until the death of publisher Jules Roques in 1910.

1898
Villon lived on Rue Caulaincourt, Montmartre, where his neighbors were Renoir, Steinlen, Jourdain (and Kupka in 1900).

He continued to contribute to newspapers (cartoons and lithographed supplements), and frequented Moulin Rouge.

1899
Villon made posters for cabarets in color lithography. He learned technique from Jourdain. These were printed by Eugène Delâtre.

Edmund Sagot became his sole publisher for color aquatints until 1913.

1901
He exhibited two prints at the Société Nationale, his first participation in a salon.

Villon's portrait appeared in a drawing by Widhopft, in the *Le Courrier Français*, June 30th. In the same issue, he was praised by Hugues Delorme for his technique and humor.

1902
He illustrated an entire issue of *l'Assiette au Beurre* (no. 46, February 15th) entitled "La Vie Facile."

1903
Villon helped to organize the drawing section of the first Salon d'automne.

1904
He became a life member of Salon d'automne, where he exhibited yearly. Villon served on the committee until 1912, when he resigned because of his colleagues' hostility toward cubism.

Marcel lived with him for one year.

Villon studied at Académie Julian from October 1904 until August 1905, painting in the neo-impressionist manner.

He also made elegant engravings in the manner of Helleu. He later disavowed this period.

1904-1905
Villon married Gabrielle Bouef.

1905
He had his first exhibition at Galerie Legrip, Rouen, with Raymond Duchamp-Villon.

1906
For a year, sometime between 1904-1906, Villon returned to Rouen to live.

Back in Paris, he resumed living at rue Caulaincourt, and then moved to Puteaux, 7 rue Lemaître, where he lived for the rest of his life. He later remarked that if he hadn't left Montmartre, he would never have got away from the cartoons and engravings which occupied him during those early years in Paris.

1907

Villon began his association with "Les XXX," founded in Rouen by Pierre Dumont. In 1910 the artistic and literary organization became *le Société Normande de Peinture Moderne*; its exhibitions were prototypes for the Salon of the Section d'Or.

He was beginning to devote more time to painting, with a change in graphic style and technique.

1909-1910

Villon gradually withdrew from making satirical cartoons.

1910

With the death of Jules Roques of *Le Courrier Français*, Villon ceased altogether to collaborate on newspapers. He said that if he could live life over he would not work for newspapers again, but it was financially difficult to break away from it. From this time he devoted himself to painting.

1910-1911

Villon shared a studio with Raymond Duchamp-Villon in Puteaux. On Sunday afternoons he began to meet with other artists and writers such as Georges Ribemont-Dessaignes and wife, Maggy, and Henri-Martin Barzun. He met Gleizes, Metzinger, Léger, and Le Fauconnier in the spring of 1911; their friendship developed rapidly in the fall, bringing together several circles of friends into the Artists of Passy.

1911

Raymond Duchamp-Villon was in charge of hanging Salon d'automne in the central room of Grand Palais.

Clovis Sagot, the brother of Edmund, became the publisher for Villon's cubist engravings.

1912

Villon met Walter Pach through Raymond Duchamp-Villon. Artists met on Sundays at Puteaux, and on Mondays at Gleizes' home in neighboring Courbevoie. Kupka, Metzinger, Picabia, Léger, Duchamp, Suzanne Duchamp, Delaunay, Marie Laurencin, Apollinaire, Walter Pach, Joachim Gasquet, Roger Allard, Valensi, André Mare, André Salmon, La Fresnaye, Le Fauconnier, Mercereau were part of this circle, which occasionally met at the rue Franklin apartment of the architect Perret brothers as well as at the regular Tuesdays of Paul Fort, at the *Closerie des Lilas*.

1912

Villon gave the name "Section d'Or" to a projected group exhibition.

The café in Place de l'Alma became the meeting place for monthly "dinners of Passy" — Paul Fort presided at the first one in September 1912. The three Duchamp brothers, Gleizes, Metzinger, M. Laurencin, Le Fauconnier, Léger, Picabia, Roger Allard, Valensi, André Mare and Apollinaire were members of the group. Meetings continued chez Villon, and chez Gleizes. The first exhibition of Section d'Or was held at the Galerie La Boétie, October, 1912. It was accompanied by lectures and one issue of a new journal entitled *La Section d'Or*.

Exhibition of the Maison Cubiste at Salon d'automne.

1913

Villon showed nine paintings at The Armory Show in New York, all of which were sold.

1914

On August 2nd Villon was called up for military service in the 21st Infantry Regiment. In October, he was sent to the front. He took part in the battle of the Somme, and was then moved to Champagne.

1915

Marcel Duchamp departed for New York.

1916

Villon was transferred to the camouflage service in Amiens, and then returned to the front.

1918

He was discharged from military service at Chartres.

Raymond Duchamp-Villon died of typhoid fever, in the Cannes Military Hospital.

1918-1921

Villon was in charge of the production of *Architectures,* a collective effort published by Louis Süe and André Mare (1921). This included plates by de La Fresnaye, Segonzac, Boussingault, Laboureux and others. *Table d'échecs, La Table servie* and *Buste de Baudelaire* were published in *Die Schoffenden*.

1919-1920

Villon's art was moving towards geometric abstraction. Gleizes' attempt to revive the Section d'Or failed.

1921

Villon's first American one man show was held in the Galleries of the *Société Anonyme* in New York.

1922

For his exhibition with Latapie, at the Galerie Povolozsky, Paris, the critic Maurice Raynal gave Villon favorable notice.

1922-1930

Financial need and his reputation as a master engraver conspired to engage Villon to do a series of color aquatints from paintings by Cézanne, Renoir, Van Gogh, Rousseau, Matisse, Picasso, Rouault, Braque, Suzanne Duchamp, Jean Crotti, Marcel Duchamp, Marquet, Gleizes, and Metzinger, They were published by Bernheim-Jeune.

1925

Both of Villon's parents died; his mother on January 29th and his father on February 3rd.

1932-1933
He exhibited with the Abstraction-Création group.

1934
On a trip to Provence, Villon's serious interest in landscape began.

1936
On a trip to the U.S. with Mme Villon in the spring, Villon stayed at the apartment of Mrs. Gerda Stein, 300 Central Park West, New York. From these windows he designed lithographs of the New York skyline. He also made trips through New England to visit Katherine Dreier and Walter Pach, who was then teaching at Bowdoin College.

At this time Villon was better known in the United States than in France.

1937
At the International Exhibition, Paris, he won two diplomas of honor and the Gold Medal for painting and engraving.

1938
Louis Carré was introduced to Villon by Madame Mare-Vène.

1939
He became a Chevalier de la Légion d'Honneur.

Villon left Paris at the beginning of the war. He spent three months in Beaugency on the Loire.

1940-41
He left Puteaux for an extended sojourn in the country, and buried Duchamp-Villon's sculptures in his yard before he left.

He and Mme Villon stayed first at Bernay, the home of André Mare, then at La Brunié (Tarn), with M. and Mme Mare-Vène.

1942
Villon returned to Puteaux.

During the war, Louis Carré sought him out, and became Villon's exclusive dealer. Carré bought the contents of Villon's studio, with some exceptions.

1944
After the extreme hardships of the war, his first exhibition in a liberated Paris was held at Galerie Louis Carré. Thirty-nine paintings were included, with a catalogue preface by René-Jean. It was a great success.

1945
By now Villon was honored and imitated by the younger generation. His influence began to spread to England through an article in *Horizon* by Raymond Mortimer.

1949
Villon won the Grand Prix de la Gravure, Lugano, at the International Print Exhibition.

1950
At the Pittsburgh International Exhibit of Paintings, Carnegie Institute, Villon was awarded first prize.

He was also chosen for the first volume of a series of books on great French painter-engravers, by Jacqueline Auberty and Charles Pérusseaux. This was the first attempt to compile a *catalogue raisonné* of Villon's graphic work.

Pierre Cailler dedicated an issue of *Art Documents* to Villon, with text by Jerome Mellquist.

1953
He was promoted to Commandeur de la Légion d'Honneur and Commandeur des Arts et Lettres.

1955
Villon designed stained glass windows for Metz cathedral.

1956
Francis Poulenc set poems of Paul Eluard to music in *Le Travail du Peintre.* One melody was dedicated to Villon. Other artists similarly honored include Picasso, Chagall, Braque, Gris, Klee, Mirò.

At the XXVIII Venice Biennale, Villon was awarded the Grand Prix for painting. This was his first trip to Italy.

1958
Villon was awarded the Grand Prize for painting at the Brussels World's Fair, 1958-1959.

1961
Galerie Charpentier, Paris, *Cent Tableaux de Jacques Villon,* reunited works which had been sold and dispersed all over the world. With this exhibition and its notices, Villon's international reputation was secured.

1963
He was elected Grand Officer de la Légion d'Honneur.

June 9, 1963
Villon died at Puteaux, age 87. He was buried in Cimetière Monumental, Rouen.

INTRODUCTION: COLOR, FORM, AND FAMILY
by Daniel Robbins

A study of Villon without reference to the lives and works of his younger brothers Raymond Duchamp-Villon and Marcel Duchamp is neither possible nor desirable. The ideas of the three men — rooted in their common background, close harmony, and affectionate relations — are like three aspects of the same, rational, civilized being, the culminating product of nineteenth-century French civilization. Certain distinguishing qualities of each brother (Raymond's optimism and social concern, Marcel's irony, Jacques's reflection) as well as the complexities of the oeuvre of each, tend to obscure the similarities.

There have been many exhibitions devoted to the three brothers, and some that also included the work of their sister Suzanne, and her husband Jean Crotti. We should stress not merely the fact that the Duchamp family was remarkable in producing three artists of major importance, but also that the family was the first and most influential audience for each of its members. Twentieth-century artists are usually seen to be creating for themselves, as opposed to earlier artists who so often worked for a more public purpose, or for a specific destination. The Duchamp brothers seem to have worked in considerable measure for each other, their wives, their sisters, parents, in-laws, and close friends. This expanding circle ultimately grew to include almost the whole world interested in modern art, but the widening sector found it necessary to penetrate, especially in the case of Marcel Duchamp, an arcane set of references, a private language which seems to have been a code for special communication among the Duchamps.

Jacques Villon (born Gaston Duchamp) was not as obscure as his youngest brother; nor was he as willing to share his feelings and ideas with society as his sculptor brother, Raymond. Villon, mentor to both Marcel and Raymond, first made the decision to be an artist. Within the context of turn-of-the-century humorous illustration, he developed the practice of punning on words and images with references readily understandable by a sophisticated audience, often including as well the special signals which made sense only to his family and close friends. The passage from public to private meaning and back again, and the development of visual ideas from one sphere into another is one of the consistent characteristics of Villon's art throughout his long and productive career.

Although Villon, the first master punster in the Duchamp family, gave up humorous illustration for the newspapers around 1910, he neither renounced humor nor the practice of private communication with his very special audience. Initially, his brothers, sisters, parents, and close friends were the only audience who could appreciate the relationship between his light efforts and his more serious ones, who could comprehend and enjoy the sources of images so often drawn from objects and surroundings well known to this magic circle. Thus chairs and stools, tables and mantles, faces and poses, music, games, sculptures, seaside scenes, ultimately even landscapes — and always titles — may be assumed to have special significance, some extra node of meaning at the secret core of each work and each variation, understandable at first only to the initiated. For Villon, proof of initiation was membership in the family; Duchamp's private audience was more complex, a kind of ever-growing secret society.

One can be sure, however, that although Raymond Duchamp-Villon knew and used the codes, he was the only brother who deliberately wished to create an art that was accessible to others. When he died in 1918 the effect on Jacques was critical. Villon was not only left with the physical and financial responsibility for his brother's artistic legacy, but also it seems he felt a growing sense of responsibility toward Raymond's convictions about the role of art in society. These were attitudes which Villon shared, as his role in the Section d'Or and the Maison Cubiste testifies, but evidently not to the same extent.

Despite their residence in Paris, Jacques and Raymond remained involved in the artistic activity of their native Normandy, and both were members of Pierre Dumont's literary and artistic organization l'Association des XXX, which held its first exhibition in October-November, 1907. This organization changed its name, in 1910, to the Société Normande de Peinture Moderne and became the group which, as William Camfield demonstrated 10 years ago,[1] furnished the basis for

[1] William A. Camfield, "La Section d'Or," unpublished Masters thesis, Yale University, 1964. See also William A. Camfield and Daniel Robbins, *Albert Gleizes and the Section d'Or* (New York: Leonard Hutton Galleries, 1964).

the widely expanded cubist manifestation in Paris that was called, in 1912, the salon of the Section d'Or. The founding of Dumont's society in 1907 followed the period when Villon had lived for approximately a year in Rouen, after he and Raymond had shared an exhibition at the Galerie Legrip in 1905 (where in 1906 Dumont also had shown paintings[2]). Villon was vice-president of Les XXX which Dumont, dissatisfied with exhibitions at Legrip, had created for the purpose of uniting avant-garde artists who opposed routine and regulations, and whose aim was not only collective exhibitions, but a forum for the discussion of the purposes of poetry and art. We know that from Rouen, Dumont followed closely the activities of both elder Duchamp brothers. Being younger (b. 1884), he probably looked up to them, envying their presence in Paris. Dumont signaled attention to the activities of the Salon d'Automne (where Villon was on the committee), and even wrote an article on Villon for the first issue (May 28, 1910) of the *Rouen-Gazette,* a weekly paper dedicated to arts and letters and financed by a friend, Dr. André Thibault. Although the ideas that dominated the discussions and lectures of the Norman Society were varied, certain strains are of special importance for the intensity, continuity, and frequency of their appearance. It seems reasonable to infer that Duchamp-Villon and Villon would have been familiar and in general agreement with them. One theme was the equation of the aims of modern art with the popular dynamism of the Middle Ages, the art of the cathedral and the poetry of François Villon.[3] Another was the possibility of creating an art that could be understood, loved, and important to all the people.[4] Still another concerned the sophisticated accomplishments of late nineteenth-century science, which were immediately available artistic and poetic inspirations. Of the scientific discoveries discussed in lectures presented at the salon of the Norman Society, no principle was more fascinating than the new conception of matter as energy and movement, described in the lecture of A. M. Gossez as the "movement of rotating particles." Art was to be renewed at the foundation of philosophical concepts.

While these interests were not unique to the Rouen group, they were surely endorsed by Jacques as well as Raymond. Villon had demonstrated his admiration for François Villon and the Middle Ages in the late 1890s, when he adopted his pseudonym. But it was Raymond, rather than Jacques, who took the lead in organizing the dissident cubist artists at the Salon, and Raymond who deliberately attempted to extend modern art into people's lives through the Maison Cubiste. Raymond — finally — translated the notion of the rotation machine into the powerful image of *Le Cheval.*

The epic quality of modern art called for in the program of the Rouen artists, as well as by the other groups of modern artists who united in the Section d'Or was in fact only hesitatingly advanced by Jacques Villon in the subjects and treatments he developed before the First World War. The *Atelier méchanique, L'Équilibriste,* and *Soldats en marche* do demonstrate Jacques's community of interest with the consciously significant subjects of other Right Bank cubists, but these works are not deliberately-built symbolic structures on the order of Gleizes' *Harvesters,* Delaunay's *Ville de Paris* or Duchamp-Villon's *Cheval.* However, one of the distinguishing features of Jacques Villon, stemming as much from his working method as his own meditative nature and his sculptor-brother's spiritual legacy, was the fact that he continued to develop and rephrase pre-war cubist subject concerns, deepening and compounding them until, as André Chastel remarked twenty years ago,[5] his work assumes a "Mallarméen" resonance.

Chastel was referring to the fact that Villon's paintings and prints went beyond his occasional specific references to poetry or drama to become steadily more emblematic, until with abstractions such as the early 1930s series of canvases entitled *L'Architecture, Allegresse,* and *L'Espace* he achieved a total equation of idea and means. There is continual growth in Villon's work, demonstrated by his perpetual reworking of

2 See P. Varenne, *Pierre Dumont, 1884-1936* (Paris: Galerie Denis, 1944-1945).

3 See A.-M. Gossez, "L'Expression: le Dynamisme Poétique," in *Essai d'expansion d'une esthétique* (Le Havre, 1911), pp. 27-58.

4 Philéas Lebesque, *L'Inspiration: Walt Whitman et la Poésie contemporaine* (Le Havre, 1911) pp. 5-26.

5 André Chastel, "Un Artiste Mallarméen," in *Exposition Jacques Villon* (Albi: Museé Toulouse-Lautrec, 1955), pp. 13-18.

subject and intensification of method; yet there is also an easy shuttling back and forth among ideas with reference to a universal hierarchy of importance. Therefore there is no conflict between the abstract treatment of some ideas, and the almost representational treatment of others; nor is there tension between different aspects of the same theme treated abstractly or realistically, as a consideration of the Globe series makes clear (see cat. no. 142).

The relationship of these life-long concerns of Villon to attitudes of the Right Bank cubists can be traced at various stages during the artist's career; sometimes they center on as modern a theme as sport: the horse race pictures fit in with Delaunay, Metzinger, Gleizes, Lhôte, and Tobeen who depicted bicycle racing, running, football, and even jai-alai. The *Globe* series has parallels in de la Fresnaye (Mappemonde) and in a host of paintings by the cubists, including the port pictures of Gleizes, Metzinger, and Lhôte, which reveal the geographical mania caused by their generation's awareness of a shrunken world. The airplane series is a tardy statement of the exhilaration that de la Fresnaye and Delaunay (and Villon, and even Picasso) caught from the idea of flight in 1912-1913. Above all, the landscapes of Villon, a genre he developed late in life, summarize a reverence for French soil which had begun to appear in the pictures of Gleizes and de la Fresnaye before World War I. This apparent continuation of late symbolist attitudes toward the land took on an extra dimension as cubism permitted a new means of stressing both the antiquity and physical extent of the earth.

Villon's work has a special quality of reverence for the intellect — and by extension, for society's need to meditate. Thus the work of art is defined as a vehicle for communication. The recognition Villon's pictures and their themes received during and directly after the Second World War may have been the sign of society understanding at last the significance attached by the cubists to a set of mental attitudes. By this time the ideas had ceased to be new and controversial.

The relationship between Villon and the epic intentions of the Right Bank cubists is focused in the obvious and continuous responsibility that he assumed with regard to his dead brother's work and — to a lesser extent — Raymond's role in French art. This is one important philosophic boundary of Villon's oeuvre. However, it is Villon's method that distinguishes his own art, and best reveals his measured, but profound, personality. In examining the steady expansion of this means and suggesting the sources of this growth, we encounter a number of problematic areas where not only Villon's approach to form, but even his *consciousness* seems to shift. In these regions, as we shall see, speculation — his and ours — arises on the work and activity of his other brother, Marcel Duchamp, giving definition to the opposite boundary of Villon's creativity.

Villon began as a printmaker. He learned every aspect of his craft in a systematic and meticulous manner. Each line and each color was tried, often many times, before he was satisfied with the result. He was careful; he was cerebral; yet by the same token he was also experimental. In early drawings and trial proofs, Villon reversed images, traced, took out motifs, recombined them, enlarged some, reduced others. It was the beginning of a method that became ever more complex as he grew older and continued to expand his techniques. He used not only mirror images, as would be expected of a master printmaker, but inverted images as well, sometimes only of parts of previous works. And he would sometimes rotate a design only half-way, or ninety degrees. But every reversal, inversion, or partial rotation is completely systematic, as organized as the series developed in connection with *La Table servie* of 1912-1913 (cat. nos. 42-48). In this group Villon used the traditional "squaring up" method for enlarging or reducing designs, which allows a draughtsman/artist to find his way when transcribing a complicated motif from one version to another.

After World War I, however, a new element appeared to enrich this pattern of transcription. In the *Jockey* series (cat. nos. 86-98) the use of the coordinate grid can be traced, along with the complicating factor of multiplying the coordinates. Thus a drawing scheme four boxes high is made five boxes high with a resulting change in proportion. In some cases, reference is made to an apparently irregular polygon, which further distorts the transcription of the original, earlier design. Tracing Villon's generation of formal design variations in the development of the *Jockey* series is an exercise in close reasoning. However, we must consider the possibility that the process of systematic distortion evident in this group is but an obvious instance of a far more complex system already functioning in works such as *Jeu* (cat. no. 69) and the *Baudelaire* series (cat. nos. 70-80).

If this is the case, it would strengthen speculation that Villon had studied D'Arcy Thompson's *On Growth and Form,* first published in 1917, and that he was particularly impressed with its most celebrated chapter, "On the Theory of Transformations, or the Comparison of Related Forms." The mathematics of this famous chapter is not particularly difficult. It begins with a discussion of Cartesian coordinates, and reinforces its method by reference to Henri Poincaré's conception of the valid function of mathematics as a tool for understanding the relation of simple to composite (natural) phenomena. Thus it falls well within the orbit of Villon's education, and is entirely consistent with his long-standing interest in numbers. Thompson used the coordinate method to recognize the permutations and malformations of one biological form in another. His famous chapter is complete with diagrams, based originally on Descartes, which show the systematic alteration of a circle in a square into an oval within a rectangle, simply by changing the dimensions of the orthogonal net, very much as Villon does in *Jeu.* Many types of consistent distortion are suggested by the extension or constriction of systems of rectangular coordinates; even more elegant systems of radial coordinates, or circular coordinates (as in polar projections), are described and diagrammed. Thompson also made reference to, and reproduced, several diagrams after Albrecht Dürer, citing the French edition, *Les Quatres livres d'Albert Dürer de la proportion des parties et pourtraicts des corps humains* (Arnheim, 1613), where "the manner in which the human figure, features, and facial expression are all transformed and modified by slight variations in the relative magnitude of the parts is admirable and copiously illustrated."[6] The fact that elementary applications of the principles of coordinates "was in common use in the sixteenth and seventeenth centuries by artists in their study of form"[7] raises the possibility that Villon may have independently read Dürer's *Treatise on Proportion,* which would have been a logical consequence of his interest in the same subject sharpened by his familiarity with Leonardo. Or, Thompson's use, in 1917, of examples from Dürer, may have had particular appeal to Villon.[8]

The system of rectangular equidistant coordinates which Villon used in "squaring up" versions of *La Table servie* in 1912-1913, then, lends itself to the most fantastic variations, simply by inclining the axes or by using ordinates which come closer and closer together. In general, any network or grid of systematically arranged lines might be used, if one draws into the system, point for point, an outline corresponding to the original design. Furthermore, two or three different coordinate systems can be superimposed, as, for example, an oblique system and an orthogonal one, with a radial system interpolated between. This seems to be similar to the method Villon employed in a series of drawings based on the bust of Baudelaire, particularly *Figure par plans* (cat. no. 78) and *Etude de tête* (cat. no. 79), which yielded the flat, angled sections ultimately translated into the painting *Figure* (cat. no. 80). The systematic tilting or rotation of planes, orderly vertical sections in the earlier *Abstract Construction* (cat. no. 77), results from the interposition of an intermediate coordinate system. One such intermediate system is suggested by the marks visible along the edges of each section in this drawing. These argue for a new set of axes at forty-five degrees to the original; but other drawings which are equally rigorous indicate the probable use of oblique and converging systems as well, parts of which were

[6] D'Arcy W. Thompson, *On Growth and Form,* abridged edition, edited by J. T. Bonner (Cambridge, England, 1961), p. 290.

[7] *Ibid.,* p. 292.

[8] Thompson, in a footnote that might have appealed to Villon, cites the influence of Dürer on Peter Camper, who used the oblique coordinate system to develop his notion of "facial angle" as an index to general deformation in *On the Connexion between the Science of Anatomy and the Arts of Drawing, Painting and Sculpture* (1768?). He also called attention to the French edition of Camper (Paris, 1791) and to a late 19th-century article by P. Topinand, "Etudes sur Pierre Camper, et sur l'angle facial dit de Camper," *Revue Anthropologique* II (1874).

combined in the different versions that occupied Villon during 1920 and 1921.

This systemization of approach to a severely limited group of subjects characterizes Villon's first abstract period[9] in the years from 1919 to 1923-1924. It is accompanied by an equally rich and intricate use of color. We know from many sources, particularly from the notebooks of Beatrice Stein (see cat. no. 128) and the evidence of Cleve Gray, that at least from the early thirties, Villon used M. A. Rosenstiehl's *Traité de la Couleur, au point de vue physique, physiologique, et esthétique, comprenant l'exposé de l'état actuel de la question de l'Harmonie des Couleurs* (Paris, 1913). We know that he urged Cleve Gray to acquire the second edition of this monumental and useful work, revised by Rosenstiehl's pupil Julie Beaudeneau. (Between the first edition of 1913 and the second, Beaudeneau had pasted up a color wheel conforming to Rosenstiehl, with the hope of providing to the color industries a complete, standardized wheel more accurate and useful than that of Chevreul, which was still widely in use just before the First World War.)

This is not the place to discuss in detail Rosenstiehl's accomplishments, but there were three in particular that Villon used in the construction of every painting. These were the fundamental color triad the aesthetic scale, and the law of surfaces. Rosenstiehl's concept of the color triad, based on Young (1802), regarded color as sensation, and established "couples of colors" as fundamental — that is, three colors and their complementaries. An essential condition was that the mixture of any two of them would produce an intermediate color, not white (or grey). "From three color sensations, (orange, yellow-green, and blue) with their combinations, we obtain all the distinctions among colors and the diverse proportions in which they may be combined leads to a number of varying tints beyond calculation."[10]

The aesthetic scale in Rosenstiehl is a ladder of tones, with the complementary present for each tone. Rosenstiehl visualized a color solid which was generally analogous to Munsell's or Pope's, systematically demonstrating variations of intensity by measurement, and showing the passages toward black or white (comparable to degrees of grey on a black-white scale) for fifty-four intermediate hues. His concept of measurement — achieved through the continuous use of rotating disks which enabled the experimenter to verify the quantity of color to be used in any combination and to express it in degrees — was basic to Villon's conviction that in any picture, a certain sum of color was required to balance or complete it. For Villon, the amounts of color were "given," once the essential triad had been selected (see cat. no. 146).

The law of surfaces was, according to Beaudeneau,[11] perhaps Rosenstiehl's most important and certainly his most original contribution to color theory. It concerned the effect of color sensations on a flat surface, examining the reasons why some jump toward the viewer while others retreat, and especially studying what happens when any combination is shifted by the exposure of the whole to a monochromatic light. In this connection Rosenstiehl formulated laws of accomodation, insisting that harmony could not be achieved unless the law of surfaces was obeyed.

There is no doubt that Villon knew Rosenstiehl's system in detail; the only question is, when did he become familiar with it? Although his palette brightened steadily after the sombre 1911 portrait of Raymond (cat. no. 29), it does not seem to have become absolutely systematic until after the war. If, for example, we look at the oval *Tête de femme* of 1914 (cat. no. 63), we see blue and yellow (complementaries) on either side of the head, but the modeled green center, split vertically and opposed to white, clearly does not obey the law of surfaces. The aesthetic scale — a careful measurement of intensities — is also absent. On the other hand, if we examine *Jeu*, 1919, Villon's first major work after the war, we can understand the entire painting in terms of Rosenstiehl's theory and practice. Two intensity scales of complementaries are operating here:

[9] If the conjecture with regard to Villon's awareness of Thompson is correct, an almost exact parallel is furnished by Villon's second abstract period in the early 1930s, where intellectual stimulation was provided by Ghyka's book (Matila Ghyka, *Esthétique des Proportions dans la nature et dans les Arts* [Paris: Gallimard, 1927]), a book that itself owed a great debt to Thompson. See cat. no. 114.

[10] Rosenstiehl, p. 113.

[11] Rosenstiehl, 2nd edition, 1934, introduction.

one is based on yellow, yielding the variations of brown that deepen toward the base of the painting; and the other is based on intervals of blue, which rise in diamond shapes to the brightest at the top. According to Rosenstiehl, if one wants to use a modified red-orange, as Villon did in the chess board, the yellow hues must be dulled to little more than browns or olives, because of the greater intensity of red-orange. In *Jeu*, the luminosity of the red is reduced by surrounding it with black, and Rosenstiehl's dictum[12] that the combination should be accompanied in the reduction of intensity by a number of rich, chocolate browns, is obeyed.

Further proof that Villon had made a close study of Rosenstiehl at the end of the war is offered by the 1921 *Équilibre rouge* (cat. no. 85), which (insofar as can be determined from color reproduction and slides) is virtually a painting based on Chapter VIII of the *Traité*. Through careful experimental studies, always using the rotating disk, Rosenstiehl established that with red alone, all tonal variations possess the same complementary. He produced a curve of intensities for red (including all the intermediaries between red and grey at the same level), and demonstrated that the intervals follow an arithmetic progression, as they do not for any other color. This, he pointed out, was due to the fact that red is the only color that does not vary when diluted by black! (With blue and yellow, for example, because all the intermediaries between these colors and grey are of another complementary, there is no common measure to determine variation of intensity.)

Rosenstiehl gave experimental proofs verifying that among the unique qualities of the color red is its ability to produce essentially the same effect in either pigment or colored glass. He provided formulas demonstrating, color for color, what would happen under a monochromatic red light: green and blue going to black, violet becoming dark red, yellow and orange appearing bright red. He showed how the same effect could be achieved through mixing pigment. Finally, he announced at every opportunity his concept of balance, harmony, or equilibrium — a desired condition, the achievement of which could be tested by reference to spinning disks. Although ac-

companying his discussion of accommodation with tables of refrangibility, he did not pretend that the tendency of color sensations to recede or jump was due to anything other than the psychological nature of color.

If *Équilibre rouge* (cat. no. 85) appears to be a startling example of Villon's familiarity with Rosenstiehl, other works of the first abstract period are only slightly less susceptible to close comparison with the ideas of the color theoretician. *Repliement*, 1921 (cat. no. 84), from the same series as *Équilibre rouge*, is an illustration of the laws of accommodation, demonstrating specifically how red always appears to stay back or withdraw. In *Composition jaune et bleu* or *Galop*, 1921 (fig. 97a), the use of complementaries may be contrasted with the roles of yellow and blue in *Tête de femme*, 1914 (cat. no. 63): "When any two colors of the chromatic circle are brought into competition, the effect produced is to move them further apart."[13] If the colors are already complementary, they appear more brilliant and saturated. This is indeed the case in *Galop*, an experiment and expression diametrically opposite to the operation of colors in *Jeu* (concerned with small intervals) and *Équilibre rouge* (concerned with the law of surfaces and the shift in colors, achieved in paint, as if they were bathed in a red light).

It seems highly probable that Jacques Villon was obliged to study Rosenstiehl — and other theoreticians as well — in his work[14] for the French Army camouflage unit to which he was transferred in Amiens in 1916. This theory will remain speculation until we know more specific details of Villon's life, or about the (then) surely classified aspects of the French Army camouflage service. In any case, among the artists who were also assigned to this unit were Jean Boussingault, Forain, Dufresné, and Dunoyer de Segonzac, all entering the section either late in 1915 or early in 1916. We must conclude that either the unit was in the process of formation, or someone in the war department had the bright idea of transferring a group of artists into a sector where they could be useful. We do know

---

12 *Ibid.*, pp. 211-212.

13 Rosenstiehl, p. 246.

14 Cleve Gray has remarked on Villon's familiarity with Ogden N. Rood's *Modern Chromatics* (1881). He owned a copy and recommended to Gray that it be studied.

from Villon's chronology, however, that the camouflage unit, with which he served until the end of the war, engaged in work both behind the lines, and subsequently in highly practical and dangerous work near the firing zone.

The art of camouflage was developing rapidly during World War I, since the use of airplanes and balloons had greatly expanded the likelihood of enemy observation. Measures developed in the camouflage service to retard or confuse air-spotting included creating the illusion of fields where none existed, of woods and shadows where fields existed; painting roads across buildings, nets over huts, etc. Applications involved two cardinal propositions: the continual awareness of a view from above (which entered Villon's work after the war), and the manipulation of color and design.

Rosenstiehl was published just before the war. In addition to theoretical and historical studies, his book was complete with practical applications; for example, how from one point of view a color can be almost invisible, yet from another, clearly distinguished. His advice to manufacturers of veils would be useful to soldiers charged with the construction of a net to conceal an airfield. Rosenstiehl's book contained practical observations on dilution of color, the effect of thickness of pigment in differing lights, the penetration of pigment by metal, and the effect of layers of color on the amount of light reflected from different materials. However, in order to determine such practical consequences, it was always necessary to refer to, recapitulate, or re-create new experiments with rotating disks of color combinations — or else the proportions of any mixture to produce a desired effect would be incorrect, given the variables of quantity and intensity. In short, the necessity of measuring these aspects of color sensation must have been of primordial importance to the camouflage service.

For the present, the foregoing must remain in the area of probable conjecture. Yet there is one further, telling, unverified coincidence that joins Villon and his younger brother Marcel in a related pursuit of the consequences of color study, most likely inaugurated by Villon. The use of diamond-shaped, receding color samples figures prominently, although without satisfactory explanation, in Marcel's *Tu' M* of 1918 (see fig. 69b). Furthermore, Duchamp's first motorized disk machine

(five plates in glass) dates from 1920; the second set of disks was produced in Paris, 1923. The third set (with the disks inscribed with puns) was made for the 1926 film *Anemic Cinema*. This set evolves from two related 1925 experiments in Paris, the *Precision Optics* and the *Rotative Demisphere* (see the Philadelphia Museum Duchamp catalog, 1973, no. 148) where Duchamp used a disk made of black velvet. Rosenstiehl outlined a series of experiments with rotating disks using black velvet to measure the regular diminution of white and of colors toward black. Velvet was employed because it absorbs the most incidental light.

Whatever else these parallel activities may someday demonstrate (we must remember that Duchamp's *Tu' M* was created when he was in the United States, and Villon still in the camouflage service), one fact is clear: the paintings and constructions of each brother had a special meaning for the other. Villon could not look at Duchamp's work without at least privately referring to his own experience and knowledge of color, without a reflective chuckle, perhaps, on the fact that Rosenstiehl, Chapter XXI, gives a detailed description on how to build spinning disk machines, together with a justification of why such a machine must stand vertically. Nor is it likely that Duchamp could look at the paintings Villon produced in the immediate postwar years without recognizing the profound master of color his brother had become.

After the war, and following the tragic death of Raymond, the relationship between Marcel and Jacques continued to develop as a secret dialogue in their art. It had begun in a perfectly straightforward way, and up to 1911 was entirely clear. Marcel learned much of his drawing style from Jacques, as well as a great deal about visual and written puns. The next phase of paintings from 1909 through 1911-1912, from *Nu debout bras en l'air* (cat. no. 23) through *Puteaux: Fumées et arbres en fleur* (cat. no. 33), continues to prove numerous similarities in both subject and treatment.

By 1911-1912 influence between the brothers had become a two-way street. It is difficult to demonstrate the sequence or order in which it operated, but certain features are so salient that speculation is invited. In catalogue nos. 35-37, it is suggested that the dynamic, cinema-like movement introduced in

Villon's *Jeune femme* series was probably a result of Duchamp's *Nude Descending a Staircase*. In nos. 54-57 a similarity between the *L'Équilibriste* series of Villon and *La Mariée* of Duchamp is tentatively suggested. *La Mariée* dates from 1912, while only one drawing for *L'Équilibriste* is known from that year. (The final versions were executed in 1913 and 1914, although the theme is one that Villon began ten years earlier.) It could well be that there was some hidden meaning for the brothers not only in the generally similar disposition of forms in the two design schemes, hinting perhaps at a common origin in an earlier and as yet undiscovered acrobat drawing by Villon; but also in the titles: the word *L'Équilibriste* is potentially an acrostic full of puns, and some are in tempting consonance with *La Mariée* — for example, *ET QUI EST LIBRE* or *ET QU'IL LIBRE*. Such a possibility, although far-fetched, would be out of character for neither brother.

We are persuaded that almost nothing in the works of Jacques Villon is accidental. Although he was perfectly candid in interviews, he was not out-going but prudent and reserved. In light of these two facts, it seems likely that he may have particularly enjoyed the very private, reciprocal understanding with Marcel of their art and its sources. With this in mind we make the tentative suggestion in catalogue nos. 105 and 106, that *Le Philosophe*, 1930, is a portrait based on Marcel. In 1951, he again entitled one of half a dozen portraits of his brother, *Un Philosophe*. Although after the Second World War and well into the 1950s, Jacques was still far more recognized as an artist than was Marcel,[15] perhaps he sensed and even relished the shift of interest that was occurring. This must have pleased Villon, as he recalled in his very old age the treasured recollections of Raymond and the revolutionary ideas of matter and rotating motion held so dear by the Rouen group early in the century. Once again, art was to be renewed at the foundation of philosophical concepts.

[15] See Pierre Cabanne, *Dialogue with Marcel Duchamp* (first published in Paris, 1967), translated from the French by Ron Padgett, New York, 1971, p. 86. Talking to Duchamp about the late 1940s, Cabanne asked if he regretted "not being known." "*Cabanne:* compared with Jacques Villon, who at that time was considered a very great painter? *Duchamp:* I was delighted that Villon held that position for our family."

The arrangement of the catalogue is both chronological and thematic. Where Villon's interest in a particular visual area carried across many years, the related works have been grouped together, regardless of date. A large number of supplementary illustrations, designated as "figures" (fig.) in the text, have been integrated into the entries, enabling the student to compare exhibited examples with related works, some not by Jacques Villon. "Catalogue number" (cat. no.) denotes only exhibited items. To simplify the information included with each entry, the Bibliography and Exhibition History have been numbered, and only the relevant numbers appear under the titles of works in the present exhibition, with those corresponding to the latter list italicized. We hope that both lists are reasonably complete up to the middle of 1975. A Chronological List of Writings on Jacques Villon has been included to facilitate historical study of the subject. The abbreviation AP refers to the *Catalogue de l'oeuvre gravé de Jacques Villon* by J. Auberty and Ch. Pérussaux (bibl. 26). The number following AP refers to the number assigned to each of Villon's prints by the authors. Most titles of works are given in French, except where Villon titled the work in English or common usage has replaced or modified an earlier version. Where dimensions are given, height precedes width. Each entry is signed with the initials of its student author.

1

1

Portrait du père de l'artiste 1891

Etching touched with black crayon,
pen and ink

14 x 12.2 cm.

COLLECTION: The Museum of Modern Art,
New York, Lent anonymously

PUBLISHED: AP 1

2

Portrait du peintre-graveur Emile Nicolle
1891

Etching

17.6 x 12.8 cm.

COLLECTION: Print Department, Boston
Public Library

PUBLISHED: AP 2

2

In his first two etchings, done at age sixteen, Villon represented the two most influential persons in his decision to become an artist: his father and grandfather.

Villon's father, Justin-Isidore Duchamp, was a notary. At his insistence Villon attended classes at the Faculty of Law at the University of Paris for a year, and then worked for a few months as a notary clerk in Rouen. When it became clear that his son was interested only in art, Duchamp reluctantly relented, but asked him to change his name. For many years, however, he supported Villon with a small allowance.

The profile portrait (cat. no. 1) lacks tonal dimension, but demonstrates Villon's fine handling of line and his ability to capture a likeness. Villon recalled the experience of pulling his first print:

In 1891 I made my first print. We were in the country and had neither ground nor mordant for biting copper. I prepared my plate and purchased acid at the pharmacist's. I used the acid undiluted and the result was catastrophic. I was obliged to begin all over again. After some reflection I diluted the turbulent solution with water. The result was a portrait of my father, signed and dated G. Duchamp, 1891.[1]

Emile Frédéric Nicolle (1830-1894) was Villon's maternal grandfather. A shipbroker who lived in Rouen, he turned to engraving after retiring from business and produced several series of prints, published by Cadart. *Cent tours de Rouen, Vieux Rouen* (fig. 2a) and *Le Rouen pittoresque* are among the works which gained him recognition. Some of his prints are housed in the *Chalcographie* of the Louvre.

Villon's decision to become an artist in spite of his father's opposition must be attributed in part to the example and encouragement of Nicolle, from whom he received his earliest training. While Villon was a boarding student at the Lycée Corneille in Rouen, under the guardianship of his grandfather, Nicolle taught him the basic techniques of etching.

In the portrait of Nicolle (cat. no. 2), done several months after the portrait of Duchamp, Villon's technical progress is evident. Done in the grandfather's traditional style, this etching forecasts Villon's subsequent handling of black and white, as well as his precocity as a draughtsman. Both of these early works illustrate two values which remained constant throughout the artist's career: his love of the portrait and use of family members as models.

Raymond Duchamp-Villon also honored his grandfather in one of his early works — a posthumous portrait bust in plaster, done in 1906.[2] The striking similarity between the bust and Villon's etching indicates that Duchamp-Villon's work was derived from the etching.

It is significant that Villon's artistic beginnings were in etching; his reputation as a printmaker was established long before he was known as a painter. After this promising beginning, however, he did no more etching until 1898.

S G

[1] *(60)* Jean Cassou, Simone Frigerio, and Peter A. Wick, *Jacques Villon, Master of Graphic Art (1875-1963)* (Boston: Museum of Fine Arts, 1964), p. 37.

[2] See reproduction in *(421)* George Heard Hamilton and William C. Agee, *Raymond Duchamp-Villon* (New York: Walker and Co., 1967), p. 28.

2a

EMILE NICOLLE

Rue du Gril (quartier Marlainville), from *Vieux Rouen-X croquis* 1878-1881

Harvard University Library, The Houghton Library, Cambridge, Massachusetts

3
Pan, pan, pan
Illustration for *Le Courrier français*
December 17, 1897, page 9

Photogravure

32.5 x 19.5 cm.

COLLECTION: Harvard College Library,
Cambridge, Massachusetts

PUBLISHED: 36

3

Jacques Villon launched his professional career with satirical cartoons for the newsprint journals, first submitting illustrations in 1894 to the Rouen publications *Rouen Artiste* and *L'Étudiant*. These were so well received that his father finally acquiesced and allowed the nineteen-year-old Villon to abandon legal studies for art. In 1895 he enrolled in Cormon's studio. Two years later he made his debut in the Parisian illustrated journals (probably beginning with *Le Rire*, April 24, 1897). Soon Villon's work could be found in *La Revue parisienne, Cocorico, Le Chat noir, Gil Blas, Quartier latin, Le Frou-Frou, L'Assiette au beurre,* and the highly respected *Courrier français.*

Although Villon usually amused his readers with the salacious wit displayed in *Pan, pan, pan,* he also created a number of satirical caricatures, notably of types from the art world. A number of Villon's artistic contemporaries also turned to caricatures early in their careers. Both Kupka and Juan Gris were associated with *L'Assiette au beurre* at about the same time as Villon.

A few of Villon's early illustrations were signed 'Gaston Duchamp,' which he soon gave up according to his father's request that he not sign the family name to illustra-tions. In 1908, Villon began again to sign a few cartoons 'Gaston Duchamp,' and continued this practice with increasing frequency, until he gave up cartoon-illustration altogether in 1910. This reversal may have been an attempt to dissociate the cartoons from his reputation as a serious painter and engraver.

Pan, pan, pan typifies both the graphic style and bawdy humor of Villon's contributions to the journals. The caption translates: "Knock, Knock, Knock." "Come in! . . . Oh! I beg your pardon, I thought it was the laundress." As was customary, the artist supplied the caption as well as the drawing. Although Villon later had misgivings about having made these illustrations, they significantly improved his facility for acute observation and quick sketching, as he himself admitted.[1]

J D F

[1] Unpublished biographical manuscript, dated August 28, 1954 by Francis Steegmuller, with the collaboration of the artist, page 1.

4

Le Grillon, american bar 1899

Color Lithograph

131 x 92 cm.

COLLECTION: Bibliothèque du Musée des
Arts décoratifs, Paris.

PUBLISHED: AP 459

Courtesy of the Museum of Modern Art,
New York.

4

The popularity of color posters by Bonnard,
Chéret, and especially by Toulouse-Lautrec,
which advertised the bars and cabarets of
Montmartre in the 1890s, gave tremendous
impetus to the color-printing industry in
Paris. Villon had worked with black and
white lithography since 1895, but he took
up color printing seriously only in 1899.
Malfeyt et Cie of Montmartre, printed his
work. By 1907 he had made eight colored
lithographic posters.[1] This experience
helped him advance technically as it contributed to his financial resources.

Le Grillon is the largest and one of the
finest of Villon's posters. Although Auberty
and Pérusseaux's catalogue raisonné dates
it to 1900, the poster is dated 1899 in the
stone. M. J.-M. Levey, a poet, posed for the
picture in 1897.[2] A decade later Marcel Duchamp executed the pen and ink drawing
Au bar using a figure dressed and posed
similarly to Villon's Levey (fig. 4a). In his
early years as an artist Duchamp often took
his older brother's work as his model.

Levey was a well-known personage in
Montmartre, noted for his eccentric and
flashy way of dressing. His friends included
Villon and the literary figures Jules Fargue
and Francis Jourdain.[3] The *grillon,* or
cricket, that gave the bar its name appears
in the lower righthand corner of the poster,
lifting his beer mug to offer a toast. The
sharply diminished figure in the background
heightens the monumentality of Levey on
his bar stool. His rakish silhouette and the
Art Nouveau lettering combine in a bold
and arresting pattern. In 1947 Villon
reworked this print, adding a portrait of his
friend Camille Renault, the restaurateur.

J H

[1] *(75)* Riva Castleman, *Jacques Villon: A
Collection of Graphic Work 1896-1913 in
Rare or Unique Impressions* (New York:
Lucien Goldschmidt, Inc., 1970),
Introduction.

4a

MARCEL DUCHAMP

Au bar 1909

Pen and ink drawing

The Mary Sisler Collection, New York

Courtesy Fourcade Droll, Inc., New York

[2] *(235)* Jerome Mellquist, "Jacques Villon,"
L'Oeil, II (February 15, 1955), p. 6. In the
French version of this exhibition (*Jacques
Villon,* Editions de musées nationaux, 1975,
no. 5), J. M. Levey is identified as J. M.
Levet.

[3] *(70) Jacques Villon,* Hôtel Drouot (Paris:
April 12, 1967), no. 105.

5
La Boudeuse 1900
Color aquatint
17.8 x 28.8 cm.
COLLECTION: Museum of Fine Arts, Boston,
Gift of Mr. and Mrs. Peter A. Wick
PUBLISHED: AP 18

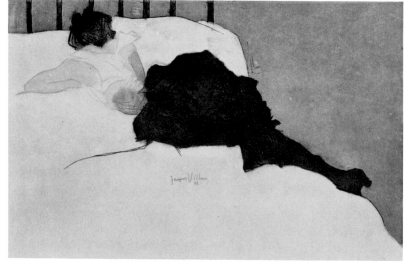

5

La Boudeuse, the sulker, originated as part
of a larger composition, a cartoon published
in *Le Sourire* in October, 1899. Entitled "La
Mélomanie," it showed a man playing a
violin and a partially undressed woman
sprawled on a bed. In the caption the
woman is saying, "As for me, I need music
to open my mind!"[1]

In *La Boudeuse* Villon transposed the
satirical illustration into a concise, independent image. Only its title hints at its
original anecdotal interest.

Villon resumed this subject in a 1905
aquatint, the *Petite boudeuse* (AP 97) in
which the woman is replaced by a little girl;
and in 1907 with the aquatint, *La Grande
boudeuse* (AP 121).

Until 1910 when he abandoned the
humorous journals, Villon's satiric contributions remained rich sources of ideas for
his independent work.

J H

[1] See reproduction in (36) Jerome Mellquist,
Les Caricatures de Jacques Villon (Geneva:
Pierre Cailler, 1960), no. 70. "Moi, la
musique, il me faut ça pour m'ouvrir les
idées!"

6
Portrait de R. Duchamp-Villon 1900-1901
Oil on canvas
93 x 65 cm.
Private collection, France
PUBLISHED: 27, 40, 342
EXHIBITED: *38, 49*

7
Conspuez Le Calicot, Conspuez
Illustration for *Le Courrier français*
January 16, 1898, page 9
Photogravure
27 x 24 cm.
COLLECTION: Harvard College Library,
Cambridge, Massachusetts
PUBLISHED: 36

6

7

Although Villon began to realize his serious intentions in art when he entered Cormon's studio, he did very few oil paintings until after 1900. Apparently in the early years he considered himself primarily an illustrator and graphic artist with an amateur's interest in painting. This was beginning to change by 1902 when Villon exhibited at the Galerie B. Weill;[1] in 1903 he entered a painting in the Salon Nationale des Beaux Arts for the first time.[2] Until 1908 or 1909 he modestly restricted most of his canvases to subjects of personal or family interest.

This handsome portrait of his brother Raymond Duchamp (before he assumed the name Duchamp-Villon) is one of the first in a long sequence of oil portraits of Villon himself, his family, and his friends. It offers another elegant example of the transformations Villon made to images developed for posters and cartoons, for the pose relates to *Le Grillon, American Bar* (cat. no. 4) and especially to *Conspuez* (cat. no. 7). This 1898 cartoon for *Le Courrier français* shows a young professional man with an amused expression interviewing a stylish, but simple young lady. Behind him on the blackboard is written a list of medical terms: "bone

tissue, muscular tissue, . . ." Using the familiar *"tu,"* the girl exclaims, "What! You're in dry goods?! . . . I thought you were a medical student." Villon puns on the French word *tissu* which translates as both "tissue" in the medical sense and, in more general usage, "fabric" or "material." In the slang of this period, reference to a woman who works with *tissus* could connote questionable morality, and it also has the meaning of "made up."[3] To avoid any possibility of his reader missing the point, Villon adds the heading "Down with Calico!" — another *double entendre*. Calico — an inexpensive unbleached muslin — may allude to the purity and simplicity of children's clothing, for which it was frequently used, but in slang a *calicot* was a sales girl in a fancy goods store, often implying loose morals.

In the upper right corner of the illustration, Villon also included another in-joke for his family and friends by dedicating the illustration: "to Raymond Duchamp, fraternally, J.V." A comparison of this caricature with the 1900 *Portrait of Raymond Duchamp-Villon* and with contemporary photographs reveals that the medical student is indeed a portrait of Raymond, who

had come to Paris as a medical student some years earlier and did not abandon his studies until 1898, when he was afflicted with rheumatic fever.

J D F

1 From June 2-15, 1902, Galerie B. Weill, 25 rue Victor-Masse; Villon showed an "aquarelle" in a group exhibit which also included works by Picasso, Marquet, Matisse, and Maillol.

2 No. 1312 — *Portrait de Mme H. . . .* He began entering color etchings in 1901, watercolors in 1902, and drawings in 1903.

3 As in the English expression 'painted woman.' It was common in Europe at this time to associate prostitution with some of the lowest paid occupations for women.

8

8a
PIERRE BONNARD
Le Fiacre 1898
Oil on canvas
Location unknown
Reproduced from T. Natauson, *Le Bonnard que jè propose* (Geneva: Pierre Cailler, 1951)

8

Maquis rue Caulaincourt 1901
Color aquatint and etching, trial proof
42 x 57.5 cm.
COLLECTION: Mrs. Frances W. Kelly, Cambridge, Massachusetts
PUBLISHED: AP 29

From 1898 to 1906 Villon lived on the rue Caulaincourt in Montmartre, where his neighbors were Renoir, Steinlen and Francis Jourdain.[1] *Maquis,* meaning thicket, referred to an adjacent tangle of shacks where drifters and small traders congregated.

Villon's compositional source for the *Maquis rue Caulaincourt* was a cartoon he had drawn for *Le Rire,* No. 357, in 1900.[2] This shows in full length a couple preparing to ride bicycles. Lightly sketched in the background are the buildings, horse cart, and tree which appear in the 1901 print. While giving the background greater prominence and finish in the new version Villon also changed the character of the couple, cutting them off at three-quarter length and placing the man upright and nearly behind the woman. Villon never carried the *Maquis* to completion, leaving only this trial proof dominated by blue.

Street scenes of Paris were common from the early 1890s on and Villon's choice of the subject and its arrangement suggests an awareness of the work of the *"Intimistes,"* Bonnard and Vuillard. Moreover, the *Maquis* makes one think specifically of Bonnard, who frequently used as motifs a cart in the middle ground and a figure in the foreground to one side, partially cut off

by the picture edge. An example is *Le Fiacre,* which Bonnard painted in 1898 (fig. 8a). According to Villon's own recollection he was not a conscious follower of the *Intimiste* school, but was indirectly influenced by them through the engraver Louis Legrand:

I knew vaguely, but very vaguely indeed, the names of Maurice Denis, Bonnard, Vuillard. And that's all. Yet there was in the Nabis painting all that graphical side which should have attracted me, had I known of them. I realised all that much later, when I heard that the engraver, Louis Legrand, who also worked for the "Courrier Français" and whom I had greatly admired, was a follower of the Nabis. The truth of the matter was that through him I had in fact admired the Nabis.[3]

J H

[1] (40) Dora Vallier, *Jacques Villon, oeuvres de 1897 à 1956* (Paris: Cahiers d'Art, 1957), p. 119. See also *Prints by European Masters* (New York: Lucien Goldschmidt, Inc., 1974), where *Maquis Caulaincourt* is identified.

[2] (36) Mellquist, *Caricatures,* No. 68.

[3] (40) Vallier, *Villon,* p. 117.

9

9a

JACQUES VILLON

La Parisienne 1902-1903

Etching and aquatint in black, AP 38

The Cleveland Museum of Art, Gift of The
Print Club of Cleveland

9

La Parisienne 1902-1903

Color aquatint

46.5 x 33.9 cm.

COLLECTION: Museum of Fine Arts, Boston,
Lee M. Friedman Fund

PUBLISHED: AP 38

The fashionable Parisian, with her full
skirts and wide hat, appeared in a variety of
poses in Villon's early prints and drawings
— gossiping with friends, caressing her pets,
or relaxing in a park. Often a sister of the
artist served as his model; in this case the
sitter was Yvonne Bon, sister of Jacques
Bon, painter friend of the Duchamps. Subsequently she married Raymond. The many
states of *La Parisienne* are prominent in Villon's early graphic work.[1]

Villon worked on this plate from 1902 to
1903. An early version shows an ornate fire-
place supported by caryatids, a fire screen, a
full length mirror and an Art Nouveau poster of figures and a peacock (fig. 9a). Gradually the artist simplified the fin-de-siècle
interior and finally eliminated it. At the
same time he reduced the number of colors
from six to two. In making these changes
Villon minimized the incidental aspects of
the composition in favor of sharpened
focus on the silhouette of the model. This
outline is as refined as the lady herself, and
is given high relief by the contrasting green
and rose that Villon finally chose to represent her.

J H

[1] Early states are reproduced in *(75)* Goldschmidt, *Villon,* nos. 11-15; and *(60)* Cassou,
Frigerio, and Wick, *Villon,* no. 18.

10

Les Cartes 1903

Color aquatint

34.8 x 44.8 cm.

COLLECTION: Museum of Fine Arts, Boston,
Bequest of W. G. Russell Allen

PUBLISHED: AP 44

10

In the print medium as well as in cartoons,
Villon not only portrayed stylishly dressed
ladies like *La Parisienne* (cat. no. 9), but also
the less respectable women of the Paris
demi-monde.[1] He seems to have been fascinated by the emergence of women into
public life at the beginning of the century.
This interest was undoubtedly stimulated
by the example of Toulouse-Lautrec, whose
influence he acknowledged.[2]

While the woman stares blankly at the
cards which tell her fortune, the little male
dog contributes a degree of anecdotal interest. Villon's early prints of women frequently include a pet, and this same dog is
found again in *Le Potin* (AP 85), an aquatint
of 1905. The woman's awkward posture, as
she leans over the bed, may be attributed to
the artist's effort at diagonal composition.
This composition, the flattened planes of
space, and the irregular silhouette of the
woman all reflect *La Boudeuse* (cat. no. 5)
of the previous year. Bright pink, red, green,
and yellow accentuate the garishness of this
picture of a prostitute in disarray.

J H

[1] Some other examples are *La Cigarette*, AP
30, aquatint, 1901; *Cabaret de nuit*, AP 32,
aquatint, 1902; *La Faute*, AP 64, brush
aquatint, 1904; and one unknown to AP,
Café with Three Young Female Couples,
drypoint, 1904, reproduced in *(75)* Goldschmidt, *Villon*, no. 48.

[2] *(40)* Vallier, *Villon*, p. 116.

11a

JACQUES VILLON

En Visite 1905

Drypoint and color aquatint, AP 68

Location unknown

Courtesy Lucien Goldschmidt, Inc.

11

11

11
Le Cake-Walk des petites filles 1904
Color aquatint and drypoint, Second state
(edition of 30)

30.8 x 42.3 cm.

COLLECTION: Museum of Fine Arts, Boston,
Stephen Bullard Memorial Fund

PUBLISHED: AP 56[II]

Children, usually the artist's young sisters
and their friends, occupy an exceptionally
important place in Villon's repertoire of
subjects. He shows them at play, as in *Sur la
plage, Le Tréport,* 1905 (cat. no. 15), *Sur les
cochons,* 1909 (cat. no. 22) and at home, as
in *Minne étendue dans un fauteuil,* 1907 (fig.
16a). But he often represents them in attitudes which are incongruously adult, as in
En visite, 1905 (fig. 11a) and frequently
highly sexualized as in the "Minne" series
(cat. no. 16) of 1907, and *Les Petites baigneuses,* 1908 (cat. no. 18). This print shows
two little girls doing the 'cake-walk,' a popular dance of the period. The frilly pink
dresses act as a foil, highlighting peculiarly
adult postures and heads, and also a sugges-
tive display of leg which seem inappropriate
in representations of children.

Le Cake-Walk des petites filles may reflect an element of sarcasm about the adult
world as well. The stance of the child at
right relates closely to the female figure in
an illustration Villon made for *Le Courrier
français* the previous year (March 15, 1903,
page 5), showing an immodest young
woman dancing with abandon while her
older male companion stands timidly at her
side. The cartoon (fig. 11b) entitled *Le*

Cake-Walk, has the caption *"Marche du
Gât . . . eux"* which makes a triple play on
words: *"Marche du gâteau"* would literally
translate as "cake-walk"; the adjective *gâ-
teux* means senile; and there may be reference to the verb *gâter* which means to spoil
or taint, suggesting the probable activities
toward which this couple seems to be
marching. The clearly sexual associations of
the theme of the 'cake-walk' in the cartoon
are also present in the depiction of the children in the aquatint.

The first state of this print (in an edition
of ten) is in blue. Auberty and Pérussaux list
only two states (the second in an edition of
30) but Goldschmidt demonstrated the existence of intermediate trials.[1] The decorative,
tapestry-like rectangle in the background of
the later states resembles the flickering pattern of light in the background of *La Chèvre*
of 1908 (AP 152), another print with evident
sexual overtones.

J D F

[1] *(75)* Goldschmidt, *Villon,* nos. 23, 24.

11b
JACQUES VILLON
Le Cake-Walk
Illustration for *Le Courrier français,* 1903
Photogravure
Harvard College Library, Cambridge,
Massachusetts

12

Portrait de Marcel Duchamp 1904

Drypoint and etching

39.2 x 30.1 cm.

COLLECTION: Bibliothèque Nationale, Paris, Cabinet des Estampes

PUBLISHED: AP 62

12

Marcel Duchamp, seventeen years old in 1904, had just come from Rouen to live and share a studio with Villon on the rue Caulaincourt in Montmartre. Villon's influence is evident in both Marcel's quick sketches and etchings during his first years in Paris.[1]

The youngest brother of the artist is portrayed here in an elegant, linear style, typical of Villon's work of this time, which is beginning to be influenced by Helleu. His publisher, Edmund Sagot, had encouraged Villon to work in this fashionable manner. The aura of romanticism and sentimentality is strangely contrary to Duchamp's image of later years. Already apparent in this stylized work, however, is an awareness of the underlying structure of the head. Emphasis is given to the planes and angular outline of Marcel's face, suggesting the reduction of form that Villon will pursue in the future.

S G

[1] (395a) Anne d'Harnoncourt and Kynaston McShine, eds., *Marcel Duchamp* (New York: Museum of Modern Art and Philadelphia Museum of Art, 1973), p. 235.

13
La Partie d'échecs 1904
Drypoint
30.3 x 39.2 cm.
COLLECTION: The Museum of Modern Art,
New York, Purchase
PUBLISHED: AP 65

13

The young figures playing chess are Marcel
and Suzanne Duchamp. *La Partie d'échecs*
was exhibited at the Salon d'Automne of
1904, and a related painting was shown in
the Salon d'Automne of the following year,[1]
indicating Villon's early estimation of the
chess theme so popular with both Villon
and Duchamp. The previous year Villon
had executed the etching and aquatint *La
Partie de jacquet* (fig. no. 13a), showing
Raymond Duchamp-Villon playing back-
gammon, possibly with one of his sisters, or
more likely, with Yvonne Bon. He used almost the same arrangement for the *Partie
d'échecs,* but gave a narrower focus, tighten-
ing the space around the figures.

Marcel Duchamp adopted the subject in
1910 with his painting *La Partie d'échecs,*
depicting Villon and Duchamp-Villon playing chess and their wives drinking tea in
their Puteaux garden. The next year he produced a series of drawings and paintings of
the *Joueurs d'échecs* in a radically different
style, cubism.[2] For Duchamp, the family
fondness for games eventually became a
passion. Villon himself repeated the chess
theme in *Jeu* of 1919 (cat. no. 69) and *Table
d'échecs* of 1920 (AP 203).

Until 1904 Villon had favored color aquatint, but now he began to turn frequently to
drypoint and etching. Trial proofs and the
regular edition of *La Partie d'échecs* contain
small areas of aquatint, but in subsequent
impressions the aquatint areas are replaced
by drypoint.[3] This evolution indicates Villon's renewed interest in black and white,
which he was to pursue in the increasingly
austere prints of the next ten years.

J H

13a
JACQUES VILLON
La Partie de jacquet 1902-1903
Color etching and aquatint, AP 65
The Museum of Modern Art, New York

[1] *(24) Jacques Villon, oeuvre gravé* (Paris:
Galerie Louis Carré, 1954), no. 13, p. 28.

[2] (395a) d'Harnoncourt and McShine,
Duchamp, no. 44, p. 247; nos. 59-65, p. 253-
254.

[3] *(75)* Goldschmidt, *Villon,* no. 29.

14

Lili, ou la femme au chat (caresse) 1905

Drypoint

41 x 33 cm.

COLLECTION: Mrs. Frances W. Kelly, Cambridge, Massachusetts

PUBLISHED: AP 95

This is one of the most successful of a group of drypoints of young women done around 1904 and 1905. Trial proofs of the print in color show Lili seated in an armchair, but in the final state Villon transformed the chair back into the cat.[1] In the same year Villon completed several other prints of women with pets, such as the drypoint *Femme au chien colley,* AP 94 (fig. 14a). The collie appears to have been a Duchamp family pet, seen in a 1912 photograph of the brothers.[2] A 1907 portrait by Marcel Duchamp of his sister-in-law Yvonne (Bon) Duchamp-Villon includes the same dog, partially erased from the canvas (fig. 14b).

Unlike the dog in *Les Cartes* (cat. no. 10), which is used for formal and anecdotal reasons, Lili's cat is a comment on her sensual nature. The word *caresse* in the title is ambiguous. One cannot be sure whether it is an imperative verb, a reference to the cat's movement, or to Lili's stroking of the cat. It might even have been the name of the family cat.

Lili is one of the "elegant" prints Villon made in the manner of the popular artist Helleu. He abandoned the flattened planes of *Les Cartes* and *Le Cake-Walk des petites filles* (cat. nos. 10, 11), in part to please his printer, Edmund Sagot. Always a severe critic of himself, Villon later disavowed this period.[3] Yet in spite of his purposeful imitation of Helleu's sentimental style and subject matter, Villon gave Lili a strong characterization. His incisive handling of the hatching, particularly in the area of the skirt, hints at stylistic developments of the following years.

J H

[1] *(75)* Goldschmidt, *Villon,* nos. 60-62.

[2] *(322) Jacques Villon, Raymond Duchamp-Villon, Marcel Duchamp* (New York: The Solomon R. Guggenheim Museum, 1957), Frontispiece.

[3] " . . . with all those engravings for Sagot, I think I made a mistake. I have even a period I daren't mention, somewhere around 1904-5, when I made elegant engravings in the manner of Helleu which Sagot liked. To think that in my sketchbook I had all that was needed to make some really good stuff . . ." *(40)* Vallier, *Villon,* p. 117.

14

14a

JACQUES VILLON

Femme au chien colley 1905

Drypoint, AP 94

Collection of Mr. and Mrs. James Swan II, Chicago

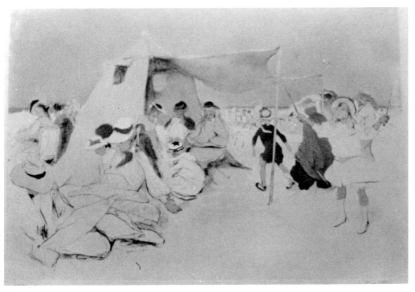

15

14b
MARCEL DUCHAMP

Portrait of Yvonne Duchamp-Villon 1907

Oil on canvas

The Mary Sisler Collection, New York
Courtesy Fourcade Droll, Inc., New York

15

Sur la Plage (Le Tréport) 1905

Aquatint and etching

Signed on the plate at lower left "Jacques Villon"

39.3 x 59.3 cm.

COLLECTION: Bibliothèque Nationale, Paris, Cabinet des Estampes

PUBLISHED: AP 79

We may assume that Villon spent many holidays on the Normandy coast. Although he never produced actual seascapes, he frequently recorded his impressions of people on the beach in 1904-07,[1] and also in 1927-31. His interest in this genre followed the 19th century tradition of beach scenes, exemplified by Boudin, although Villon's interpretations usually focused on single figures or small groups of figures reading, sewing or quietly conversing with less attention paid to the beach itself. *Sur la plage (Le Tréport)*[2] is a combination of some of these individual studies, such as the group of three vacationers under the tent, and the woman sitting in the chair behind the tent.[3] This aquatint may even form a collective image of many years of Duchamp family outings. The large tent resembles one erected in the yard of the family's house at Blanville,[4] and one of the women under the tent flap may possibly be Gabrielle (Gaby) Boeuf, Villon's future wife.[5]

Villon occasionally portrayed human interaction, and even humor, on the beach, as in *La Mer vient à nous, tandis que la montagne . . .* (fig. 15a). However, in *Sur la plage* he has left each figure in the group as psychologically isolated as in the single figure

15a

JACQUES VILLON

La Mer vient à nous, tandis que la montagne 1907

Etching, AP 114

Print Department, Boston Public Library

15b

JACQUES VILLON

Femme sur la plage a la robe bleu 1902-1904

Watercolor

Collection of Mr. and Mrs. Paul Mellon

studies from which they derive. The little girl, absorbed in her game, pays no attention to anyone around her, while the adults concentrate on their own thoughts. Except for the small child running under the flap of the tent, the scene is static and silent.[6]

In *Sur la plage,* Villon not only makes his most complete compositional statement of the beach theme, but he also exploits aquatint with greater technical finesse than in any of the other known 1904-07 seaside scenes, handling it with the soft and airy qualities of watercolor, vividly evoking the atmosphere of the beach. Early in his career, Villon did not use watercolor often, but its appropriateness for the seashore yielded at least two watercolor sketches of women, including *Femme sur la plage à la robe bleu* (fig. 15b). Villon used the medium again to heighten the hats of the women in *Sous la tente, sur la plage,* 1905 (AP 80).

M S S

[1] One of Villon's earliest treatments of this theme, a painting entitled *Sous la tente, sur la plage,* 1904 (reproduced in [40] Vallier, *Villon,* p. 28) was exhibited at the Salon d'Automne of that year. Another, rather caricaturish, sketch was published in *Le Courrier français,* September 4, 1904 (reproduced in [36] Mellquist, *Caricatures,* no. 28).

[2] Le Tréport is a resort town north of Dieppe on the English Channel.

[3] In addition to our figs. 15a and 15b and to the 1904 painting referred to in note 1, the following studies of figures closely resemble those in the Tréport aquatint: *Femme sur la plage à la robe rose* 1902-04, watercolor, coll: Paul Mellon, on loan to National Gallery of Art. *Devant la mer* 1901, lithograph AP 400.

[4] d'Harnoncourt and McShine, *Duchamp,* p. 13. Marcel at age 9.

[5] *(75)* Goldschmidt, *Villon,* no. 44. Goldschmidt identifies the three figures in *Sous la tente, sur la plage* as Gaby, Bouzine, and Felix Barré.

[6] Villon maintains this lack of communication in several later beach scenes (1927-29) depicting figures on the rocks near Cannes: *Sur les rochers* 1927, etching AP 212. *En Vacances sur les roches,* etching 1927, not in AP. *Famille sur la plage de Cannes* 1928, lithograph AP 426. *La Veillée* 1928, oil on canvas, location unknown. *Sous la tente* 1929, oil on canvas (?), location unknown. *Le Paradis* 1929, oil on canvas, private collection, New York.

16

16

Renée à bicyclette 1906

Drypoint and aquatint

40 x 30 cm.

COLLECTION: The Art Institute of Chicago,
Gift of Mr. Frank B. Hubachek

PUBLISHED: AP 107

Renée, the daughter of one of Villon's cousins, posed for a number of his prints from 1906 to 1911. He depicted her in *Renée à bicyclette* and *Renée au canapé* (AP 107 and 111), in the series of thirteen prints listed in AP as *le Bain de Minne* (AP 122-134), and in a later series of portraits (AP 180-183). All of the *Bain de Minne* group show the little girl in seductive attitudes, as in *Minne étendue dans un fauteuil* (AP 122, 1907, fig. 16a).[1] In *Renée à bicyclette*, the combination of innocence and sexuality is particularly effective as the girl stretches to reach the pedals of the bicycle.

J D F

[1] Auberty and Pérussaux do not list this print. Villon appears to have rejected it as a variant on *Minne étendue dans un rocking chair* (AP 122). Villon's interest in subjects with sexual overtones first emerges in his journal illustrations, continues into the prints, most numerous around 1907, and finally trails off as the artist enters his Cubist phase, although it never totally disappears. While female poses similar to *Minne étendue* are frequent in the works of other artists of the period, especially Bonnard, Villon differs from the convention in his depiction of young girls. It has recently been suggested (Museum of Modern Art, June-July 1975, *Jacques Villon*) that the *Minne* titles were developed to illustrate the novel by Colette.

16a

JACQUES VILLON

Minne étendue dans un fauteuil 1907

Etching, not in AP

Private Collection, New York

17

17
L'Aide gracieuse 1907
Etching
19.7 x 14.7 cm.
COLLECTION: Print Department, Boston
Public Library
PUBLISHED: AP 117

This strangely awkward etching — the title may be ironic — marks a profound shift in Villon's graphic work. From 1907 he virtually abandoned the vignettes of fashionable young ladies, soldiers, and townspeople. *L'Aide gracieuse* and two other etchings, *Trois femmes sur l'herbe* (AP 118), and *Les Femmes de Thrace* (AP 119), go further than the series of Minne etchings (cat. no. 16) in eliminating details of physiognomy and in minimizing anecdote.

Similarly, as the influence of Helleu receded and the example of Anders Zorn came under the artist's consideration, elegant and intricate contour also ceased to occupy Villon. Villon told Cleve Gray that Zorn's use of line gave him an impetus to allow the long hatching lines themselves to run over the outlines, disintegrating them and establishing a surface texture enmeshing both figures and background.[1]

By 1907 Villon was working in his new studio in Puteaux next to the sculpture studio of his brother Raymond. Raymond's drawings, often from the same models, show a concern for sober volumetric analysis that parallels and may also have influenced Villon's rejection of the decorative arabesque. *Chanson*, a sculpture by Duchamp-Villon of 1908, shows two seated women clasping hands in a pose distinctly reminiscent of *L'Aide gracieuse* (fig. 17a). Villon himself was to paint a version of this sculpture in 1926.[2]

J H

[1] Cleve Gray in conversation, December, 1974.
[2] The painting is in the Solomon R. Guggenheim Museum, New York.

17a
RAYMOND DUCHAMP-VILLON

Chanson 1909
Wood sculpture
Courtesy of The Art Institute of Chicago

18

L'Éternelle actualité, l'art d'être Grand-père

Illustration for Le Courrier français

September 26, 1907, cover

Photogravure

21.8 x 20.4 cm.

COLLECTION: University of Minnesota Libraries, Minneapolis

PUBLISHED: 36

19

Les Petites baigneuses 1908

Drypoint and softground etching

26.5 x 35.4 cm.

COLLECTION: Mr. and Mrs. Dimitri Sevastopoulo, New York

PUBLISHED: AP 143

In *Les Petites baigneuses* Villon portrays little girls bathing naked in the privacy of the woods. Women in the forest, the subject of other works by Villon (*Trois Femmes sur l'herbe;* 1907, *Les Femmes de Thrace;* 1907, and *Dans la forêt,* 1909) is a theme that was to become important for early Cubism (as in Picasso, Braque, Léger, Le Fauconnier, and Picabia). The figures first appeared in an illustration made for *le Courrier français* (September 26, 1907) entitled *"L'Art d'être grand-père; l'éternelle actualité"* ("The Art of being a grandfather; the eternal present"). In the *Courrier* engraving, Villon shows the same three nude girls before an older man. Two of the figures in the etching are reverses of the two foreground figures in the illustration, while the right hand figure, seen from behind in the etching, is posed as the child between her grandfather's knees in the *Courrier* illustration. The middle figure is in turn taken from a Villon print of 1907, *Minne jouant avec un chien dans un panier,* AP 124, (fig. 18a).

The entire composition in the journal is surrounded by a circular wreath of leaves, and this — like the dedication "à Belleville" — remains unexplained: however, these three images suggest the frequent and complex interrelationship between Villon's early fine art prints and his popular illustrations.

J D F

18a

JACQUES VILLON

Minne jouant avec un chien dans un panier 1907

Location unknown

Courtesy Lucien Goldschmidt, Inc.

18

19

20

20

Les Haleurs 1908

Oil on canvas

Signed lower left "Jacques Villon 08"

65 x 92 cm.

PROVENANCE: Jacques Villon; Louis Carré
et Cie, Paris; E. V. Thaw and Co., New York;
Margaret McLennan Morse, Santa Barbara

COLLECTION: The Twenty-Four Collection,
Miami, Florida

PUBLISHED: 27, 32, 34, 40, 117, 233, 342;
Important Impressionist and Modern Paint-
ings, Drawings, Sculpture, New York:
Parke-Bernet Galleries, Inc., November 20,
1968

EXHIBITED: *15, 18, 38, 49, 92, 367*

Derived from a 1907 aquatint (AP 120)
inspired by a group of workers observed
along the banks of the Seine, *Les Haleurs*
marks a shift in Villon's style. Earlier, his
painting had treated subjects either in a late
impressionist or *intimiste* manner. In *Les
Haleurs,* however, the artist developed more
abstract concerns for formal problems of
tension, direction, and movement. "In
1908," Villon said, "I was relying on quick
sketches for my painting. What was then
capturing my attention was the inner line
of a movement — and that enabled me to
find, as for instance in *Les Haleurs,* a synthesis of movement."[1]

This search for a synthesis of movement,
form and subject, may be indebted to the
great Cézanne retrospective exhibition of
1907. In *Les Haleurs* Villon approaches
Cézanne's use of constructive brush-work
in order to establish contrasting directional
forces on the painted surface. This emphasis on the brushstroke becomes increasingly important in Villon's work of 1908-10
(see cat. no. 21) and is the first indication of
his later preoccupation with structure and
geometry in painting.

Les Haleurs is also an important step in
the development of Villon's subject matter.
The theme of figures in active tension —
workers or athletes — is one to which the
artist frequently returns. Indeed *Les Haleurs*
itself provides the source for several later
works (figs. 20a and 20b and a lithograph
of 1931, AP 431).

A M

1 (40) Vallier, *Villon,* p. 119.

20a

JACQUES VILLON

Les Haleurs c. 1929-1930

Oil on canvas

Location unknown

Photo from the archives of the late Mrs.
J. C. Guggenheimer

20b

JACQUES VILLON

Les Haleurs 1930

Etching, AP 222

Print Department, Boston Public Library

21

21

Mon portrait 1909

Oil on canvas

Signed on the right "Jacques Villon"

21 x 15 cm.

PROVENANCE: Pearl C. Holbein, New York

COLLECTION: Gerson Nordlinger, Jr.,
Washington, D.C.

PUBLISHED: *American, French and other
Modern Paintings and Drawings,* New
York: Parke-Bernet Galleries, Inc., December 1, 1967

Villon's portraits of himself, his family, and
his friends are his most intimate paintings,
and perhaps because of the freedom he felt
in this genre he often experimented with
new stylistic concepts in portraiture. Three
self-portraits capture the moment of transition to the constructive mood of 1909-1914.
The more naturalistic representation of
1908 (fig. 21a) has the brick-like brush
strokes which Villon discovered in neo-
impressionism, but like Matisse, Metzinger,
and Delaunay, Villon used the stroke not
chiefly to achieve optical color mixture but
rather to emphasize pictorial structure.

The somber-toned 1909 *Portrait de
l'artiste* (fig. 21b) shows virtually the same
view, but there is greater expression of both
emotion and the internal structure of the
face rendered in broader, irregular brush-
work. *Mon Portrait* (cat. no. 21) is another
closely related and still looser self-portrait,
where the description of the chin and beard
is very close to the 1924 *Portrait of the
Artist's Father* (fig. 21c).

J D F

21a

JACQUES VILLON

Portrait de l'artiste 1908

Oil on canvas

Location unknown

Reproduced from (40) Dora Vallier, *Jacques Villon:* Oeuvres de 1897 à 1956 (Paris: Editions Cahiers d'Art, 1957)

21b

JACQUES VILLON

Portrait de l'artiste 1909

Oil on canvas

Collection of Mrs. Bertram Smith, New York

21c

JACQUES VILLON

Portrait du père de l'artiste 1924

Oil on canvas

The Solomon R. Guggenheim Museum, New York

22

Sur les cochons 1909

Aquatint, intermediate state in black
and white

39.2 x 30.5 cm.

COLLECTION: Print Department, Boston
Public Library

PUBLISHED: AP 159

22

Villon brought a number of children's toys
— merry-go-rounds, wooden horses, and
airplanes — into his studio, using them as
models or sometimes even as subjects.[1] In
this etching, Villon shows a child riding a
pig on a merry-go-round.[2] Like Delaunay,
he was fascinated with such subjects. Earlier, in his 1904 *Manège rue Caulaincourt*
(AP 54), he showed children on wooden
horses; he returned to the theme in the
Petit manège of 1905 (AP 77); in *Manège
des cochons* of 1907 (AP 113); and in later
works.

In *Sur les cochons* (cat. no. 22), powerful contrasts between flat areas of varying
intensity develop a sense of drama and
movement, while the strong parallel strokes
— a major feature of Villon's later graphic
style — transform the representational aspects of this print into a pattern of light and
dark abstract planes. Villon heightened
both effects in the second state and further
reduces the image into simple planes, an-
ticipating his 1911 cubist works.

J D F

[1] Dora Vallier, *l'Intelligence de Jacques
Villon* (Paris: *Cahiers d'Art*, 1957), p. 116.

[2] In French carousels, children often ride
wooden pigs rather than horses.

23

Nu debout, bras en l'air 1909

Drypoint

55 x 41.6 cm.

COLLECTION: Museum of Fine Arts, Boston,
Lee M. Friedman Fund

PUBLISHED: AP 163

24

Femme debout, de dos (nue) 1910

Etching

31.8 x 19.3 cm.

COLLECTION: R. S. Johnson-International
Gallery, Chicago

PUBLISHED: AP 166

23

24

In *Nu debout, bras en l'air* Villon carried volumetric analysis so far that it verged on distortion of the twisting, reaching figure. The same tendency is evident in the etching *Dans la forêt* (AP 162) of the same year. Rigorous use of hatched lines shading the legs and torso explores value gradations through slight variations in the width and spacing of lines that extend beyond the contour.

Young Man and Girl in Spring of 1911 by Marcel Duchamp (fig. 23a) used figure types very similar to the *Nu debout*. Perhaps both artists worked from the same model in the Puteaux studio; or, Villon's etching may have served as a source for his brother's painting.

In the *Femme debout, de dos (nue)* of the next year, the model may have been the girl Renée, subject of the *Minne* prints and the busts *Renée de face* and *Renée de trois-quarts* (cat. nos. 16, 25, 26). The attenuated limbs of the earlier figure are now filled out, and the subject treated with monumentality. While sharp contrasts of light and dark define the forms sculpturally, they are distributed in such a way as to establish an ample and complex rhythm. This rhythm is seen also in *La Table servie* of 1912-1913 (see cat. nos. 42-48). The *Femme debout*

contains the germ of what was to become Villon's mature drawing method based on encircling highlights and shading beneath them.

Etching, with its limits of calligraphic possibilities and all the technical precision it requires, was a boon to Villon. From 1907 to 1914 he responded to the exacting nature of the medium with increasing discipline, and was rewarded by an increasing range of expression and power.

J H

23a
MARCEL DUCHAMP
Young Man and Girl in Spring 1911
Oil on canvas
Galería Arturo Schwarz, Milan

25

Renée de face 1911

Drypoint

54.5 x 41.5 cm.

COLLECTION: Print Department, Boston
Public Library

PUBLISHED: AP 180

26

Renée de trois-quarts 1911

Drypoint

56 x 41 cm.

COLLECTION: Lucien Goldschmidt, Inc.,
New York

PUBLISHED: AP 181

27

Renée de trois-quarts 1911

Oil on canvas

Signed lower right "Jacques Villon"

60.5 x 49.5 cm.

PROVENANCE: Gift of Jacques Villon

COLLECTION: Galerie Camille Renault, Paris

EXHIBITED: 56

In 1911 Villon made four prints of the bust
of Renée. They represent a high point in his
sculptural treatment of the human figure.
The two large drypoints exhibited here
achieve intense presence. Villon never finished the shoulders of *Renée de face,* but
developed the same theme more fully in the
smaller format of *Renée de face (petite
planche)* (AP 182).[1] He restated the three-
quarter view in the small *Petite mulatresse*
(AP 183), and in the 1911 painting *Renée de
trois-quarts* (cat. no. 27).

Four years earlier, Renée as a young girl
had been the subject of the *Minne* etchings
(see cat. no. 16, fig. 16a). In that group and
in the works that followed, such as *L'Aide
gracieuse* (cat. no. 17) and the *Nu debout,
bras en l'air* (cat. no. 23), Villon began his
volumetric approach to form. Gradually the
elegant, fragile line of his earliest works
gave way to the power and immediacy of
sculptural mass, and delicate color gradua-
tions gave way to angular black hatching.
This sculptural style developed simultaneously in Villon's painting, as may be seen
from an oil portrait of Renée of 1908-1909,[2]
as well as the self portraits (see cat. no. 21,
figs. 21a and 21b).

The drypoint version of *Renée de trois-
quarts* is remarkable for the consistent way
in which hatching lines defining the body
extend into the surrounding field. The space
around the figure is not atmospheric, nor is
it rationally structured as it was to be in
Villon's later work; yet this treatment, a
development of a tendency first evident in
L'Aide gracieuse (cat. no. 17), is another
sign of change in his conception of space.

J H

[1] *(75)* Reproduced in Goldschmidt, *Villon,*
no. 103.

[2] The *Portrait de jeune fille,* reproduced in
(40) Vallier, *Villon,* p. 37.

25

26

27

28
Duchamp-Villon 1911
Pencil drawing on white paper
Signed lower right 'Duchamp-Villon par
Jacques Villon 11"
25.8 x 16.8 cm.
PROVENANCE: Jacques Villon
COLLECTION: Louis Carré et Cie, Paris
PUBLISHED: 446
EXHIBITED: 60; 1964, Cassel, *Documenta III*

28

At the time Jacques Villon made these portraits, his brother Raymond was reaching the height of his artistic powers. The painting (cat. no. 29) relates not only to the drawing of Raymond by Villon (cat. no. 28) but also to Raymond's own sculptured head of Baudelaire of the same year (see fig. 70a); which contains elements of a self-portrait. Villon, now applying geometric principles which he found in Leonardo da Vinci's *Trattato della Pittura,* breaks up surfaces into rectangular planes and reinforces the architectural solidity of the forms.

Theories in Leonardo's book are open to different interpretations, and Villon does not claim to have understood them fully; but the *Trattato* strengthened Villon's interest in using geometric construction in his treatment of subject matter. This tendency was already becoming evident in his work, and it was now also reinforced by his contact, beginning in 1911, with other cubist artists. Discussing his reading of Leonardo around 1911, Villon mentioned the emphasis placed on the "golden section."[1] Although the golden section itself does not appear in the *Trattato,* much of the theory ascribed to Leonardo was known through the writings of Luca Pacioli, who, by the end of the 15th century, had interpreted Leonardo's writings with great emphasis on the golden section.[2] Furthermore, the translation Villon read was by the occult artist Josephin Péladan,[3] a founder of the Salon de la Rose-Croix, who attached great mystical significance to the golden proportion and to other geometric configurations.

Villon seems to have drawn encouragement from all of this literature for his application of geometry to painting and for the idea that abstraction in art should develop from the analysis of nature. Yet, if Leonardo had a theoretical interest for Villon, his technical evolution nevertheless proceeded

29

Portrait de Raymond Duchamp-Villon 1911

Oil on wood panel

Inscribed and dated lower left "Portrait de
R. Duchamp-Villon 1911"; signed lower
right "Jacques Villon"; signed and dated on
the back of the panel

35 x 26.5 cm.

PROVENANCE: Gift of Jacques Villon

COLLECTION: Centre National d'Art et de
Culture Georges Pompidou, Musée National
d'Art Moderne, Paris

PUBLISHED: 27, 28, 32, 34, 40, 91, 130, 342,
401, 413, 437, 439

EXHIBITED: 15, 26, 34, 38, 45, 47, 49, 55, 208,
220, 252, 322, 348, 379, 409, 433, 447, 459,
463, 494, 497

29

in a pragmatic fashion. The description of
the volumes in Raymond's face follows the
method developed in the etched portraits of
Renée, circumscribing the highlights into
simple abstract areas. It was typical of
Villon to emphasize dramatic lighting first
in etching, before committing himself to it
in painting.

J D F

1 (40) Vallier, *Villon*, p. 62. Vallier quotes
Villon: "J'ai lu le *Traité de le Peinture* de
Léonard, et j'ai vu l'importance qu'il don-
nait à la section d'or. Mais c'est surtout en
parlant que nous avons arrêté nos idées,
sans trop nous encombrer de science." Mentioned again on page 81. (See also footnote
2, cat. no. 143, herein. -Ed.)

2 Leonardo's treatise was never completed by
the artist but assembled later from notes
and first published in 1651. Pacioli wrote *La
Divina Proporzione*, Venice, 1509; and
Summa de Arithmetica, Venice, 1494.

3 Leonardo da Vinci, *Traité de la peinture*, tr.
Josephin Péladan, Paris, 1910.

30

30

Service de café 1911

Porcelain ceramic, 5 pieces (hot water pot, creamer, sugar bowl, coffee cup and saucer)

PROVENANCE: Gift of Jacques Villon

COLLECTION: Mme Anne-Françoise Mare-Vène, Paris

PUBLISHED: 200, 236, 274, 421

EXHIBITED: *99, 101*

Villon's contribution to the decorative arts exhibition known as the "Maison Cubiste" was a porcelain coffee service for six. The "Maison Cubiste" was a collaborative attempt of artists, decorators, and designers to raise the status of the decorative arts and to relate them to advanced art. Raymond Duchamp-Villon and André Mare were the key figures in the inception and planning of the "Maison," and many artists of the Puteaux or Right Bank cubist group, including all three Duchamp brothers, participated in this effort which took place at the 1912 Salon d'Automne. The center of attraction was the living room, complete with furniture, rugs, curtains, artworks, and a table laid with Villon's coffee service. Duchamp-Villon designed the rooms themselves and a façade for the building which housed them, the first story of which was exhibited. The name "Maison Cubiste" was suggested by the planes of the façade, and by the fact that the collaborators who aimed to reconcile decorative art with their own newly emerged styles, were identified as cubists by the public.

Villon's service includes a coffee pot, hot water pot (fig. 30a), a sugar bowl (fig. 30b), and creamer, and six cups and saucers. The decorative motif is a running deer, a theme which the artist first explored in a 1901 engraving, and which later appeared in a drawing, *Les Daims surpris* (cat. no. 31) and a 1914 etching of the same name (AP 200). The cups and sugar bowl are painted with these whimsical animals, and the coffee pot is actually in the shape of a deer, the spout being its long neck, and the handle its tail. The service is done in orange and purple. The bright colors and animal designs may indicate Villon's awareness of the contemporary German expressionist group, especially the work of Franz Marc, which may have been brought to his attention by Robert Delaunay, who was identified with both the Blaue Reiter and Passy groups.

Once before Villon had ventured into ceramic work, executing a tea service and a set of plates in 1904.

S G

30a

JACQUES VILLON

Hot Water Pot 1911

Porcelain ceramic

Collection of Mme Anne-Françoise Mare-Vène, Paris

30b

JACQUES VILLON

Sugar Bowl 1911

Porcelain ceramic

Collection of Mme Anne-Françoise Mare-Vène, Paris

31

Les Daims surpris 1913

Pencil drawing on tracing paper

Signed and dated lower right "Jacques Villon 13"

20.3 x 16.4 cm.

PROVENANCE: Jacques Villon

COLLECTION: Louis Carré et Cie, Paris

EXHIBITED: *55, 433*

31

32

Étude pour Puteaux (No. 1) 1912

Oil on canvas

Signed upper right "Jacques Villon"

38.1 x 53.5 cm.

PROVENANCE: Miss L. Parsons
Private Collection, New York

PUBLISHED: 386

EXHIBITED: *103, 429*

33

Puteaux: Les Fumées et les arbres
en fleur 1912

Oil on canvas

Signed and dated lower left
"Jacques Villon"

114.9 x 147.9 cm.

PROVENANCE: Arthur B. Davies, New York;
Duncan Chandler, Litchfield, Connecticut

COLLECTION: Mr. and Mrs. Dan R.
Johnson, New York

PUBLISHED: 86, 386

EXHIBITED: *102, 103, 322, 336, 429, 461*

32

Around 1910, Jacques Villon ceased to work for the illustrated journals and began, for the first time, it seems, to regard himself as a serious avant-garde artist. His paintings increased in number and grew more ambitious. The years 1911-1913 were particularly significant for the varied experiments that characterized his transition to cubism. *Puteaux: Les Fumées et les arbres en fleur,* one of the rare landscapes before 1934 and also one of the largest paintings in his oeuvre, was executed in 1912, in the distinct cubist vernacular of Villon's circle. Its monumentality, advanced style, and its important contributions to our understanding of Villon's creative method make it a key painting from this period.

A large blue and pink figure lies across the foreground with head and back near the left edge of the canvas (see fig. 33a). Villon outlines the figure with the kind of free black line which, in his *Table servie* of 1912, he described as *le vol d'une mouche* (the flight of a fly).[1] This summary of the figure also resembles the linear forms derived by Villon's neighbor Kupka from analysis of the trajectory of a bouncing ball, developed in Kupka's 1912 *Amorpha: Fugue in two colors* exhibited in the 1912 Salon d'Automne (fig. 33b).

Horizontal tiers of houses in the village of Puteaux occupy the background of *Puteaux: Les Fumées et les arbres en fleur,* along with verdant trees and what appears to be a large black factory chimney, emitting a transparent cloud of smoke, in the middle of the painting. To the left of the central chimney is what may be another industrial smoke stack, and further to the left are more houses. Wisps of white cloud float at the top left. The superimposed layering of planes in this landscape anticipates Villon's 'constructive decomposition' of the years following the First World War. The overall rhythmic movement of geometric forms — suddenly so abundant here — is characteristic of Villon's subsequent style and may relate to Futurist works such as Boccioni's *Stati d'Animo* (shown in Paris in February 1912). The radiant waves of energy and especially the treatment of the fluffy white clouds over Puteaux seem to have a particularly close affinity with the Boccioni; on the other hand, the interweaving of organic and geometric shapes (smoke and clouds played off against figures and landscape) appears earlier in the works of Léger, as well as Gleizes, de la Fresnaye, and Delaunay.

By this time, the monumental nude in a

landscape was already well established in Right Bank cubist tradition. Perhaps inspired by Cézanne's *Bathers,* the theme occurred frequently after 1910 in such cubist paintings as Le Fauconnier's *L'Abondance* (1910), Delaunay's *La Ville de Paris* (1910-1912), and Gleizes' *Bathers* (1912). Derain had employed the theme earlier in his 1908 *Bathers;* Matisse's large figure compositions of 1907-1910, though not cubist, presented several figural and spatial ideas that may have influenced the cubists. Villon doubtless knew these pictures, but in *Puteaux: Les Fumées et les arbres en fleur* a reference to the great masters — to Titian and Giorgione in particular — is not only unmistakable but consistent with his study of Leonardo. Jacques Villon was a cautious artist, and at this moment, as he takes a bold step toward the forefront of cubism, he simultaneously looks back — like Delaunay — to Renaissance prototypes. The contrast of the grand tradition -- the Venetian nude or the Baroque *fête champêtre* — against an anecdotal suburban setting imbues this picture with a kind of tension that recalls Seurat and Manet as well as the more contemporary cubist compositions. In addition, Villon's *Puteaux* has the languid feeling of Manet's *Olympia*, as the figure seems to

33

rest casually in the shade of a tree on a Sunday afternoon.

The carefully-drawn study which Villon made after Manet's *Olympia* during this same year of 1912 (fig. 33c) is evidence of Villon's interest in Manet at this time. The drawing has many lightly sketched-in geometric forms which resemble the shapes in *Puteaux: Les Fumées et les arbres en fleur*. Several specific correspondences seem to exist. The half blue, half green loop in the lower center of the painting, for example, relates to the fold of the sheet which hangs over the edge of the bed from the figure's mid-thigh to heel in Villon's sketch. The black crescent behind the head in the landscape finds its parallel in a lightly-indicated shadow across the pillow behind the Olympia's neck. The triangular glimpse of the mattress in the lower left of the drawing, the angle of the curtain in the upper left, and the long verticals in the background behind the Olympia's legs may also have counterparts in *Puteaux*. The configuration in the lower right of the canvas may even suggest a cat. The position of the head in the painting, however, differs from that in the study after Manet, as do other features of the composition. Irrespective of the connections which may exist, it is not suggested here that Villon made the drawing as preparatory to the painting.[2]

Four preparatory studies for *Puteaux* were exhibited in the Armory Show of 1913: one is in the Walter Arensberg Collection (fig. 33d) at the Philadelphia Museum, a second is exhibited here, and the third is in a private collection in Maine (fig. 33e). We know that the study was sold in 1913; however its location is now unknown. Each seems to focus more naturalistically on a smaller section of the final conception, but the exact inter-relationship is difficult to discern.

J D F

[1] Francis Steegmuller, unpublished manuscript of questions put to Jacques Villon, question 18. July 1954.
[2] See also his later print after the *Olympia* (AP 514) of 1926.

33c

JACQUES VILLON
Drawing after Olympia (by Edouard Manet) 1912
Private collection, London

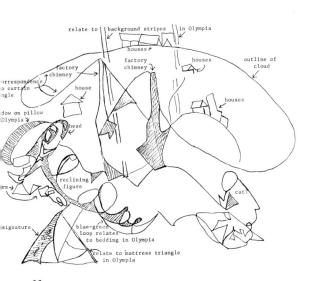

33a

Diagram of **Puteaux: Les Fumées et les arbres en fleur** by Jonathan D. Fineberg

33b

FRANTIŠEK KUPKA

Amorpha: Fugue in Two Colors 1912

Oil on canvas

Narodni Gallery, Prague

33d

JACQUES VILLON

Étude pour Puteaux (No. 2) 1912

Oil on canvas

Philadelphia Museum of Art,
Arensberg Collection

33e

JACQUES VILLON

Étude pour Puteaux (No. 3) 1912

Oil on canvas

Collection of John Laurent, York, Maine

34

Fillette au piano 1912
Oil on canvas (oval)
Signed lower left "Jacques Villon"
129.5 x 96.5 cm.
PROVENANCE: John Quinn, New York
COLLECTION: Mrs. George Acheson,
New York
PUBLISHED: 386, 392, 417, 427, 438
EXHIBITED: 102, 103, 138, 181, 311, 343,
461, 482

Fillette au piano, the earliest of three oval
canvases (see cat. no. 64, fig. 40a) executed
in 1912-1914, is one of the most beautiful
and sensitive of the artist's cubist works.
The oval format is traditional in French portraiture, particularly of the 18th century.
The shape was revived for the cubist idiom
by Braque, Picasso and Mondrian out of
compositional necessity; Villon reasserted
its traditional function for portraits.

Fillette au piano is a portrait of Villon's
youngest sister, Magdeleine Duchamp. It is
similar to an earlier print, *Jeune fille au
piano,* 1908 (fig. 34a), and the pose appears
to be related to the left central figure in
Marcel Duchamp's painting, *Sonata,* 1911,[1]
which depicts the three Duchamp sisters
and their mother.

Formally, the *Fillette au piano* sums up
the artist's concerns of the previous year,
1911, and goes even further in developing a
curvilinear geometry from a language associated among most of the cubists with
more exclusively rectilinear elements. It is
close in both rhythm and mood to *Puteaux:
Les Fumées et les arbres en fleur* (cat. no.
33) and *La Table servie* (see cat. nos. 42-48).

The painting is tightly composed, and the
curves, harmoniously dispersed throughout
the composition, confirm and repeat the
oval edge of the canvas. These fluid movements are in counterpoint with the more
angular shapes of the background which
conform to an implied grid of vertical, horizontal and diagonal elements.

A M

[1] Reproduced in (395a) d'Harnoncourt and
McShine, *Duchamp,* no. 57, p. 252.

34

34a
JACQUES VILLON
Jeune fille au piano 1908
Drypoint, AP 144
Print Department, Boston Public Library

35

35a
JACQUES VILLON
Portrait de jeune femme 1913
Drypoint, AP 193
Courtesy The Museum of Fine Arts, Boston

35
Étude pour Jeune femme 1912
Oil on canvas
Signed right center "Jacques Villon"
61 x 50.8 cm.
PROVENANCE: John Quinn, New York;
Howard L. Gray, Bryn Mawr, Pennsylvania
COLLECTION: Mr. and Mrs. Alister
Cameron, Cincinnati
PUBLISHED: *386, 438*
EXHIBITED: *103, 138, 314, 408, 429, 455*

All of Villon's cubist portraits began from
relatively naturalistic studies and moved
toward abstraction. The small oil *Étude
pour Jeune femme,* 1912 (cat. no. 35), is
from an early phase in the process, where
the pose and details of dress are described.
The chair also used in the 1912 portrait of
the artist's father, *Homme lisant son journal*
(fig. 38a) is still recognizable in *Jeune
femme,* 1912, seen here (cat. no. 36). The
1913 print after the first painting (fig. 35a)
shows further decomposition of the forms
into cubist facet planes, but in the second
1912 painting *Jeune femme* (cat. no. 36)
Villon employed a more radical formula: he
determined the location and shape of the
forms by a compositional scheme based on
geometry, forcing observations of reality to
conform. He also repeats shapes — like the
curve of the figure's back and seat — creating a kinetic effect similar to Marcel's *Nude
Descending the Staircase* done in 1911 and
1912. The 1913 *Portrait de Mlle Y.D.* (cat.
no. 37) emerges out of the 1913 *Femme
assise* (not illustrated) and the closely related etching of the same year, *Yvonne D.
de profil* (fig. 36a). Another small oil, called
Étude pour portrait de Y.D. (not illustrated)
and a wood engraving *Jeune fille de profil*

36

Jeune femme (Jeune fille) 1912

Oil on canvas

Signed right center "Jacques Villon"

146 x 114 cm.

PROVENANCE: Arthur Jerome Eddy, Chicago; Louise and Walter Arensberg, Hollywood, California

COLLECTION: Philadelphia Museum of Art, The Louise and Walter Arensberg Collection

PUBLISHED 201, 203, 379, 386, 405, 413

EXHIBITED: 29, 102, 103, 129, 146, 199, 322, 336, 396, 491

37

Portrait de Mlle Y.D. 1913

Oil on canvas

Signed lower right "Jacques Villon"

120 x 88.9 cm.

PROVENANCE: John Quinn, New York; Leo Bing, Los Angeles

COLLECTION: Los Angeles County Museum of Art, Gift of Anna Bing Arnold

PUBLISHED: 285, 392, 438

EXHIBITED: 113, 286, 297, 317, 385, 461, 482

36

(fig. 37a) of 1913 also belong to this development. But the 1913 *Portrait de Mlle Y.D.* is in its way the definitive version. Villon achieved its shallow space and contained pose without resorting to the Futurist-like repetitions of the *Jeune femme* or the description in the *Yvonne D. de profil* etching (fig. 36a). The whole composition is constructed out of small volumetric pyramids like those Villon described having read about in the writings of Leonardo. The result is an image of crystalline monumentality, and the observed forward movement of the first study (cat. no. 35) is contained as potential, rather than described, energy.

In all these portraits, particularly rich in color, the artist's sister Yvonne Duchamp served as the model. She also sat for the highly abstract oval *Tête de femme* (cat. no. 63) which relates to this series.

J D F

36a
JACQUES VILLON
Yvonne D. de profil 1913
Drypoint, AP 194
Print Department, Boston Public Library

37

37a
JACQUES VILLON
Jeune fille de profil 1913
Wood engraving, AP 454
Print Department, Boston Public Library

38

39

38b

JACQUES VILLON

Homme lisant 1926

Oil on canvas

Location unknown

Reproduced from Finarte-Ketterer Sales
Catalogue No. 21023, 1962

38a

JACQUES VILLON

Homme lisant son journal 1912

Oil on canvas

Collection of Jean Bauret, Paris

38

Portrait du père de l'artiste 1912

Charcoal drawing on laid white paper

Signed and dated lower right "Jacques Villon 12"

62.5 x 47.5 cm.

PROVENANCE: Louis Carré et Cie, Paris

COLLECTION: The St. Louis Art Museum: Gift of The Measuregraph Company and Mr. and Mrs. George S. Rosborough, Jr.

PUBLISHED: 284

39

Portrait du père de l'artiste 1913

Oil on canvas

Signed and dated upper right "Jacques Villon 13"

61 x 50 cm.

PROVENANCE: Duchamp-Duvernoy Collection

COLLECTION: Musée des Beaux-Arts, Rouen,

PUBLISHED: Catalogue to exhibition no. 459 (not in exhibition)

EXHIBITED: 15

40

M.D. lisant 1913

Etching and drypoint

40 x 30 cm.

PROVENANCE: Peter Deitsch Gallery, New York

COLLECTION: Samuel and Dorothy Glaser, Newton, Massachusetts

PUBLISHED: AP 198

41

Portrait de E.D. 1913

Etching and drypoint

23.5 x 16 cm.

COLLECTION: The Museum of Fine Arts, Boston, Gift of Peter A. Wick

PUBLISHED: AP 191

Jacques Villon made many portraits of his father beginning with his etching of 1891 (see cat. no. 1) and ending with the 1929 *Homme lisant* (AP 219) etching after Justin-Isidore Duchamp's death in 1925. Marcel Duchamp also did an important portrait of their father in 1910 (see Marcel Duchamp, Philadelphia Museum of Art, 1973, cat. no. 35, p. 243). *Portrait du père de l'artiste,* the naturalistic drawing of 1912 (cat. no. 38), which exists in several versions and at least one facsimile, uses the now familiar parallel hatching and shows Duchamp *père* with the same stern expression as in the 1891 print. The pose resembles the 1912 painting *Homme lisant son journal* (fig. 38a),[3] but has an even closer affinity in both composition and style with the 1913 *Portrait du père de l'artiste* (cat. no. 39) for which it certainly served as a study.

The close compositional relationship of the 1912 drawing to the abstract *Homme lisant* of 1926 (fig. 38b) and to the 1929 *Homme lisant* etching (AP 219) demonstrates that these works of the 1920s also represent Villon's father. The shapes in the 1926 painting move in the same direction as in the earlier drawing: the white center of the canvas corresponds to the newspaper in M. Duchamp's lap. In the 1926 abstraction, the three pointed shadows (behind the head in the drawing) are exaggerated; the volumes of figure and face are transformed into thin planes. A round hole and a straight shadow line are all that remain of the eye and nose. As Villon said to Dora Vallier in the fifties, "my starting point is in nature, but I don't feel the need of sticking to nature."[4] The 1926 painting *Homme lisant,* done fourteen years after the original drawings which also provided the basis for the *M.D. lisant* print (cat. no. 40) and the oval shaped oil painting, *Portrait d'homme* (fig. 40a), demonstrates the truth of his comment.

The 1913 *Portrait de E.D.* (cat. no. 41) etching (Villon's father was sometimes called Eugène) is remarkable for its exquisite execution and relates formally to the highly geometricized 1924 *Portrait du père de l'artiste* (fig. 21c). Villon's interest in developing the overall surface texture out of dark and light patches of parallel lines yields a complex tapestry of small planes from which the stony profile emerges. In this way, Villon simultaneously divides and constructs the total composition of his prints, while in his paintings color is used to articulate the facet-like areas (see *Portrait de Mlle Y.D.,* 1913, cat. no. 37). Through the great variety of parallel striations, a rich coloristic effect is created in black and white. By imitating the parallel cross-hatchings as well as the dramatic highlighting that had already begun to appear regularly in his graphic work by 1911, the artist had established a fresh approach to color in cubism, one which was to continue to evolve for the rest of his career.

Even more than in the *Portrait de E.D.,* the structural organization of the 1913 oval *Portrait d'homme* and the related drypoint *M.D. lisant* takes precedence over — indeed, nearly submerges — the subject. The intense parallelism of the striations in the etching give it a veneer of deliberate non-involvement reinforced by the large crystalline planes, which dominate both compositions, and cut into one another from all angles as this interpenetration converges precisely in the middle of the picture. Occasionally the rounded forms of the sitter emerge from beneath the machinery of the style, and M. Duchamp's subdued presence, so described in the 1912 drawing (cat. no. 38), creates a distinctly cubist tension between subject and formal dynamics. The central clustering of planes, particularly insistent in the painted version, anticipates later works such as *Repliement* of 1921 (cat. no. 84): as in *Repliement* (and other paintings of the 1920s) there is total surface covering. In *Repliement,* the artist created the overall surface with a veil of deep red pigment; in the 1913 *M.D. lisant* he used the familiar screen of parallel hatchings over the whole; but in the 1913 *Portrait,* he required the oval. More and more frequently Villon covered the forms in his prints with his gossamer web of lines, but it was not until the postwar period that he consistently found a method to produce its coloristic equivalent in painting.

J D F

1 Of course the conception of even later works, like *Le Philosophe,* 1930 (cat. no. 106), may have originated in portraits of the artist's father. See especially the single eye as treated in the 1926 *Homme lisant* (fig. 38b).

2 *M. Duchamp,* pencil on paper, signed with an inscription added later but undated (22.2 x 16.5 cm.), private collection, New York; *M. Duchamp,* charcoal on white paper, signed and dated 1912, R. Jullian, Paris. *M.D. lisant* (cat. no. 40) was identified as Marcel Duchamp in *(60),* Cassou, Frigerio, and Wick, *Villon,* no. 55, p. 48; and *(77a) Jacques Villon,* Musée des Beaux-Arts de Rouen, Grand Palais (Paris, 1975), no. 47. The source, however, is clearly M(onsieur) Duchamp *père,* although a certain fusion of the character of the father and the features of the youngest son is not to be ruled out.

3 In style, *Homme lisant son journal* resembles the group of seated representations of Yvonne (see cat. nos. 35-37). In the upper right hand corner (above and behind the sitter's head) is a small face in grisaille — a picture, or possibly a reflection of the artist in a mirror. As in the 1898 *Le Courrier français* illustration, where Villon deliberately alluded to Raymond, the second face in this painting seems to be another reference intended primarily for the enjoyment of the artist's family and close friends.

4 (40) Vallier, *Villon,* p. 114.

40

41

40a

JACQUES VILLON

Portrait d'homme 1913

Oil on canvas (oval)

Collection of Mr. and Mrs. David Howald
Shawan, Columbus

42

43

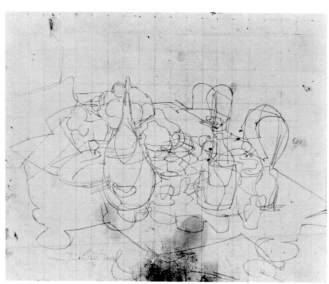

44

42
La Table servie 1912
Drawing in pencil and grey wash
Signed and dated lower left "Jacques
Villon 12"

34 x 49.5 cm.
PROVENANCE: Lucien Goldschmidt, Inc.,
New York
COLLECTION: The Art Institute of Chicago,
Gift of Mr. Frank B. Hubachek
PUBLISHED: 40, 342
EXHIBITED: *55, 72*

43
La Table servie 1912
Pencil drawing
Signed and dated lower left "Jacques
Villon 12"

29 x 42.5 cm.
PROVENANCE: Jacques Villon
COLLECTION: Louis Carré et Cie, Paris
PUBLISHED: 40, 342

45

45a

JACQUES VILLON

La Table servie 1912

Drawing, squared

Location unknown

Reproduced from (40) Vallier, *Jacques Villon*

44

La Table servie 1912-1913

Pencil drawing, squared

Signed lower left "Jacques Villon, croquis pour La Table Servie"

34 x 49 cm.

PROVENANCE: Jacques Villon; Louis Carré et Cie, Paris; Lucien Goldschmidt, Inc., New York

COLLECTION: The Metropolitan Museum of Art, Robert Lehman Collection, 1975

PUBLISHED: 40, 342

EXHIBITED: 68

45

La Table servie 1912-1913

Drypoint

28.7 x 38.1 cm.

COLLECTION: The Museum of Modern Art, New York. Purchase

PUBLISHED: AP 196

Although still life was the staple subject matter of the orthodox cubists, it was not favored by the Passy group and occurs infrequently in the work of Jacques Villon before the war. Nevertheless, it provided the basis for a fascinating series which yielded at least two of the masterworks from his early maturity, *La Table servie* of 1912-1913 (cat. no. 47), and *Déjeuner* (cat. no. 48). The sequence of the studies in relationship to the three painted versions is an interesting problem,[1] and a conjectural examination of their probable order affords another example of Villon's basic method during his subsequent career.

The table itself was an important furnishing in Villon's home, and appears in the background of earlier works, for example in *Minne jouant* (fig. 18a). The initial sketch (cat. no. 42) focuses on the table, set for lunch. In pencil and wash, the motif is naturalistically established, with an emphasis on the arrangement of the various objects. Villon once said, "I make an analysis straight from nature so that I may have time to think it over."[2]

Analysis and planning begin to be evident in the working drawing (cat. no. 43). Here meandering line and hatching clearly divide the composition into two basic areas, light and dark, which, together with "the inner line of the object"[3] become the essential formal elements of subsequent development. Although this drawing is a rough sketch, with notations written in about color and tone, it establishes basic dispositions to be explored more fully in the small painting (cat. no. 46).

This painting seems also to be a study, and although it has undergone considerable restoration, its direct relationship to the working drawing (cat. no. 43) is evident in the light patches of color representing the near part of the table top and the upper portion of the flowers. This corresponds to Villon's written notation 'clair' in the same sketch (cat. no. 43).

The next step in the series seems to be the drawing on squared-up paper (cat. no. 44). This sheet is more involved with the movement of line through object and space than with either the arrangement of shape or tone. Villon's pencil moved an even and rhythmic line across the page, following first contour, then volume, and then space, as he said, "like the flight of a fly."[4] The objects on the table are enlarged and become the focus of his attention, while he ignores

46

La Table servie 1912-1913

Oil on canvas

Signed upper right "Jacques Villon"

50.8 x 61.7 cm.

PROVENANCE: André Bernheim, Paris

COLLECTION: Stephen Hahn Gallery,
New York

47

La Table servie 1912-1913

Oil on canvas

Signed and dated upper right "Jacques
Villon 12"

65 x 81 cm.

PROVENANCE: Jacques Villon

Private Collection, New York

PUBLISHED: 34, 40, 162, 186, 342, 382, 393

EXHIBITED: 29, 149, 181, 198, 215, 252, 295,
415, 461, 482

48

Déjeuner (also called Nature morte or La
Table servie) 1912-1913

Oil on burlap

Signed lower right "Jacques Villon"

89 x 116 cm.

PROVENANCE: Jacques Villon

COLLECTION: Yale University Art Gallery,
New Haven, Gift of Société Anonyme
Collection

PUBLISHED: 142, 182, 404, 407, 419, 420, 442

EXHIBITED: 20, 29, 125, 163, 166, 174, 195,
206, 257, 322, 461

46

47

48

the background. The drawing was prepared for transfer, and the design used for the distribution of objects in the painting, *La Table servie* (cat. no. 47).

This last is a synthesis of elements that have been explored in all of the previous studies. The energy of line and compositional placing of objects are derived from the drawings (especially cat. no. 44), fused with the complex arrangement of simplified shapes of light and dark and the background design from the small oil sketch (cat. no. 46). The interaction of line and shape in *La Table servie* is more sophisticated than its predecessors. The painting is a definitive statement, but also, because of Villon's love of the print medium, it becomes a point of departure.

The drypoint (AP 196), also called *La Table servie* (cat. no. 45), is developed from the painting *La Table servie* (cat. no. 47). Villon moved his vantage point still closer to the objects on the table, further monumentalizing them as compositional elements. The concentration falls on intricate formal relationships between transparent objects, space, and light. The initial still life elements are increasingly difficult to identify as the energetic probes of line interact with

the feathery textures that establish dark and light planes.

The composition of the print (cat. no. 45), taken from both the painting (cat. no. 47) and the working drawing (cat. no. 44), is reversed by the drypoint medium. This mirror image is the source for still new variations, a second squared-up drawing (fig. 45a) and the painting, *Déjeuner* (cat. no. 48). In the squared-up drawing (fig. 45a), however, Villon modifies the flowing curves and arabesques of both the print and *La Table servie* (cat. no. 47) in favor of a more rigid geometric structure. This new angularity is particularly evident in comparing the treatment of the water bottle located just to the left of center in both versions. This drawing is also squared for transfer, and is, in fact, the preliminary plan for the painting *Déjeuner* (cat. no. 48). In each work the central axes of the vase of flowers, the water bottle and the Chianti flask are placed on the third, fifth and ninth verticals from the left side of their respective grids. The third horizontal from the bottom of each grid locates the basis of these objects.

Although the use of transfer grids is traditional, they are of special importance to Villon. His interest in grids developed early

from a familiar technical tool to a means of invention, and complex grid structures are the starting point for his painting after the First World War.

This series indicates not only Villon's process of intense re-examination and re-development of his own work, but also marks an important transition in his style. The meandering curves of line in the earlier pictures reach an apogee in *La Table servie* (cat. no. 47), and give way to the harder geometry of the drawing (fig. 45a) and the painting *Déjeuner* (cat. no. 48). This change of preference from curved to straight lines, from a loose to a tightened geometry, is Villon's final stylistic variation on cubism before the beginning of the Great War.

A M

[1] See (40) Vallier, *Villon,* p. 115 ff. for a different sequence.

[2] *Ibid.*

[3] *Ibid.*

[4] *(59)* Francis Steegmuller, *Jacques Villon, Master Printmaker* (New York: Helene C. Seiferheld Gallery, 1964), Introduction

49   50

49

Portrait de Félix Barré 1912

Drawing, black chalk over slight trace of
blue pencil on white paper

Signed lower right "Jacques Villon 12"

37 x 35.5 cm.

PROVENANCE: Stephen Hahn Gallery, New
York; Louis Macmillan

COLLECTION: The Metropolitan Museum of
Art, New York, Rogers Fund, 1963

EXHIBITED: *437*

50

Félix Barré 1913

Drypoint

16.7 x 13.7 cm.

COLLECTION: Print Department, Boston
Public Library

PUBLISHED: AP 189

The complex and varied series of portraits
of the actor Félix Barré begins naturalistically with a 1912 chalk study (cat. no. 49),
a related oil sketch (fig. 49a) which was subsequently heavily reworked, and a 1913 engraving (AP 190). In 1912-13, Villon made
three oil paintings of Barré, at least two
drawings, and three prints. In 1914 he did a
watercolor (cat. no. 52) of the actor. Thereafter the subject disappears except for an
intriguing drawing of 1919 (fig. 52a) and an
untitled painting of around 1920 (fig. 81b)
which derives from this later, presently unlocated drawing. Félix Barré was a successful if not prominent actor who played in
blood curdlers like "le crime de la rue
Morgue" and "Au Rat Mort" at the Grand
Guignol and the Théâtre Réjane in Paris.
His association with the Duchamp family
can be traced back as far as 1905, when
Villon included him in *Sous la tente, sur la
plage* of 1905;[1] Marcel Duchamp also
painted Barré, in his 1907 *Man Seated by a
Window* (fig. 49b).

In the 1912 oil sketch of Barré, the large
dark mass of the chest and shoulders gives
this slightly balding, heavy-set man an imposing presence, but despite the angular
planes in the figure and background the ar-

tist presents a relatively conventional description of a sitter whose face is devoid of
emotion. This mask-like face serves as the
basis for the 1913 etching (AP 189) (cat. no.
50) in which the artist has simplified the
planes into a composition of great elegance
and economy. Perhaps Villon even intended
this emblematic physiognomy as a reference
to the mask, traditional symbol of the
theater, for in the etching he has twisted the
features into a grin.

The more radically-geometricized etching
(AP 199) of 1913 (which relates to a 1913
painting of the same composition) is a tour-
de-force in the cubist idiom. The actor's face
— highly expressive yet totally depersonalized — emerges from animated geometric
forms. But again, the power of Villon's formal organization seems to coincide with
Barré's superficial expression, while his true
nature remains masked. The delicately-
tinted, more spontaneous watercolor of
1914 (cat. no. 52) projects a greater intimacy than any version in the Barré series,
and reveals still another expression on the
face of the actor whose fluidity of features
plainly fascinated Villon. The looplike
head closely resembles a 1913 drawing (collection Lucien Goldschmidt, Inc., New

49a
JACQUES VILLON
Portrait d'acteur (Félix Barré) 1912
Oil on canvas
Collection of Françoise Tournie, Paris

York) while the faintly drawn angle of the shoulder (upper right), the posture of the figure, and the central axis line provide important material for the remarkable drawing of 1919 (fig. 52a).

In the unlocated *Pour un portrait de Barré,* the features are lightly indicated in the background along with all the compositional lines of the *Portrait d'acteur* etching of 1913 (AP 199) (cat. no. 51). Over this delicately sketched reprise of two earlier versions, Villon placed a complex grid of concentric rectangles which describe volumes receding into space. He established a 'floor' in a perspectival 'room' with wide horizontal lines of watercolor diminishing in length and thickness as they recede into depth. Stylistically this work makes a bold advance, paralleling a type of spatial description through the use of translucent materials employed by the Constructivists. But simultaneously as Villon ventured this imaginative approach to space, he referred back to an historical prototype, alluding to the classic convention of fusing the sitter with the symbols of his profession. Instead of portraying the actor *with* his attribute, Villon constructed a spatial system which subtly transforms the actor *into* his attri-

bute: the actor mysteriously becomes the theater itself. In the 1920 painting (see fig. 81a), the Barré theme is expanded even further, and it may also be echoed in the 1932 compositions Théâtre (fig. 116c) and *L'Espace* (cat. no. 116).

J D F

1 AP 80. *(75)* Goldschmidt, *Villon,* no. 44; notes that Villon depicts the actor in this 1905 aquatint.
2 Reproduced in (40) Vallier, *Villon,* p. 41.

49b
MARCEL DUCHAMP
Man Seated by a Window 1907
Oil on canvas
The Mary Sisler Collection, New York
Courtesy Fourcade Droll, Inc., New York

Portrait d'acteur (**Félix Barré**) 1913

Drypoint, 32/32

40 x 31.4 cm.

COLLECTION: Fogg Art Museum, Harvard
University, Cambridge, Massachusetts

PUBLISHED: AP 199

51

52

Portrait de Félix Barré 1914

Watercolor on paper with pen and ink

Signed and dated lower right "Jacques Villon 1914"

21 x 16.7 cm.

PROVENANCE: Jacques Villon; Mrs. J. C. Guggenheimer, New York

Anonymous loan

52a

JACQUES VILLON

Pour un portrait de Barré 1919

Drawing

Location unknown

Courtesy Lucien Goldschmidt, Inc.

52

53

53

Soldats en marche 1913

Oil on canvas

Signed and dated lower right
"Jacques Villon 13"

65 x 92 cm.

PROVENANCE: Jacques Villon

COLLECTION: Louis Carré et Cie, Paris

PUBLISHED: 27, 28, 29, 34, 39, 40, 57, 78, 101,
122, 131, 153, 155, 167, 203, 212, 216, 227,
237, 342, 371, 381, 400, 406, 413, 417, 418,
440, 445, 450

EXHIBITED: 13, 15, 18, 19, 22, 26, 27, 34, 38,
45, 46, 47, 49, 51, 55, 133, 154, 198, 220, 235,
239, 246, 252, 274, 322, 344, 383, 387, 419,
438, 494

Although Villon occasionally drew soldiers in his early newspaper work, either poking fun at them or using them as extras loitering in the background of a street scene,[1] the true subject of *Soldats en marche* is taken from the artist's own experience on military maneuvers, and his chief interest here is movement.

In 1912-13 Villon experimented with the representation of movement in several ways. Various trials attempt progressively more rational and logically constructed bases for kinetic expression. For example, in *La Fillette au piano* (cat. no. 34) and *Jeune femme* (cat. no. 36) of 1912 he used a cinematic device in which the illusion of movement is created through the progressive change in the arrangement of a body or limb. This technique was widely used in Futurist works, and in Marcel Duchamp's *Nude Descending a Staircase* of 1912. In *La Table servie* (see cat. nos. 42-48) and the *Équilibriste* series of 1912-1913 (see cat. nos. 54-57), movement is conveyed through the pure motor energy of his *"vol de mouche"* ("flight of a fly") lines. In later, more geometric work, this black line does not disappear but serves as an outline for planes and facets. In both *La Table servie* and the

53a
JACQUES VILLON
Soldats en marche 1912
Drawing over photograph
Musée National d'Art Moderne, Paris

Équilibriste series curved lines give way to the more structured regularity of angles and planes.

In his sketch for *Soldats en marche* (fig. 53a) Villon begins with a geometrical construction of basic elements. The transition in these two years towards more rational means of construction shows the effects of the weekly discussions of the Puteaux-Courbevoie group, especially the idea of "reasoning a painting before it is begun" — a key stratagem of the group. The "reasoning" is clearly presented in the skeletal drawing of 1912 for the painting of the following year. Villon does not arrive at abstraction through a process of reduction, as in earlier work; the composition evolves from a simpler state of abstraction to a more complex one. The structure of the work originates in the most basic elements: dots, lines, and planes. An overall network of rhythmic lines drawn from "points of demarcation" begins to reconstruct a vision of marching soldiers in geometric terms. Planes, overlaid in wash, reinforce the major diagonals. A troop of soldiers seen from the rear begins to take form. Two complete bodies of soldiers in uniform toting backpacks and rifles can be distinguished on the

left. The rest of the troop merges into the shallow depth of the picture plane.

In the painting of 1913 the structure is resolved in a stronger hierarchy of form and color. Three major diagonals, in heavy black, organize the multiplicity of obliquely-set planes of various sizes. All lines are diagonal. Each plane is outlined in a solid or dotted black line, emphasizing its separateness. Color reinforces the hierarchical structure of form. Reds and blues are used for the primary carriers of motion — red for hats and blue for arms and legs. The rest of the bodies, interpenetrating with the background, are done in soft secondary tones of green, pink, orange and neutrals. Their transparency allows the planes to shift and overlap, creating ambiguous spatial relationships. This rhythmic ordering of parts through line and color determines a powerful yet rational dynamism. Each formal element makes a significant contribution to the effect of the whole.

The reduction of form into facets and shifting planes is seen in other work of 1913, including the *Équilibriste*. But in *Soldats en marche* these planes and facets are larger, clearer and crisper; they have more regular shapes and play a more integral role in the

overall composition by contributing to the movement and structure of the work as a whole, while retaining a strong sense of individual form. Motion has not decomposed form, nor is it sacrificed to stability, but movement and form are successfully combined on a new level. The synthesis of these elements was an important aim of the Puteaux-Courbevoie group, who viewed the Futurist dissolution of form through motion as naive.

S G

[1] (36) Mellquist, *Caricatures*, Nos. 17, 31

54

L'Équilibriste 1913

Pencil and watercolor

Signed at bottom "Jacques Villon 13"

12.5 x 7.5 cm.

PROVENANCE: Jacques Villon

COLLECTION: Marcel Guiot, Paris

55

L'Équilibriste 1913

Pencil and watercolor

Signed at bottom "Jacques Villon 1913"

13.5 x 9.5 cm.

PROVENANCE: Jacques Villon

COLLECTION: Marcel Guiot, Paris

56

L'Équilibriste 1913

Drypoint

40 x 20.8 cm.

COLLECTION: The Museum of Modern Art, New York, Given in memory of Peter H. Deitsch

PUBLISHED: AP 197

57

Le Petit équilibriste 1914

Drypoint

22 x 16 cm.

COLLECTION: Print Department, Boston Public Library

PUBLISHED: AP 201

The theme of the acrobat attracted Villon's attention as early as 1897, when he executed a lithograph called the *Danseuse de corde* (tightrope walker, AP 387) for a supplement of the *Nouvelle Revue Parisienne*. The theme reappears in a pen-and-ink study for the *Équilibriste* in 1912,[1] and in two related sketches of 1913. One of these shows in cursory strokes an acrobat balancing on his hands (cat. no. 54). Villon left the spatial context undefined but suggested the performer's motions. He developed his plan for the *Acrobats* painting (fig. 55a) in the second 1913 sketch (cat. no. 55). Head, arms, torso and legs are no longer distinguishable. The acrobat's motions have become more important than his physical details. 1913 and 1914 saw the fulfillment of Villon's efforts in the two prints and in two oil paintings of 1913, *L'Acrobate* (fig. 55a) and *Équilibre*.[2]

For the acrobat Villon renounced the mass he had so carefully carved out in the *Renée* series of 1911 (see cat. nos. 25-28), and instead visualized energies alone — the acrobat's dextrous movements pitted against the force of gravity. In *L'Acrobate* and the *Petit équilibriste* etching (cat. no. 57) he did this by pure linear arabesque overlaid on a concentration of triangular planes. The surrounding space is suffused with energy that emanates from the center of the picture: for the first time in a work of Villon an environment is suggested in completely abstract terms.

The color scheme of *L'Acrobate* is based on the three primary colors and gray, and appears to be a refinement of the scheme Villon used in the *Homme lisant son journal,* 1912 (fig. 38a). By the time of the *Petit équilibriste* his graphic vocabulary was so disciplined and economical that he captured the transparent, shifting, interpenetrating planes by ruled, vertical hatching alone.

The drypoint *Équilibriste* (cat. no. 56) and the oil painting *Équilibre*, both of 1913, are more angular than the others of the series. Here, the particularities of the acrobat have crystallized into the essential quality of balance. This is an early example of what was to become a practice of Villon in the 1920s: reducing a subject from life to its basic forms, and giving it the name of an abstract concept.

The *Équilibriste* series reveals the fruitful interchange between Villon and his two brothers, who were all interested in prob-

54

55

lems of portraying dynamism and force,
as expressed in Duchamp-Villon's *Horse*
sculptures and in Duchamp's *Nude Descending a Staircase,* 1911-12. Furthermore,
the composition of *L'Acrobate* (fig. 55a)
somewhat resembles *La Mariée* by Marcel
Duchamp of 1912, with its curving thrust
to the right (fig. 55b).

J H

¹ *(60)* Wick, *Villon,* no. 142, p. 29.
² Reproduced in (40) Vallier, *Villon,* p. 46.

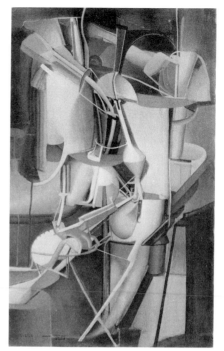

55b

MARCEL DUCHAMP

La Mariée 1912

Oil on canvas

Philadelphia Museum of Art, The Louise
and Walter Arensberg Collection

55a

JACQUES VILLON

L'Acrobate 1913

Oil on canvas

Collection of Mr. and Mrs. David Howald
Shawan, Columbus, Ohio

56

57

58

Machines 1913
Drawing in pencil and India ink on tracing paper
Signed lower right "Jacques Villon 13"
18.5 x 19.2 cm.
PROVENANCE: Jacques Villon
COLLECTION: Louis Carré et Cie, Paris

58

The role of the machine in relation to art, paralleling the dynamism of the emergent industrial era, was a major topic of discussion among the Puteaux group,[1] and all three Duchamp brothers were involved with images of the machine in different ways.

Raymond Duchamp-Villon was a strong believer in the machine and its influence on art. In a letter to Walter Pach he wrote: "The power of the machine imposes itself and we can scarcely conceive of living beings without it anymore."[2] Duchamp-Villon had visited the Galerie des Machines at the Exposition Universelle in 1900, where he viewed a dynamo as "a work filled with power and audacity, proclaiming, in a fantastic hall, the power of steel."[3] His *Cheval* of 1914, showing the metamorphosis from horse to machine summarizes his feelings on the relation between mechanization and life (see fig. 58a).

Marcel Duchamp, as so many authors have noted, was also fascinated by the machine and its implications for modern life, although he did not see the relationship in Duchamp-Villon's optimistic terms.[4] In 1911 he painted a coffee grinder with its handle in several different positions at once. Subsequently he explored a series of mechanomorphic forms in *Nude Descending a Staircase* and *The Passage from Virgin to Bride*. His interest in the rotary machine, seen earlier in the *Coffee Grinder*, reappears in the twenties in an ironic series of *Roto-Relief* works (see fig. 58b).

Not surprisingly, the machine was of sustained interest to Jacques Villon. Beginning in 1913-1914, Villon did several studies consisting of larger and smaller wheels interconnected by a bar. These are certainly related to Duchamp-Villon's preparatory drawing for *Le Cheval*, begun in the same year.[5] Here Villon, like both of his brothers, focused on the rotary machine or dynamo,

58a
RAYMOND DUCHAMP-VILLON
Le Cheval 1914
Bronze
Joseph H. Hirshhorn Museum and Sculpture Garden, Smithsonian Institution, Washington, D.C.

58b
MARCEL DUCHAMP
Revolving Glass 1920
Courtesy of Yale University Art Gallery, New Haven

59

59a

JACQUES VILLON

L'Atelier de mécanique 1914

Oil on canvas (cropped)

Collection of Henry B. Thielbar, New York

59b

MYRBACH

Illustration from **Jack** by Daudet 1889

Harvard College Library,
Cambridge, Massachusetts

59

Le Petit atelier de mécanique 1913

Oil on canvas

Signed lower left "Jacques Villon 13"

73.5 x 92 cm.

PROVENANCE: Walter Pach, New York;
Brummer Gallery, New York

The Phillips Collection, Washington, D.C.

EXHIBITED: *148, 481*

but he also placed it in a wider context, the machine shop.

In *Machines* (cat. no. 58) two rotary devices are shown side by side in a pyramidal composition. The background is broken into triangular planes. This drawing was probably done soon after the 1913 first painting of the workshop, *Le Petit atelier de mécanique* (cat. no. 59); it intervenes between the almost representational space of that work and the more complex treatment of the 1914 *L'Atelier de mécanique* (cat. no. 60). While only a small portion of the 1914 painting is shown in the drawing (cat. no. 58), it is the focal point of the work, the portion saved in the cropped version (fig. 59a) and the basis for later variations (cat. nos. 61 and 62, fig. 61a).

Villon turns from the exploration of the paths of the wheels in motion in the 1913 drawing to a more representational study of the machine itself in a drawing of 1914 entitled *La Tour* (fig. 59b). Here he gives more attention to the relation of the parts. A smaller wheel fits inside a larger one to which it is connected by a bar, and the entire machine is placed on a block and connected to the wall by a horizontal support. The title refers to the motion of the machine, and the spiral lines indicate that the wheels are in motion.

Still later in 1920 Villon made a drawing of the same machine, in a style very similar to *La Tour*. The most significant change is the title, *Globe céleste, globe terrestre*. This drawing became the source for the *Globe* series, which continued until the 1940s (see cat. no. 142 and figs. 142a-142d). The machine which had so preoccupied Villon (as well as Raymond and Marcel) initially for its mechanical might now takes on wider symbolic meaning. The force of the single dynamo which set the machine shop in motion became an expression of the mechanical power of the universe.

Villon's concern — for the machine shop as well as the symbolic implications of the machine — may stem from personal experiences. In 1913 he briefly worked in a machine shop in Asnières.[6] During Villon's youth, his favorite book was *Jack*, by Alphonse Daudet, first published in 1876, the year following the artist's birth. Gaston Duchamp was so taken with this book that when he went to Paris to become an artist, he adopted "Jack" (which he later changed to Jacques) as half of his pseudonym.[7]

In *Jack*, Daudet depicts the horrors of industrialization through its effects on a sensitive young boy forced to work in an engine room. The author's attitude is clearly communicated by the harsh terms he employs to describe machines as seen through the eyes of Jack:

Set in motion by steam they seemed to him the personification of malevolent beasts lying in wait for him as he passed, and ready to seize him, rend and cut him to pieces. Cold and motionless, they seemed to him still more menacing, as they stood with gaping jaws, their claws extended, all their instruments of destruction, motionless, concealed, they wore the air of glutted, satiated cruelty.[8]

Francis Steegmuller cited a striking correspondence between an illustration by Myrbach of the engine room in *Jack* and the 1914 version of the machine shop, *L'Atelier de mécanique*.[9] In the book illustration, a wide panoramic view of a high-ceilinged room with windows at the back is shown (fig. 59c). Pulleys traverse the ceiling in diagonal lines from left to right, and from them hang a profusion of chains, belts and hooks attached to the machines below. These features can be seen in Villon's 1914 painting. On the right, at the bottom of the illustration, is a large propeller. A propeller is also seen in profile in both the 1913 and

the 1914 paintings. In later version it is eliminated; the flywheel of the dynamo, roughly in the same position as the propeller, seems to serve the same function in terms of the design. There are obvious differences between the illustration and the painting, such as the types of machines used, but the basic structure of the room in Villon's machine shop is closely related to the illustration.

Daudet's description of the machine shop may also have played a role in Villon's conception:

All the rest of the shop was plunged in shadows in which the moon indicated objects without giving them a precision of form. All along the walls where the tools were hung up projected sharp and ragged edges of steel. The lathes stood ranged in long rows. The cords, cranks, wheels stopped and motionless crossed each other as in a network, while chips of filings of metal gleamed on the ground.[10]

Villon's machine shop series also depicts an austere, unpeopled world. Like Daudet, Villon seems to have admired the form and power of the machine, but to have viewed its effects on man with suspicion. These mixed feelings about industrialization, perhaps more typical of writers and sociologists than turn-of-the-century artists, are well-expressed in yet another passage from *Jack*, on the occasion of the launching of a gunboat with a thousand horsepower engine:

Ah well, speed on, then monster, across the world. Man has made thee so strong that thou hast nothing to fear. Be not cruel as thou art strong. Control that terrible power already put to the test. Direct thy vessel without wrath, and above all with respect to human life . . .[11]

Even in the late forties and fifties when he did a series of landscapes with farm machinery, such as *Le Grain ne meurt* (cat. no. 148), 1947, or a series on airplanes (cat. no. 159), Villon's attitude towards the machine seems unchanged. In these works, as in the *Atelier mécanique* series, huge machines dominate scenes where man is either not shown or is given a secondary role.

s g

[1] (421) Hamilton and Agee, *Duchamp-Villon*, p. 89.

[2] (434) Walter Pach, *Queer Thing, Painting* (N.Y.: Harper Bros., 1938), p. 19.

[3] (421) Hamilton and Agee, *Duchamp-Villon*, p. 89.

[4] (395a) d'Harnoncourt and McShine, *Duchamp*. Lawrence D. Steefel, Jr., "Marcel Duchamp and the Machine."

[5] (421) Hamilton and Agee, (434) Pach, and (413) John Golding, *Cubism: A History and an Analysis* (London: Farber and Farber, Ltd., 1968), are of the opinion that studies were begun for the *Cheval* in 1913, but Agee believes they were begun in 1914, footnote 3, p. 103.

[6] Told to Peter Wick in an interview in *Arts*, 1961.

[7] (59) Steegmuller, *Villon, Master Printmaker*, Introduction. The surname of the pseudonym "Jacques Villon" came from the artist's admiration for the French poet François Villon.

[8] Alphonse Daudet, *Jack*, translated by Marian McIntyre, Vol. 2 (Boston: Little, Brown and Co., 1960), p. 30.

[9] (59) Steegmuller, *Villon, Master Printmaker*, Introduction. He cites the illustration from the Flammarion edition of *Jack* (Paris: Marpon and Flammarion, 1889), p. 330. The illustration was printed by Ch. Guillaume.

[10] Daudet, *Jack*, p. 30.

[11] Daudet, *Jack*, p. 36.

60

L'Atelier de mécanique 1914

Oil on canvas

Signed lower left "JV" and on back "l'atelier de mécanique Jacques Villon"

72 x 92.7 cm.

PROVENANCE: John Quinn, New York; Ferdinand Howald, Columbus, Ohio

COLLECTION: Columbus Gallery of Fine Arts, Ohio, Ferdinand Howald Collection

PUBLISHED: 34, 373, 438

EXHIBITED: *113, 138, 169, 198, 230, 477, 478, 496*

61

Le Petit atelier de mécanique 1946

Oil on canvas

Signed lower right "Jacques Villon"

81 x 116 cm.

PROVENANCE: Jacques Villon; Louis Carré Gallery, New York

The Phillips Collection, Washington, D.C.

PUBLISHED: 27, 34, 235, 301, 333

EXHIBITED: *8, 9, 20, 29, 49, 176, 209, 221, 322, 479*

62

Un Atelier de mécanique 1955

Oil on canvas

Signed lower right "Jacques Villon 55"

89 x 116 cm.

PROVENANCE: Jacques Villon; Louis Carré et Cie, Paris; Dr. F. G. Schlatter, Zug, Switzerland

Anonymous loan

PUBLISHED: 40, 282, 342, 385

EXHIBITED: *34, 55, 62, 423*

60

61

61a

JACQUES VILLON

Atelier de mécanique tintamarre 1947

Oil on canvas

Sonja Henie-Niels Onstad Foundations,
Norway

62

63

63

Portrait de femme (Tête de femme) 1914

Oil on canvas (oval)

Signed lower right "J.V." and on the back
"Jacques Villon 1914"

55 x 46 cm.

Mounted in wooden box 79 x 70 cm.

PROVENANCE: John Quinn, New York;
Sir Roland Penrose, London;
E. V. Thaw and Co., New York

COLLECTION: Museum of Art, Rhode Island
School of Design, Providence; Mary B.
Jackson Fund

PUBLISHED: 438, 441

EXHIBITED: *113, 138*

Tête de femme, derived from Villon's sister,
Yvonne, is probably the last in a series of
three oval portraits (see *Fillette au piano,*
cat. no. 34 and *Portrait d'homme,* fig. 40a)
done in 1913-1914. Indeed it is similar
enough in shape, size and structure to *Portrait d'homme,* a portrait of the artist's
father, to suggest that the two works may
have originally been intended as oval pen-
dants, a traditional mode of French portraiture. However, *Tête de femme* and the
three-quarter figure painting *La Femme
assise* offer complex solutions to the pictorial problems explored by the earlier
series of portraits based on Yvonne (cat.
nos. 35-37); in addition, the two appear related to the 1914 sculpture *Femme assise*
(cat. no. 64a) by Raymond Duchamp-Villon.

In the 1912-1913 series of paintings and
prints of Yvonne, Villon was, as always,
fascinated with the subtle energy of his
young sister's movements, the compressed
curve of her body as she leaned forward in
a chair with her knees drawn up, the manner
in which she tilted her head above somewhat hunched shoulders, and her apparent
habit of clasping one arm, shoulder, or even
her chin with the other arm, crossing the
body to form an inverted triangle with the
elbow point at the center of the composition. This sense of urgent movement held in
check, as it were, by the sitter herself, was
refined into progressively more abstract
images in the 1912-1913 series, to which the
two paintings (cat. nos. 63 and 64) properly
belong. The *Tête de femme* goes even further in its use of rigorous rectilinear geometry, focusing attention on the girl's head,
the way in which her bangs emphasize the
structure of her forehead, cheekbones,
finely-chiseled nose, and above all, the
elegant thrust of her neck and chin, seen
in a typical cubist double view, both frontally and in profile.

It is especially this characteristic, the alert tilt upward and forward of the head rising from a long neck, that puts Jacques Villon's painting into startling relationship with Raymond's sculpture, even though the figure in the painting is clothed while the sculpture is a nude. The relationship is even clearer between the sculpture and the 1914 canvas *Femme assise* for which the more daring *Tête de femme* served as a study (cat. no. 64). Here, the figure is seen frontally, her left arm brought across the body, elbow resting on fore-shortened knee, the right arm hanging down, as in the sculpture, but holding a piece of paper or a book, more akin to the action in the *Jeune femme*, 1912 (cat. no. 36).

The *Tête de femme* is one of the best examples of Villon's intense interest in finding a means of achieving what he calls the absolute[1] in painting through geometry. From the Section d'Or exhibition onwards, Villon, according to the recollections of his brother Marcel, became "familiar with the work of geometricians from Pythagoras to Dom Verkade."[2] It seems likely that his study also led him to the work of Charles Henry, the author of *Le Cercle chromatique* and *L'Esthétique scientifique,* so important to neo-impressionist theory.[3] Most of the angles formed by intersecting lines in *Tête de femme* conform to those defined as harmonious in Henry's aesthetic protractor device, first published in 1888.

La Femme assise (cat. no. 64) retreats somewhat from the rigorous, almost rule-and-compass geometry of *Tête de femme,* yet if the shapes are a degree more spontaneous than those of the oval portraits (see cat. no. 34 and fig. 40a) they are also flatter. Diagonals extend from three hubs, the head, the elbow point, and the intersection of the legs, complemented by subordinate linear movements causing the internal composi-

tion to work as a series of star-like formations, knitting the pictorial structure to the sides of the canvas like a spider web. The use of overlapping planes is further developed, simultaneously implying spatial recession and asserting surface flatness. Along with such planes, Villon uses overlapping areas of color, alluding to transparent probes of light through space and form. This combination of opaque and transparent planes is of paramount importance to Villon's post-war style. It is seen in a drawing of 1920, *Figure-plans*[4] derived from *Tête de femme* and *La Femme assise. La Femme assise* is also a source for the 1919 painting *In Memoriam* (cat. no. 67).

A M

[1] (40) Vallier, *Villon*, p. 114.

[2] (413) Golding, *Cubism*, p. 168.

[3] Henry's work is cited by Apollinaire in connection with the work of both Villon and Marcel Duchamp in L. C. Breunig, *Apollinaire on Art* (New York, 1972), p. 588-9. Henry's interest for certain artists continued even after the war. For example, a series of lectures by Henry is reprinted in Esprit Nouveau, nos. 6-8, 1921. Albert Gleizes published an article "Charles Henry et le vitalisme" in *Cahiers des Etoiles* (no. 13, January-February 1930, pp. 112-128) several years after Henry's death. For a recent survey of Henry's theories see Arguelles, *Charles Henry and the Formulation of a Psychophysical Esthetic* (Chicago and London, 1972).

[4] Reproduced in catalogue to exhibition no. 60, p. 80.

64
La Femme assise 1914
Oil on canvas
Signed and dated lower right "Jacques Villon 1914"
126 x 60 cm.
PROVENANCE: Jacques Villon
COLLECTION: Louis Carré et Cie, Paris
PUBLISHED: 27, 29, 32, 34, 39, 48, 344, 413
EXHIBITED: 9, 15, 26, 38, 45, 47, 49, 55, 198, 220, 252, 387, 421, 494

64

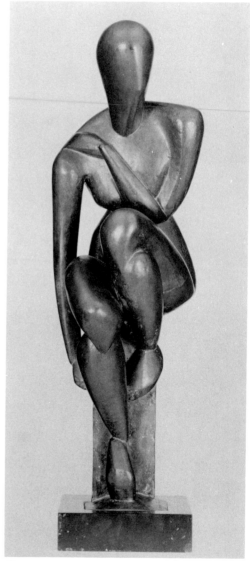

64a

RAYMOND DUCHAMP-VILLON

La Femme assise 1914

Bronze

Courtesy of Yale University Art Gallery,
New Haven

Museum of Art, Rhode Island School of
Design

65

Portrait de M. J.B. peintre c. 1914
(dated 1911)

Oil on canvas

Signed lower left "JV" and signed and
dated on back "Jacques Villon 1911"

130 x 89 cm.

PROVENANCE: The Caroll Gallery, New
York; John Quinn, New York; Pottier
Collection; Ferdinand Howald,
Columbus, Ohio

COLLECTION: Columbus Gallery of Fine
Arts, Ohio, Ferdinand Howald Collection

PUBLISHED: 373, 438, 441

EXHIBITED: *113, 138, 230, 471, 477, 496*

Portrait de M.J.B. peintre depicts the artist,
Jacques Bon, the brother of Raymond
Duchamp-Villon's wife, and a neighbor of
Villon's at Puteaux. Bon, a pupil of the
renowned fin-de-siècle portraitist and genre
painter Antonio de la Gandara, also appears in two later works by Villon, *L'Elève
de la Gandara*, 1923 (fig. 65a), and the
etching *Aventure*, 1935 (AP 271). Jacques
Bon was evidently fond of wearing a peculiarly wide-brimmed hat which accounts for
the almost cowl-like shapes that surmount
the head.

   M.J.B. peintre relates to several works
by Villon of the period 1913-1914. Its planar
geometric structure places it in close stylistic proximity to his etching *M.D. lisant* (cat.
no. 40), *Portrait d'homme* (fig. 40a), *Tête de
femme* (cat. no. 63) and *La Femme assise*
(cat. no. 64). In addition, in both the treatment of the eye and the visibility of the
transfer squaring, there is a particular affinity with *Tête de femme*. Villon may have
been planning an entire series of family
portraits, but it remains a mystery as to
why this portrait of a brother-in-law is so
unusually large.

   From the latter part of 1913 until he
entered the army in 1914, Villon's style
underwent a continuous change from the
fluid curvilinear geometry of *Puteaux: les
fumées et les arbres en fleurs* (cat. no. 33)
and *La Table servie,* 1913 (see cat. nos. 42-
48) toward the more rectilinear form seen
here. *M.J.B. peintre,* brought to the United
States in 1914, is signed and dated 1911. As
this painting bears little relationship to
other works by Villon of 1911, two explana-
tions of this dating are possible. Either this
is an isolated aberration in Villon's work,
or the picture was somehow misdated. The
latter explanation seems the more probable
given the orderly nature of Villon's artistic
evolution.

A M

65

65a

JACQUES VILLON

L'Elève de la Gandara 1924

Oil on canvas

Collection of Mrs. Frances W. Kelly,
Cambridge, Massachusetts

66

66

Femme assise 1919

Oil on canvas

Signed lower right "Jacques Villon"; signed and dated on the back "Jacques Villon 1919"

82 x 45 cm.

PROVENANCE: Jacques Villon; Suzanne Duchamp-Crotti

Private collection, Paris

67

In Memoriam 1919

Oil on burlap

Signed lower left "Jacques Villon"

129.9 x 81.9 cm.

PROVENANCE: Jacques Villon

COLLECTION: Yale University Art Gallery, New Haven, Gift of Société Anonyme Collection

PUBLISHED: 142, 182, 402, 407, 419, 442

EXHIBITED: 20, 125, 143, 163, 166, 167, 174, 195, 198, 231, 376

In Memoriam is one of the first works painted by Villon after his return from the First World War. It was exhibited in 1920 at the opening of the galleries of the *Société Anonyme* in New York.

The title undoubtedly makes it a tribute to Raymond Duchamp-Villon, who died during the war in 1918. This was the first instance of many memorial tributes which Villon would pay his brother throughout the remainder of his career.

The painting is developed from *La Femme assise*, 1914 (cat. no. 64) and *Femme assise*, 1914 (cat. no. 66), both of 1914. *In Memoriam* shares with the earlier paintings the general pose (reversed) the large vertical format, and the breaking-up of the figure into planes representing several views. It differs, however, in that the woman is nude (like the sculpture), purged of portrait characteristics, and split into two major views. The upper portion of the canvas, a three-quarter view, recalls the sinuous contours of Raymond's statue. In contrast, the lower half of the work remains frontal, more like the 1914 painting, and possibly also related to the work of Russian sculptor Alexander Archipenko. The "V" shape of the pelvis, the curve of the thighs, and the

bend of the knees recall the features of several Archipenko works, especially *Woman Combing Her Hair*, 1915 (fig. 67a). Archipenko had been drawn to the Puteaux group of artists and was particularly well acquainted with Duchamp-Villon. Villon was doubtless familiar with the work of Archipenko, which was constantly exhibited in Paris during the mid-teens; and indeed he owned Archipenko's *L'Espagnole*,[1] which he is thought to have acquired about 1919.[2]

The most pronounced change in *In Memoriam*, however, is its return to curvilinear geometry that Villon had been moving away from since 1912.

D S R

[1] Reproduced in *Les Soirées de Paris* (Paris: M. Knoedler and Co., May 16 to June 30, 1958), no. 1.

[2] Conversation with Edward Fry, January, 1973. Mr. Fry believes that Villon must have acquired the work during a time when he and Archipenko would have both been in Paris. For Archipenko, after the war, this was but a brief visit in 1919-20. *L'Espagnole* bears no resemblance to Archipenko's female statues and does not relate stylistically to *In Memoriam*.

67

67a

ALEXANDER ARCHIPENKO
Woman Combing Her Hair 1915
Bronze
Perls Galleries, New York

68

La Table d'échecs 1919

Drawing in red and black ink, black, red and blue pencil on tinted paper; signed lower left "Jacques Villon 19"

36 x 18 cm.

PROVENANCE: Jacques Villon

COLLECTION: Louis Carré et Cie, Paris

PUBLISHED: 27, 40, 342

EXHIBITED: 32, 40, 49, 55, 60, 68, 72

69

Jeu 1919

Oil on canvas

Signed lower left "Jacques Villon"

92 x 73 cm.

PROVENANCE: Jacques Villon

COLLECTION: Louis Carré et Cie, Paris

PUBLISHED: 27, 29, 34, 39, 40, 155, 227, 232, 301, 342, 440

EXHIBITED: 9, 13, 15, 22, 26, 27, 34, 37, 45, 46, 47, 49, 51, 55, 154, 198, 220, 277, 322, 432

The painting *Jeu* and a subsequent etching (fig. 69a) were developed from the drawing *Table d'échecs* (cat. no. 68), a simple architectural plan and elevation of a chess table accompanied by a small sketch at the lower left, where Villon begins to explore the possibilities of tilting the table at different angles, thus developing from it a "new object."[1] Before the war, Villon moved around objects recomposing images based on different vantage points in a typical cubist approach. He later said that, "toward the end of the war I treated the objects in successive planes. I proceeded by disposing the object in superimposed layers, and that enabled me to confer greater expression to the volume."[2] This modification of method, showing the layering of planes, was already beginning in 1914 works (see *Tête de femme and Femme assise,* cat. nos. 63 and 64), but its highly systematic use dates from after the war (see cat. nos. 70-80, 81, and 86-98).

The game of chess is not only a recurring theme in Villon's work, but also an intimate link between members of the Duchamp family, all of whom played the game enthusiastically, and appear in this activity in each other's work (see *La Partie d'échecs,* 1904, cat. no. 13, or Duchamp's *Les Joueurs d'échecs,* 1910, and Duchamp's studies of chess players, 1911).[3] An additional link between Jacques and Marcel is the motif of stacked planes, treated as receding diamonds, which appear as painted color samples in Marcel's *Tu'M* (fig. 69b) commissioned as a decoration over a bookcase by Katherine S. Dreier in 1918.

A M

[1] (40) Vallier, *Villon,* p. 115.

[2] *ibid.,* p. 118.

[3] (395a) d'Harnoncourt and McShine, *Duchamp,* nos. 13, 44, pp. 85-91.

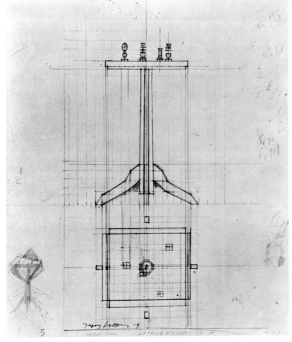

68

69

69b

MARCEL DUCHAMP

Tu'M 1918

Courtesy of Yale University Art Gallery,
New Haven

69a

JACQUES VILLON

Table d'échecs 1920

Etching, AP 203

Courtesy of Yale University Art Gallery,
New Haven

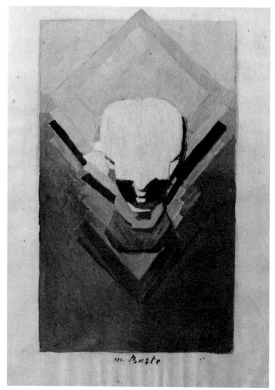

70

70a

RAYMOND DUCHAMP-VILLON

Baudelaire 1911

Bronze

Collection of Wellesley College Museum,
Wellesley, Massachusetts
Courtesy The Museum of Modern Art,
New York

70b

JACQUES VILLON

Tête 1919

Oil sketch

Location unknown

Reproduced from Sotheby sales catalogue,
*Impressionistic and Modern Painting and
Sculpture,* April 26, 1967

70

Un Buste 1920

Gouache

Signed and dated lower left "Jacques Villon 20"

16.2 x 11.8 cm.

PROVENANCE: Gift of Jacques Villon

COLLECTION: Mme Anne-Françoise Mare-Vène, Paris

In 1919, a year after the death of Raymond, Jacques Villon began working on a group of studies after his brother's powerful 1911 sculpture, the *Baudelaire* (cat. no. 70a). Although Jacques had used sculpture by his brother as models as early as *Sancta Fortunata,* 1908, variations on sculptural themes assumed a special significance after he became executor of the Duchamp-Villon artistic legacy.

An early study of *Baudelaire* was a 1919 oil sketch, *Tête* (fig. 70b). In the artist's calculated analysis, the bust is sliced into successive planes, a method Villon called "constructive decomposition."[1] (See cat. nos. 42-48, 63-64, 66-67, and 68-69.)

While *Tête* reveals systematic analysis of the subject, *Un Buste* (cat. no. 70 and fig. 70c) is its transformation into a working compositional formula, involving separation and reorganization of the planar elements. The segmented planes expand in space, to represent visually an idea Villon was to recall many years later: "I remember that about 1911, we used to say . . . that if Baudelaire's bust were to explode, it would do so along certain lines of force . . ."[2] In both versions of *Un Buste* the diamond shapes represent a table or stand, segmented in the same way as the chess table in *Jeu* 1919 (cat. no. 69). The rectangles between Baudelaire and the table suggest the base, an important feature in the etching *Baudelaire avec socle* (cat. no. 71).

Un Buste was not a final step, but rather a transitional state in Villon's cubist analysis of Raymond's bust. Several other somewhat abstracted drawings surveyed the bust frontally and in profile. Among these are *Pour "Architectures," Charles Baudelaire, Étude Pour un Baudelaire, Baudelaire au socle,* and *Baudelaire* (cat. nos. 72-76). The most revealing of all these studies are a series of pen-and-ink drawings[3] where the head ex-

70c

JACQUES VILLON

Un Buste 1920

Oil on canvas

Collection of Samuel Maslon, Minneapolis

pands upward into space along the "lines of force," as it is sliced and reorganized into a grouping of individual geometric shapes. The ridge of the nose and the cheekbones appear in *Abstract Construction*, 1920 (cat. no. 77) as protrusions into the contour of a geometric slice through the forehead just above the brow. The Duchamp-Villon sculpture of Baudelaire becomes more obscured as it is overtaken by the process of geometric simplification — that is, of abstraction. Yet, as in all of Villon's abstract works, subject matter and volume are of utmost importance; here Villon retains linear hatching and cross-hatching to express the solidity of the bust's contours.

Baudelaire is treated schematically in two more drawings (cat. nos. 78 and 79). The transformation is complete with *Figure*, 1921 (cat. no. 80), the source for a popular Villon print widely believed to be an example of non-objective abstract art. Here the head and base have become a series of stacked planes. Within this structure, an illusion of depth is created by the opaqueness of the planes, their overlap in space, and the sharp contrast between the bright yellow and orange colors, and black.

Villon's fondness for this composition was demonstrated by the fact that he used its final development as the only example of his own work to be included in the series of reproductive aquatints he produced for Bernheim-Jeune between 1922-1930. At least twice subsequently he returned to the penultimate version: in 1949 as an illustration in *Poésies de mots inconnus* and as a cover design for a Gerald Cramer gallery catalogue no. 50 (no date, but probably mid-fifties), *Oeuvres originals de peintures*, Geneva.

D S R

1 (40) Vallier, *Villon*, p. 66.
2 *ibid.*, p. 56.

71
Baudelaire avec socle 1920
Etching
41.5 x 28.1 cm.
COLLECTION: The Museum of Fine Arts, Boston, Bequest of W. G. Russell Allen
PUBLISHED: AP 204

72
Pour "Architectures" 1920
Drawing in colored pencil and purple ink on tracing paper
Signed and dated lower right "Jacques Villon 20"
19 x 14.5 cm.
PROVENANCE: Jacques Villon
COLLECTION: Louis Carré et Cie, Paris

73
Charles Baudelaire 1920
Drawing in pencil and ink on tinted paper
Signed and dated lower right "Jacques Villon 20"
14.4 x 8.5 cm.
PROVENANCE: Jacques Villon
COLLECTION: Louis Carré et Cie, Paris

74
Étude pour un Baudelaire 1921
Drawing in blue ink, pencil, and red colored pencil on paper
Signed lower left "Jacques Villon 21"
PROVENANCE: Jacques Villon
COLLECTION: Louis Carré et Cie, Paris

75
Baudelaire au socle 1920
Drawing in pencil on tracing paper
Signed in ink at lower left "Jacques Villon"
34 x 17 cm.
PROVENANCE: Jacques Villon
COLLECTION: Louis Carré et Cie, Paris

76
Baudelaire 1920
Pencil and watercolor on white paper
Signed and dated lower left "Jacques Villon 20"
20 x 12 cm.
PROVENANCE: Jacques Villon
COLLECTION: Louis Carré et Cie, Paris
EXHIBITED: 32, 54, 60

71

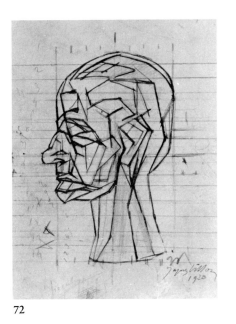

72

73

74

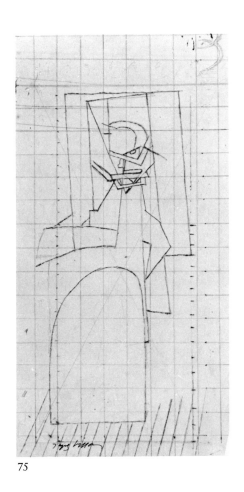

75

76

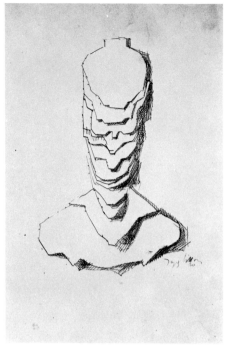

77

77

Abstract Construction 1920

Pen and ink on paper

Signed lower right "Jacques Villon 20"

21.2 x 14 cm.

PROVENANCE: Jacques Villon

COLLECTION: Yale University Art Gallery, New Haven, Gift of Société Anonyme Collection

PUBLISHED: 419

EXHIBITED: 174, 198, 206, 228

78

Figure par plans 1921

Pencil drawing on tracing paper

Signed and dated lower left "Jacques Villon 21"

21.2 x 12.5 cm.

PROVENANCE: Jacques Villon

COLLECTION: Louis Carré et Cie, Paris

79

Étude de tête 1921

Crayon drawing on tinted paper

Signed and dated lower right "Jacques Villon 21"

16.5 x 12.4 cm.

PROVENANCE: Jacques Villon

COLLECTION: Louis Carré et Cie, Paris

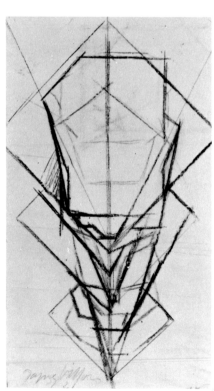

78

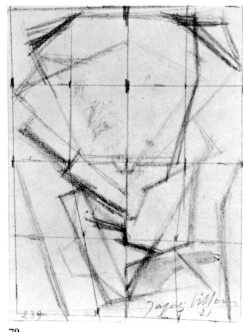

79

80
Figure 1921
Oil on canvas
Signed lower right "JV"
55 x 38.1 cm.
PROVENANCE: Louis Süe, Paris; G. David
Thompson, Pittsburgh; Galerie
Beyeler, Basel
COLLECTION: Albright-Knox Art Gallery,
Buffalo, New York, Edmund Hayes Fund
PUBLISHED: 34, 43, 109, 162
EXHIBITED: *15, 389, 397, 404, 464, 474*

80

81

Noblesse 1921

Watercolor

26.8 x 20.8 cm.

COLLECTION: Lucien Goldschmidt, Inc.,
New York

PUBLISHED: 27

EXHIBITED: *49, 55, 68*

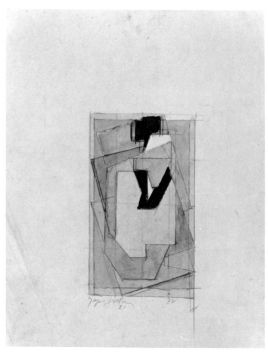

81

Noblesse (fig. 81b) is one of the most striking of Villon's postwar abstractions. The large planes in the foreground, placed along a vertical axis, are opposed to the diagonally positioned planes which serve as a backdrop. The colors, the adroit use of black, and Villon's placement of forms convey a sense of the nobility, stature, and grandeur implied by the title.

This achievement is retained in the small watercolor version (cat. no. 81) made after the oil (fig. 81b). Villon carefully studied his subject, reduced it into geometric shapes, and then redefined the formal elements by eliminating some lines and reshaping others. These changes may even be observed by comparison of *Noblesse* with a similar, probably earlier version of the composition (fig 81a). Villon's method was to simplify forms to obtain greater clarity in the expression of a subject.

The refinements from one version to the next also served to distinguish two separate identities. The earlier version (fig. 81a) shows the actor Barré transformed into a network of crossing horizontal, vertical and diagonal lines from which the shapes in the painted composition have been distilled. The geometric planes which signify head and body are widely proportioned, which

would be appropriate for the stout Barré (cf. cat. nos. 49-52).

In both the oil and watercolor versions of *Noblesse,* more slender shapes have been employed in order to convey the narrower proportions of a female body.[1] This may be the same woman who is represented in *La Femme assise* (fig. 81c), a drawing of 1921, where floral patterning (representing fabric design) accompanies the geometric planes signifying the woman's body, a motif also developed in 1914.

In *Noblesse* the black rectangular element at the top represents the woman's head in profile; the black triangular plane below conveys the contour of her upper arm. The torso and lower body have been transformed into large, brightly-colored planes. As in *Figure,* 1921 (cat. no. 80) and *Cheval de course,* 1922 (cat. no. 98), the tilted planes behind the subject stand for space itself.

D S R

[1] Many years after painting it, Villon disclosed that the point of departure for *Noblesse* was a seated woman. See (51) Simone Arbois, "Jacques Villon," *Volontés,* December 27, 1944. We wish to thank Hélène Lassalle for calling Villon's statement to our attention.

81a

JACQUES VILLON

Untitled c. 1920

Location unknown

Reproduced from (43) *Abstraction-Création, art non-figuratif* I, 1932 (reprinted by Arno Press, 1968)

81b
JACQUES VILLON
Noblesse 1920
Oil on canvas
Collection of Ragnar Moltzau, Jr., Oslo

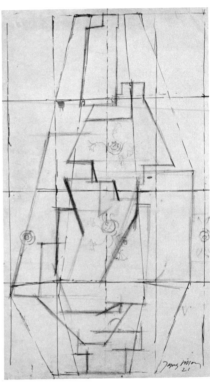

81c
JACQUES VILLON
La Femme assise 1921
Drawing
Private collection, Braintree, Vermont

L'Athlète de Duchamp-Villon 1921
Pen drawing in red and green
Signed lower left "Jacques Villon 21"
31.8 x 24.2 cm.
COLLECTION: Mr. and Mrs. Lucien
Goldschmidt, New York
EXHIBITED: *63, 443*

82

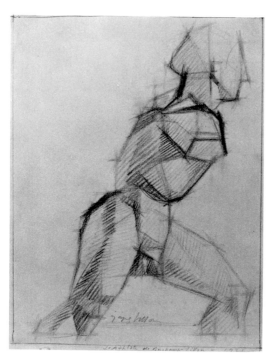

82a
JACQUES VILLON
L'Athlète de Duchamp-Villon 1921
Drawing
Courtesy Museum of Fine Arts, Boston

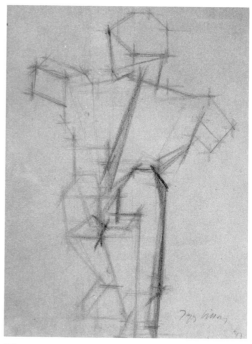

82b
JACQUES VILLON
Le Jeune homme 1937
Drawing
Private collection, New York

Of the many sculptures by Raymond Duchamp-Villon which Jacques Villon used as subjects, the *Torse de jeune homme, 1910*, often called *L'Athlète* appears the most frequently over the longest period of time. Marcel Duchamp is said to have posed for the head.[1] At least two drawings were done in 1921 (cat. no. 82, and fig. 81a). In addition, *L'Athlète* is seen innumerable times in the background of studio scenes.

In figure 82a the cubist planes of the sculpture are defined volumetrically through the use of hatched line shading. This method is consistent with other work of this period. *L'Athlète* is seen from the front without its base.

The position has been reversed in the Goldschmidt version, catalogue no. 82, and the figure is seen on its base, a long rectangular cube. Line and motion, rather than volume, are emphasized. The powerful striding torso is represented in jutting, overlapping planes which carry the motion of the body. There is no shading.

The drawing is divided in half vertically and horizontally, and to the right of the torso is a proportional study of squares within squares. Villon may have been squaring off the drawing for transfer to a painting: however, no version of *L'Athlète* in oil is known until the 1938 *Nature morte au buste de jeune homme* (fig. 82b) where the massive planes of the torso are outlined in crisp straight lines drawn from points marked by Xs. Once again, there is no shading or unnecessary detail; Villon's concern is the exact location of these planes in space. Compared to the earlier drawings of 1921 (cat. no. 82, fig. 82a), Villon is more concerned in this rear view with the direct rendering of form in an almost diagrammatic manner, than with reinterpreting it.

The torso faces front in the 1938 painting (fig. 82c) but the unmodeled planes and their clear, black outlines bear some relation to the drawing of the previous year. This sculpture is placed on a table with other objects which are not clearly identifiable (although the gold rectangular shape on the right side of the table may be a palette). The still life and table are set in a shallow geometrical space, the structure of which is reminiscent of Villon's second group of abstract paintings of the early thirties (see cat. nos. 114-117), where the sense of receding space is created by placing a smaller rectangle inside a larger one and connecting their corners with diagonal lines, exactly as in the pencil study to the right of *L'Athlète* in cat. no. 82.

S G

[1] (421) Hamilton and Agee, *Duchamp-Villon*, p. 50.

82c

JACQUES VILLON

Nature morte au buste de jeune homme

1938

Oil on canvas

Private collection, New York

83

Joie 1921

Oil on canvas

Signed lower left "JV", dated on back "21"

60 x 92 cm.

PROVENANCE: Jacques Villon

Private collection, France

PUBLISHED: 27, 34, 40, 41, 153, 342

EXHIBITED: 49, 55

84

Repliement 1921

Oil on canvas

Signed lower right "JV"

73 x 92 cm.

PROVENANCE: Jacques Villon

COLLECTION: Louis Carré et Cie, Paris

PUBLISHED: 27, 34, 40, 132, 153, 227, 342, 443, 456

EXHIBITED: 13, 15, 26, 27, 34, 38, 45, 46, 47, 49, 51, 55, 198, 220, 322

85

L'Équilibre rouge 1921

Oil on canvas

Signed lower right "JV"

81 x 60 cm.

PROVENANCE: Jacques Villon

COLLECTION: Louis Carré et Cie, Paris

PUBLISHED: 27, 40, 153, 342, 418, 456

EXHIBITED: 17, 19, 34, 38, 49, 51, 55, 299

83

While some of Villon's most abstract paintings can be traced unequivocally through drawings to their subject origins, others will remain problematic until related sketches are discovered. As Villon was a methodical artist, it is likely that the compositions of *Joie*,[1] *Repliement* and *L'Équilibre rouge* resulted from his usual procedure of analyzing a subject and then geometricizing it until the source is no longer immediately recognizable. Like *Noblesse*, 1920 (fig. 81b) *L'Équilibre rouge* may derive from a human model. Even though shapes of planes and their general arrangement are almost purely orthogonal, a general similarity to *Noblesse* is retained. *Joie* may belong to the many jockey representations (see cat. nos. 86-98) of 1921. The diagonal elements which project from the center outward to the corners resemble the shape of the horse's leg found in *Jockey Study No. 4* (fig. 89b). *Repliement* bears some relationship to the right-hand side of *Soldats en marche* (cat. no. 53), inverted.

Repliement and *L'Équilibre rouge* both demonstrate Villon's interest in color study, which became intense in the early 1920s when he may have begun to use the system of M. A. Rosenstiehl.[1] In these two paintings he restricted his palette to variations in value and intensity of red. His most obvious concern is the manipulation of lights and darks, which he first mastered within the monochromatic framework of black and white etchings.

Beyond complex demonstrations of color relationships, however, these paintings convey a deeper meaning, suggested by the titles "Joie" and "Repliement" are abstract qualities which — judging from Villon's consistent working method — are embodied by the shapes employed, somehow distilled from the nature of each original subject. (Another 1921 painting is titled *Peine*.[2]) If *Joie* does relate to a horse race, then the title reflects the artist's conception of the event as one of pleasure. *Repliement* is more complicated and speculative, as it can be translated "retreat" as well as "withdrawal." Since the late 19th century, color theorists (with whose work Villon was familiar)[3] related the color red with blood and death. Because *Repliement* seems compositionally related to *Soldats en marche* (cat. no. 53), and was painted only three years after Villon's brother Raymond's death as a consequence of military service, the choice of title and color may be a ref-

84

erence to the war and the withdrawal of troops. *L'Équilibre rouge*, a more literally meaningful title, may only express Villon's affirmation of the harmony and balance of shapes within a specified color scheme; yet given the artist's consistent practice of developing visual ideas, there is probably a deeper theme here as well.

D S R

[1] M. A. Rosenstiehl, *Traité de la couleur . . . ,* 1st edition (Paris, 1913).

[2] Reproduced in (35) Jacques Lassaigne, *Jacques Villon* (Paris: Editions de Beaune, 1950), p. 47.

[3] See cat. nos. 99, 100.

85

86

86a

RAYMOND DUCHAMP-VILLON

Le Petit cheval 1914

Bronze

The Joseph H. Hirshhorn Museum and
Sculpture Garden, Smithsonian Institution,
Washington, D.C.

86

Le Cheval de course 1921

Pencil drawing with red ink on
tracing paper

Signed in ink at lower right "Jacques
Villon" and dated below "21"

22.5 x 33.7 cm.

PROVENANCE: Lucien Goldschmidt, Inc.,
New York
COLLECTION: The Art Institute of Chicago,
Gift of Mr. Frank B. Hubachek

EXHIBITED: 60

The race course furnished a popular theme in late nineteenth-century French art, stimulating some of the finest achievements of Manet, Degas, and Toulouse-Lautrec. Jacques Villon did not take an active interest in this genre until the 1920s. In his earlier works, race horses were present only in subsidiary roles; for example, in *Autre temps*, 1904,[1] the emphasis is on the foreground figures, rather than on the race itself.

The major impetus for the jockey series, perhaps the largest concentrated group of drawings executed by Villon, may once again have been the death of his brother Raymond. Duchamp-Villon's most monumental sculpture was *Le Cheval* of 1914 (fig. 58a), preceded by many drawings and studies (see fig. 86a). The similarity between some of Raymond's sketches (see figs. 86b, 86c) and one of Villon's drawings, *Le Cheval de course*, 1921 (cat. no. 86), suggests that Villon began this project as a continuation of his brother's interrupted work. These three drawings (figs. 86, 86b, 86c) share a mechanical conception of the horse's movement. Though Villon did not go as far as Duchamp-Villon in transforming the horse's anatomy into machine parts, he nevertheless retained the strong diagonal axis which, like a piston rod, propels the horse's movement. *Le Cheval de course* is probably the first of Villon's jockey drawings, since he took a different approach in all of the others. *Le Cheval de course* was to suit his needs in another project, however; two years later, when he turned the compositional arrangement ninety degrees counter-clockwise, it became *Le Perroquet* (fig. 86d).

The "jockey series," so called because of the relationship between the eight drawings (cat. nos. 87-90, 92, 94, 96, and fig. 89b) and a painting of 1924 entitled *Le Jockey* (fig. 93a), was published by George Heard

Hamilton in 1948,[2] but several additional drawings have been discovered since. The fact that only the Yale drawings are numbered, while all but one are dated 1921, suggest that Villon numbered the Yale drawings subsequent to their execution,[3] probably trying to recall the sequence when he sold them, along with the 1924 painting, to the Société Anonyme in 1924.

The jockey drawings are characteristic examples of the way Villon scrutinized a subject before painting it. In *Study for the Jockey Nos. 1, 2, and 3* (cat. nos. 87-89), he examined both horse and rider in profile and from above. Plotted on intersecting lines which give them the quality of an architectural plan or blueprint, the elements are lined up on the same axis in preparation for subsequent combining of different views. Also evident in these early studies is the process of geometric clarification: shapes that are to be further developed are emphasized. For example, the ears, nose, tail and withers of the horse have been slightly geometricized in *Study No. 1*. The rider in *No. 3* betrays its origin as a toy model: Villon admitted to using toys often when preparing for certain paintings.[4]

Le Jockey en course (fig. 89a) was the first attempt to combine the different views of the horse and rider into a single drawing. The solution for the horse's head, attained in this drawing, appears at the upper left, isolated from the other parts. Of the five shapes making up this head, the top two components derive from *Study No. 1*, where the head was viewed from above, while the lower three parts are a modified version of the nose in profile, originating from *Study No. 2*.

Having determined the essential shapes for horse and rider in *Le Jockey en course*, Villon appears to have thought out the total composition in *Study No. 4* (fig. 89b). The

horse and jockey have been traced from *Le Jockey en course* (fig. 89a) but here pencil and watercolor has also been used to activate the surrounding space by means of the now familiar diamond shapes.

The remaining drawings are variations of *Study No. 4*, modified according to the needs of two different compositions Villon was developing. He seems to have been working simultaneously on two approaches, a narrow format and a broader, larger one. For the narrow format, he tightened up the shapes until they could all be inscribed nearly within a rectangle. In *Study No. 5* (cat. no. 90) he traced only the subject portion of *No. 4*, and divided it into sixteen unequal polygonal units. In *Composition* (cat. no. 91) he transformed these differing units into sixteen equal rectangles, adjusting the internal shapes accordingly. For example, in order to fit the horse's head into the space now provided, he was forced to slant it. In both drawings he also considered color relationships, indicated by hatching with colored pencil, and, in *Composition* (cat. no. 991) he sketched in background planes. *Study No. 6* (cat. no. 92) and *Le Jockey* (cat. no. 93) show the transitional and final refinements of this design. Part of the rider's head did not fit into the delineated rectangular area, and thus it was dropped in *Le Jockey*. This final drawing for this format is the basis for the 1924 painting *Le Jockey* (fig. 93a).

The drawings which established the large format include *Study No. 7* (cat. no. 94), *Cheval de course* (cat. no. 95) and *Study No. 8* (cat. no. 96). Since these are on tracing paper and approximately the same size, it is likely that there is an unknown drawing from which *No. 7* was traced. This group employs a combination of forms which appeared in *Study No. 4* (the background planes) with those of *Composition, No. 6*

86b

RAYMOND DUCHAMP-VILLON

Drawing for Le Cheval c. 1914

Location unknown

Reproduced from (421) George Heard
Hamilton and William C. Agee, *Raymond
Duchamp-Villon* (New York: Walker and
Co., 1967)

86c

RAYMOND DUCHAMP-VILLON

Drawing for Le Cheval c. 1914

Location unknown
Reproduced from *Ibid.*

and *Le Jockey* (the slanted horse's head).
It is also probable that the 1922 date inscribed on *Cheval de course* is inaccurate,
probably added years later, since the drawing is so close to *No. 7* and both seem to
have preceded *Study No. 8*. These drawings show Villon again systematically
refining the formal arrangement. When he
was dissatisfied with a line, for example the
triangle below the rider's arm in *Cheval de
course,* he crossed it out, much as an author
pencils out words in a manuscript. In *No. 8*
(cat. no. 96) the subject and the background
planes are both compacted to fit tightly
within a rectangular space (the same procedure as in *No. 5*), indicated by a grid of
horizontal and vertical lines now in proportion of 10:16. Where the horse's head
was slanted in order to fit into the narrower
(proportion 1:2) framework of *Composition,* it now reemerges upright, expanded to
the shape of the earlier drawings (figs. 89a,
89b), both harmonizing with the larger
format and allowing the inclusion of the
rider's head.

The paintings which derive from *Study
No. 8* are *Les Courses,* 1922[5] and *Color
Perspective,* 1922 (cat. no 100). In both, the
subject, background, and grid lines become
fused and are synthesized into finished
compositions. They appear as groupings of
stacked-up colored planes, the typical
Villon formula for abstract painting in the
early 1920s.

Knowledge of the drawings furnishes
clues to traces of figuration in *Color
Perspective* (cat. no. 97); here, the rider has
been transformed into a single wedge-
shaped plane, center and uppermost in the
composition. The rider's head (i.e., the top
of the plane) has again been removed, but
it remains visible in the underpainting. The
silhouette of the horse's lower leg is a
contrast of light and dark in the lower left

of the canvas.

There is another group of works related to the jockey series where the elements have been rearranged differently from those discussed in the above preparatory drawings. In two paintings, *Composition en jaune et bleu* or *Galop*, 1921 (fig. 97a) and *Galop*, 1921,[6] and an etching of the same year, *Le Cheval*,[7] horse and rider are both present, but the horse's tail has been displaced from the upper right hand corner to the upper left. It may be identified as three long narrow planes with curving contours. Of these Galop paintings, *Composition en jaune et bleu* or *Galop* (fig. 97a) is the most complex and therefore probably the first. In the patterning of the background, the horizontal lines may recall racetrack railings. The plane dominating the bottom portions of these works shows Villon experimenting with a different triangular pattern for each. This was the first time Villon employed repetitive patterning in painting, although he used similar devices in early aquatints, for example in *Les Cartes*, 1903 (cat. no. 10) and *Le Cake-Walk des petites filles*, 1904 (cat. no. 11).

One additional painting derived from the series concentrates on horse without rider. This is *Cheval de course*, 1922 (cat. no. 98), which derives from a watercolor sketch, *Outsider*, 1921 (cat. no. 98a). For the study, the shapes originate in the drawings with slanted horse's head, now freed from the limitations of a linear grid. In the painting, Villon has monumentalized the horse, enthroning it atop the diamond shaped planes. In the transition from watercolor to oil, the color scheme has been modified: contrast of yellow and blue was used in both the watercolor and the painting, but these complementaries have been transferred from horse to surrounding planes in the latter. The only color location which

remains the same is the red in the lower portion of the horse.

Although the development of the jockey series was completed by 1924, Villon returned from time to time to one of his favorite motifs. *L'Aumone*, 1943[8] and *Aux Courses*, 1952 (fig. 98b) are among the many examples where the race horse, with or without rider, darts across the canvas once again.

DSR

[1] AP 72

[2] (181) George Heard Hamilton, "The Dialectic of Later Cubism: Villon's Jockey," *Magazine of Art*, XLI/7 (November, 1948), p. 268-273. Professor Hamilton did not question Villon with regard to when he numbered the Yale drawings.

[3] Letter from George Heard Hamilton to David S. Rubin, June 26, 1974.

[4] (40) Vallier, *Villon*, p. 116. "Sometimes, I have brought with me to the studio children's toys, merry-go-rounds or little aeroplanes. I used them as references for my works. I liked having under my eyes when I was painting races or more recently, aeroplanes. Of course, I have been to real races and I have seen real planes." — Jacques Villon.

[5] Reproduced in (40) Vallier, *Villon*, p. 55.

[6] Reproduced in *Ibid.*, p. 54.

[7] AP 206.

[8] Reproduced in *Tableaux modernes*, Galerie Motte (Geneva, June 28-29, 1968), p. 76.

86d

JACQUES VILLON

Le Perroquet 1923

Oil on canvas

Location unknown

Reproduced from (400) *Henie-Onstad Collection* (Stockholm: Moderna Museet, 1961)

87

Study for the Jockey (No. 1) 1921

Pencil drawing

Signed lower right "Jacques Villon 21"
and lower left "n. 1"

7.3 x 3.6 cm.

PROVENANCE: Jacques Villon

COLLECTION: Yale University Art Gallery,
New Haven, Gift of the Société Anonyme
Collection

PUBLISHED: 181, 182, 419

EXHIBITED: *20, 29, 60, 174, 194, 198, 206, 449*

88

Study for the Jockey (No. 2) 1921

Pencil on paper

Signed lower right "Jacques Villon 21"
and lower left "n. 2"

15 x 36 cm.

PROVENANCE: Jacques Villon

COLLECTION: Yale University Art Gallery,
New Haven, Gift of the Société Anonyme
Collection

PUBLISHED: 181, 182, 419

EXHIBITED: *20, 29, 60, 174, 194, 198, 206, 449*

89

Study for the Jockey (No. 3) 1921

Pencil on paper

Signed "n. 3"

32.5 x 41.5 cm.

PROVENANCE: Jacques Villon

COLLECTION: Yale University Art Gallery,
New Haven, Gift of the Société Anonyme
Collection

PUBLISHED: 181, 182, 419

EXHIBITED: *20, 29, 60, 174, 194, 198, 206,
357, 449*

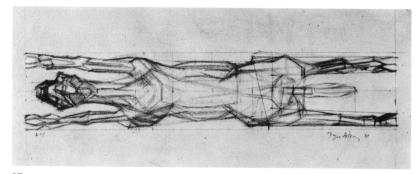

87

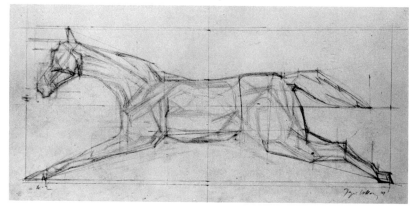

88

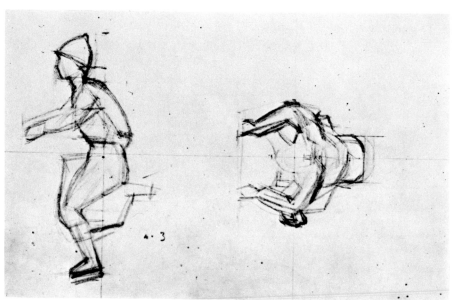

89

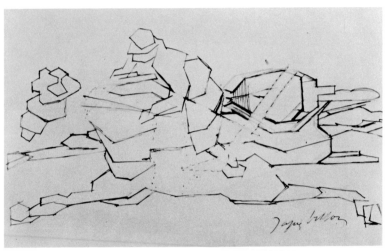

89a

JACQUES VILLON

Le Jockey en course 1921

Drawing

Collection of Mr. and Mrs. Richard Victor,
New York

89b

JACQUES VILLON

Study for the Jockey (No. 4) 1921

Drawing

Courtesy of Yale University Art Gallery,
New Haven

90

Study for the Jockey (No. 5) 1921

Black and red pencil on tracing paper

Signed lower left "Jacques Villon n. 5"

39.5 x 55.5 cm.

PROVENANCE: Jacques Villon

COLLECTION: Yale University Art Gallery,
New Haven, Gift of the Société Anonyme
Collection

PUBLISHED: 181, 182, 419

EXHIBITED: *20, 29, 60, 174, 194, 198,
206, 449*

91

Composition 1921

Drawing in India ink, colored pencil,
and watercolor

Signed lower right "Jacques Villon"

20 x 40 cm.

COLLECTION: Private collection, Brussels

92

Study for the Jockey (No. 6) 1921

Pencil on paper

Signed lower right "Jacques Villon" and
lower left "n. 6"

14 x 36 cm.

PROVENANCE: Jacques Villon

COLLECTION: Yale University Art Gallery,
New Haven, Gift of the Société Anonyme
Collection

PUBLISHED: 181, 182, 419

EXHIBITED: *20, 29, 60, 174, 194, 198, 206,
357, 449*

93

Le Jockey 1921

Pen and wash

Signed lower right in pencil "Jacques
Villon 21"

15.8 x 38 cm.

PROVENANCE: Jacques Villon

COLLECTION: Louis Carré et Cie, Paris

PUBLISHED: 27

EXHIBITED: *32, 49, 55, 60*

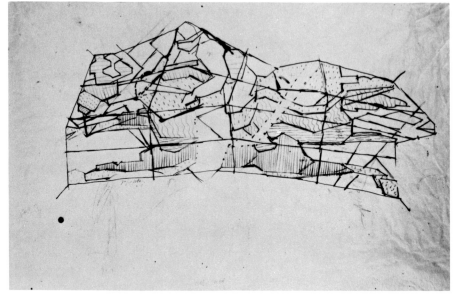

90

91

92

93

93a

JACQUES VILLON

Le Jockey 1924

Oil on canvas

Courtesy of Yale University Art Gallery,
New Haven

94

Study for the Jockey (No. 7) 1921

Pen and ink on tracing paper

Signed lower right "Jacques Villon n. 7"

27 x 45 cm.

PROVENANCE: Jacques Villon

COLLECTION: Yale University Art Gallery, New Haven, Gift of the Société Anonyme Collection

PUBLISHED: 181, 182, 419

EXHIBITED: 20, 29, 60, 174, 194, 198, 206, 357, 449

95

Cheval de course 1922

Pen and ink drawing on tracing paper

Signed lower right in pencil "Jacques Villon 22"

26.3 x 43.8 cm.

PROVENANCE: Jacques Villon

COLLECTION: Louis Carré et Cie, Paris

EXHIBITED: 366

96

Study for the Jockey (No. 8) 1921

Red and blue ink and pencil on tracing paper, squared

Signed lower right "Jacques Villon" and lower left "n. 8"

28.5 x 48 cm.

PROVENANCE: Jacques Villon

COLLECTION: Yale University Art Gallery, New Haven, Gift of the Société Anonyme Collection

PUBLISHED: 181, 182, 419

EXHIBITED: 20, 29, 60, 174, 194, 198, 206, 357, 449

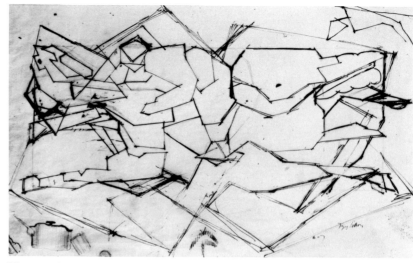

94

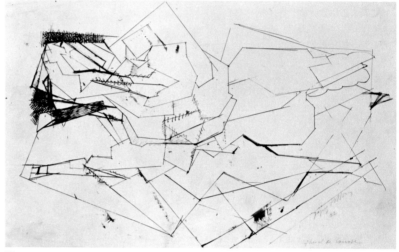

95

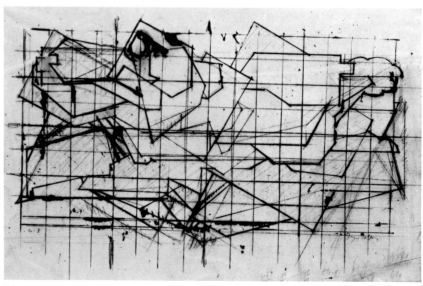

96

97

Color Perspective 1922

Oil on canvas

Signed lower left "J.V." and on back
"Jacques Villon 22"

60 x 92 cm.

PROVENANCE: Jacques Villon

COLLECTION: Yale University Art Gallery,
New Haven, Gift of the Société Anonyme
Collection

PUBLISHED: 182, 407, 419, 420

EXHIBITED: *20, 166, 174, 177, 191, 206*

98

Cheval de course 1922

Oil on canvas

Signed lower left "J.V."

46 x 98 cm.

PROVENANCE: Jacques Villon

COLLECTION: Louis Carré et Cie, Paris

PUBLISHED: 27, 29, 34, 122, 132, 138, 139,
153, 396, 449

EXHIBITED: *15, 17, 18, 19, 22, 26, 27, 34, 37,
45, 46, 47, 49, 51, 55, 220, 322, 459*

97

97a

JACQUES VILLON

Composition jaune et bleu or Galop 1921

Oil on canvas

Collection of Gérard Bonnier, Stockholm

98

98a
JACQUES VILLON
Outsider 1921
Pencil and watercolor
Location unknown
Courtesy Louis Carré et Cie, Paris

98b
JACQUES VILLON
Aux Courses 1952
Oil on canvas
Private collection

99

Figure par plans 1921

Drawing in India ink, squared

Signed lower right "Jacques Villon 21"

25.5 x 17.5 cm.

PROVENANCE: Jacques Villon

COLLECTION: Louis Carré et Cie, Paris

PUBLISHED: *28*

EXHIBITED: *32, 49*

100

Color Perspective 1922

Oil on canvas

Signed lower left "J.V." and on back "Jacques Villon 22"

73 x 60 cm.

PROVENANCE: Katherine S. Dreier, New York

COLLECTION: The Museum of Modern Art, New York, Katherine S. Dreier Bequest, 1953

PUBLISHED: *133, 382*

EXHIBITED: *149, 248, 260, 280, 302, 441*

"Color Perspective" was a title which Villon used for several of his abstractions in the early 1920s. Even though these paintings were ultimately based on observation, as in the Yale *Color Perspective* (cat. no. 97), each represented for Villon a new experiment in the juxtaposition of different forms and colors. Not all the paintings entitled "Color Perspective" belong to the same series. By 1920 at least, Villon determined his colors by reference to the chromatic system developed by M. A. Rosenstiehl,[1] and its use enhanced his delight in creating and manipulating endless color possibilities:

But, you tell me, does not all the richness of color lead to mere fugues? That is an idea which may be defended as, indeed, one may defend abstract art, since it offers to him who employs it, if not to him who contemplates it, the joy of the commander-in-chief organizing his reserve troops.[2]

Although the absence of many preparatory drawings makes it difficult to be certain, *Figures par plans* and the 1922 *Color Perspective* probably belong to a series of related works; they share a vertical format and a double diamond-shaped planar structure. *Figures par plans* is a study for a painting known only through reproduction (fig. 99a). It derives directly from *Espaces*, 1920 (fig. 99b), a study of the fusion of planes intersecting two spherical objects, perhaps the globes Villon kept in his studio (see discussion cat. nos. 58-62 and 142). In this version (fig. 99a) the two stacked planar units have been merged into one central cluster.

Another lost painting, known only through photographs (see fig. 100a), provides a likely link between *Figures par plans* (cat. no. 99) and *Color Perspective,* 1922 (cat. no. 100). This lost work appears to stand midway between them in degree of formal complexity. As Villon simplified his forms and progressed from version to version in a series, he usually enlarged the planar elements. Finally, *Color Perspective* and the lost painting also share a lightly-painted frame around the canvas perimeter, further suggesting that one is a later manifestation of the other.

D S R

[1] Rosenstiehl, *Traité.* "This book expands upon the author's important brochure, *Les Premiers éléments de la science de la couleur* (Mulhouse, 1884) which had helped spread knowledge of Maxwell color discs, the adjustable colored discs which when spun at high speed form a single color." Robert L. Herbert, The Faber Birren Collection in Color, *Yale University Library Gazette* XLIX/1 (July, 1974), p. 44-45. In 1934, the same publisher, Dunod, brought out a second edition *"revue et mise à jour"* by Julie Beaudeneau. This edition contained remarkable chromatic circles and detailed color charts, and Villon used these to establish his palette. He urged his young painter friend Cleve Gray in 1945 to be sure to obtain the second edition of Rosenstiehl's work.

[2] (263) Jacques Villon, quoted in Walter Pach, "This is Cubism Cultivated," *Art News* XLVIII, 3 (May, 1949), 51.

99

99a

<small>JACQUES VILLON</small>

Untitled c. 1921

Oil on canvas

Location unknown

Reproduced from (38) Walter Pach, *Villon*
(New York: Société Anonyme, Inc., 1921)

99b

<small>JACQUES VILLON</small>

Espaces 1920

Oil on canvas

The Peggy Guggenheim Foundation, Venice

100

100a

JACQUES VILLON

Untitled c. 1921-1922

Oil on canvas

Location unknown

Photo from the archives of the late
Mrs. J. C. Guggenheimer

101

101

Papiers 1923

Oil on canvas

Signed lower right "Jacques Villon 23"

38 x 46 cm.

PROVENANCE: Jacques Villon; Louis Carré et Cie, Paris

Private collection, France

PUBLISHED: 27, 28, 29, 32, 34, 40, 153, 155, 237, 342

EXHIBITED: 13, 15, 26, 27, 34, 38, 49, 55, 198, 220

In *Papiers,* a final step in the development of Villon's abstractions of the early 1920s, the geometric design originated — as always — from observation. Here a stack of papers is well suited to the compositional format of layered planes characteristic of all the works of this period. While the works of 1920 and 1921 contained a wider variety of smaller, more intricate, and more opaque geometric shapes, 1922 and 1923 saw a move towards larger planes, greatly simplified and more transparent.

Commenting on *Papiers* many years later, Villon reaffirmed his purpose to unite subject and form: "The essential is that the object is willfully incorporated into the canvas."[1] By this he meant that the rectangular shape of the papers, of the planes representing them, and of the canvas itself become almost indistinguishable in the painting. He also recalled his procedure. The smaller rectangles were drawn first, and then enlarged as they were repeated from the center outward: "I have taken a small measure in the middle of the painting and have accordingly established larger planes towards the edge of the canvas."[2]

He then modified the design, using color to transform the rectangles into polygonal and triangular elements. The bright palette is typical of the artist's color experimentation of the early 1920s, though this combination of pastel greens, purples, pinks, and yellows appears here for the first time and would not be seen again for many years, until *Les Grands fonds,* 1945 (cat. no. 145).

DSR

[1] (40) Vallier, *Villon,* p. 118.
[2] *Ibid.*

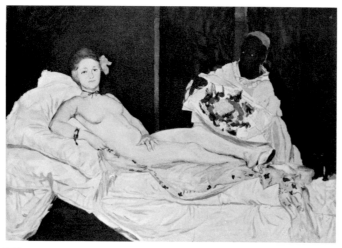

102

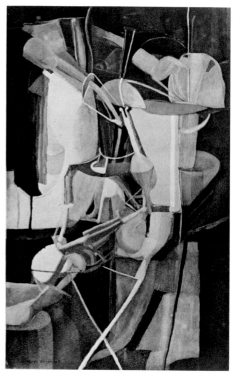

103

102

Olympia (After Edouard Manet) 1926

Color aquatint and etching

40.5 x 58.6 cm.

PROVENANCE: Jacques Villon

COLLECTION: Yale University Art Gallery, New Haven, Gift of the Société Anonyme Collection

PUBLISHED: AP 514

103

La Mariée (After Marcel Duchamp) 1930

Color aquatint and etching

50 x 31.3 cm.

COLLECTION: Fogg Art Museum, Harvard University, Cambridge, Massachusetts, Gift of Theodore Stebbins, Jr., in honor of Jacob Rosenberg

PUBLISHED: AP 538a

In 1922, Villon was persuaded by a group of Bernheim-Jeune artists who admired his skill as a printmaker to make a series of reproductive engravings after well known modern works.[1] Continuing with this series until 1930, Villon made prints after approximately 40 paintings. Each original edition of 200 was signed by Villon and co-signed by the original artist, if possible.

The earlier aquatints were by the most popular masters — Matisse, Picasso, Derain, Braque, Renoir, Vlaminck, Dufy, Cézanne, Bonnard, and Manet, to name a few. In 1926, the Louvre acquired Villon's rendition of Manet's *Olympia* for *La Chalcographie du Louvre*.[2] The odalisque theme had appeared in Villon's early aquatint prints, such as *La Boudeuse,* 1900 (cat. no. 5); and in *Les Cartes,* 1903 (cat. no. 10), the woman's pet rests on her bed much as does the cat in *Olympia*. It seems certain that Villon was attracted to Manet's *Olympia* since he sketched it in 1912, probably in connection with his monumental landscape *Puteaux: Les fumées et les arbres en fleur* (cf. cat. no. 33 and fig. 33c). In the reproductive aquatint, Villon has faithfully and carefully copied Manet, sensitively retaining the inti-mate mood and the figure's piercing gaze.

By 1927 Villon had apparently had a stronger voice in the decision of whose paintings he would engrave, for many of the reproductions after this date are of works by artists in Villon's circle of family and friends — Marcel Duchamp, Suzanne Duchamp, Jean Crotti, Katherine Dreier, André Mare, Albert Gleizes, Jean Metzinger, and Villon himself (a reproduction of *Figure,* 1921, cat. no. 80). Finally, in 1930, he made an aquatint after Marcel Duchamp's 1912 *La Mariée,* itself possibly related to one of his own compositions (see cat. nos. 54-57, fig. 55b).

D S R

[1] Letter from Gilbert Gruet (for Bernheim-Jeune et Cie) to David S. Rubin, December 1, 1972.

[2] Angoulvent, P. J., *La Chalcographie du Louvre: histoire et description des collections* (Paris: Musées Nationaux, Palais du Louvre, 1926), reproduced p. 140.

104

Nature morte aux noix 1929

Etching, second state

22.3 x 27.7 cm.

COLLECTION: Print Department, Boston
Public Library

PUBLISHED: AP 220[11]

104

During the late 1920s, a period generally
hostile to cubist derived abstraction, Villon's
best energies were once again largely absorbed by printmaking. The graphic power
infused into this commonplace subject
through two old etching techniques, drypoint and stipple, justifies Villon's reputation as one of the great printmakers of
the century. Although the etching is closely
related to a small painting (fig. 104a), it
helps to demonstrate why, at the time, many
of his fellow artists considered him exclusively as a printmaker.

Particularly evident here, and the source
of the initial impact of *Nature morte aux
noix,* is the eccentric nature of the design.
It is simultaneously symmetrical, yet dis-
jointed because of the contrast between
light and dark areas, and between line and
mass; above all because of the scale of the
pears, knife and chestnuts in relation to the
angled, erratically tilted table top, sug-
gestive of the stacked planes developed in
Villon's abstract work early in the decade.

A M

104a

JACQUES VILLON

Nature morte aux noix 1929

Oil on canvas

The Baltimore Museum of Art

105

Le Philosophe 1930

Etching

21.3 x 15.3 cm.

COLLECTION: Print Department, Boston
Public Library

PUBLISHED: AP 226

106

Le Philosophe 1930

Oil on canvas

Signed lower left "Jacques Villon "30"

100 x 78.5 cm.

COLLECTION: The Brooklyn Museum,
Gift of Mrs. Gerda Stein

PUBLISHED: 40, 262, 342, 370

EXHIBITED: 4, 5, 6, 29, 298, 242, 443

Even while he was giving up eight months each year to the Bernheim reproductive engraving project (see cat. nos. 102, 103), Villon found the time to produce individual work, mostly still lifes (see cat. no. 104) or figure studies. Many of the figures seem to have their origins in drawings made in 1927, or even earlier of men and women relaxing by the seashore, standing, seated or lying down on rocks (see AP 212). Some of these were developed into paintings almost immediately (e.g., *Sur les rochers,* 1927, now in a New York private collection); others appear in 1930 in single figure paintings like *Femme debut* or *Femme assise* (see *Cent tableaux de Jacques Villon,* Galerie Charpentier, Paris, 1961, n.p. reproduction), which retain the quality of a study.

We may hypothesize that these studies of men and women on holiday also served for some more complex prints and paintings executed as late as 1938 or 1939. Two of these, *L'Appel de la vie* (AP 320, fig. 105a) and *D'où on tourne l'épaule à la vie* (AP 327, fig. 105b), have metaphysical titles, one deriving from Mallarmé. This elevation of genre themes to subjects of greater significance, paralleling the formal evolution of Villon's early 1920s painting from observa-

tion to abstract idea and construction, is first evident in *Le Philosophe.* Probably *Le Philosophe* began as the study of a seated male bather, half wrapped in a towel, reading a newspaper.[1] Removed from the context of life, it suggested a classical figure, wrapped in a toga, studying a scroll. A standing male, similarly wrapped, appears in *L'Appel de la vie;* reversed and still more simplified, he appears in *D'où on tourne l'épaule à la vie.* The similarity of the rocks, as well as the arrangement and dress of the figures, points to a common origin for all three prints, as well as *Sur les rochers* (AP 212), in an outing by the sea.

D S R

[1] Yale University Art Gallery possesses a small oil study for *Le Philosophe* (see fig. 106a) which has been catalogued and titled *Le Philosophe, Study for a Self-Portrait.* Although the canvas bears no inscription, a note among Katherine S. Dreier's papers indicating that *Le Philosophe* was a self portrait is the basis for the label. If this were the case, the pose would suggest the artist drawing, and *Le Philosophe* would be a source for the series of self portraits beginning in 1935, including *Petit dessinateur*

105

105c

JACQUES VILLON

Drawing for Le Philosophe 1929

Location unknown

Reproduced from (34) Jacques Lassaigne, *Jacques Villon* (Paris: Les Editions de Beaune, 1950) (cat. no. 121), *Home dessinant* (cat. no. 122), and culminating in the *Signature* or *Scribe* series (cat. no. 154).

Yet, the features of the drawing for *Le Philosophe,* as well as the carriage of the body, do not suggest Villon, but a younger man. A suggestion has been made linking the final version of *Le Philosophe* (cat. no. 106) with the series of portraits of the artist's father (see cat. nos. 38, 39, 40, 41); it seems still more probable to link this image initially with a portrait of Marcel, bearing in mind that one of Villon's 1951 portraits of his younger brother also bore the title *Un Philosophe* (see cat. no. 155).

106

105a

JACQUES VILLON

L'Appel de la vie 1938

Etching, AP 320

Print Department, Boston Public Library

105b

JACQUES VILLON

D'où on tourne l'épaule à la vie 1939

Etching, AP 327

Print Department, Boston Public Library

106a

JACQUES VILLON

Study for Le Philosophe 1929

Oil sketch

Courtesy of Yale University Art Gallery, New Haven

123

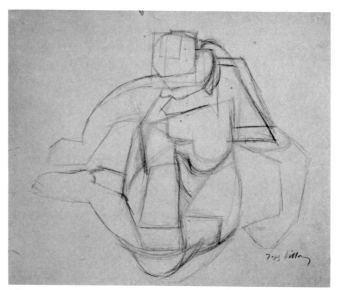

107

107a

RAYMOND DUCHAMP-VILLON

Femme assise 1909

Wood sculpture

Collection of Niels Onstad, Oslo

107

Femme assise c. 1931

Pencil drawing on white paper

Signed lower right "Jacques Villon"

37.9 x 27.5 cm.

PROVENANCE: Mrs. J. C. Guggenheimer, New York

Anonymous loan

108

La Bonne aventure 1931

Drawing in India ink on tracing paper

Signed lower right "Jacques Villon 31"

33.5 x 25.5 cm.

COLLECTION: Lucien Goldschmidt, Inc., New York

Exhibited: 63

In these two drawings of a female nude, based on Raymond Duchamp-Villon's *Femme assise*, 1909 (fig. 107a), Villon returned to the strict isometric approach he first developed in the early 1920s. Once again the subject is transformed into a geometric design of planes overlapping each other in space. In *La Bonne aventure* the planes are viewed from the top, and the title may refer to the intricate formal game that results from the systematic division of the figure into sections. Some of the shapes in these drawings may be found as early as *Noblesse,* 1920 (fig. 81b) and *Repliement,* 1921 (cat. no. 84). The upper half of the configuration in *La Bonne aventure* is similar to the *Color Perspective,* 1921, in the Solomon R. Guggenheim Museum, New York. Villon referred to *Femme assise* and *La Bonne aventure* in preparing *Abandon,* c. 1946-1950 (fig. 108a), where the variety of shapes is allowed to play freely with a vivid display of color.

D S R

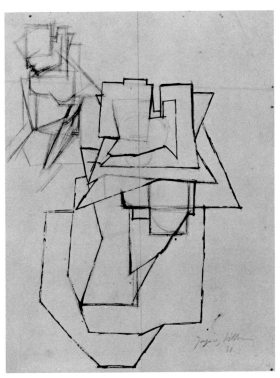

108

108a
JACQUES VILLON
Abandon 1946-1950
Oil on canvas
Collection of Ragnar Moltzau, Oslo

109

Sculptures 1931
Etching and drypoint, 48/50, third state
18.8 x 12 cm.

COLLECTION: The Art Institute of Chicago,
Gift of Mr. Frank B. Hubachek

PUBLISHED: AP 234

Two of Duchamp-Villon's 1911 busts, *Maggy* (fig. 109a) and *Baudelaire* (fig. 70a), dominate this simple studio scene. They both rest on stands, with *Baudelaire* below, and *Maggy* directly behind. Two preparatory drawings of this composition from the same year are known (fig. 109b), and there are two versions of the subject in oil — *Le Masque*, 1931 (fig. 109c), and *La Stèle aux bustes*, 1933.

The proximity of the busts fuses them together in the design; *Baudelaire* appears at first to be the base or neck of *Maggy*. The drawings indicate that the two sculptures were intended to be merged within a single contour. In the etching the two pieces are slightly more independent. From the drawing we can infer that the vague forms on the shelves above the paintings were also sculptures.

The mature etching technique is typical of Villon's work at this time, which had already begun to influence many of his contemporaries from Morandi to Picasso. Here as in *Le Philosophe*, 1930 (cat. no. 105), he uses a delicate network of intersecting horizontal, vertical and diagonal lines which in some areas are intensified for rich, dark tones. The figures emerge from dark into

109a
RAYMOND DUCHAMP-VILLON
Maggy 1911
Bronze
The Solomon R. Guggenheim Museum,
New York

109

light. Unlike *Le Philosophe*, however, the
entire ground of *Sculptures* is not dark; a
long rectangular area of white divides the
sheet geometrically into dark and light. In
previous etchings, the light areas were used
primarily for highlighting objects.

The etching is arranged in steps, descending from left to right. All objects are placed
parallel to the picture plane and *Maggy* and
Baudelaire face the viewer frontally. This
view, emphasizing symmetry and the most
stable characteristics of the heads, suggests
religious objects or cult objects, an impression strengthened by the altar-like stands,
and the stacking of the busts one above the
other like a monument. As in many other
works in which the sculptures of Raymond
Duchamp-Villon are used, this work com-
memorates the dead brother and his artistic
legacy. In the title of the 1933 painting, *La
Stèle aux bustes,* the use of the term *"stèle"*
makes the commemorative aspect even
more explicit.

S G

109c
Le Masque 1930
Oil on canvas
Private collection

109b
**Maggy, Baudelaire, sculptures de
Duchamp-Villon** 1931
Drawing
Private collection

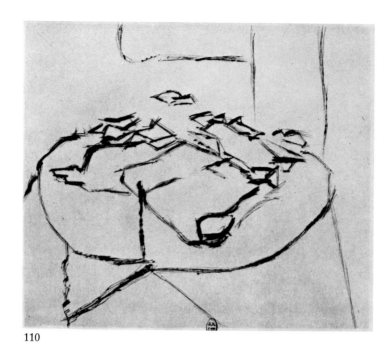

110

110

Papiers sur une table 1931

Drypoint, first state

13 x 15.7 cm.

COLLECTION: Bibliothèque Nationale, Paris, Cabinet des Estampes

PUBLISHED: AP 233[1]

111

Papiers sur une table 1931

Drypoint and etching, second state

13 x 15.7 cm.

COLLECTION: Bibliothèque Nationale, Paris, Cabinet des Estampes

PUBLISHED: AP 233[11]

112

Papiers sur une table 1931

Drypoint and etching, third state

13 x 15.7 cm.

COLLECTION: Bibliothèque Nationale, Paris, Cabinet des Estampes

PUBLISHED: AP 233[111]

The three states of *Papiers sur une table,* 1931, demonstrate both Villon's creative method and his technical mastery of the graphic process. The first state (cat. no. 110) seems an initial response to the motif, an almost spontaneous selection of shapes achieved by scratching directly into the plate with a fine drypoint stylus. The feathery quality of the line is the result of the ink interacting with the burr produced by the needle's digging into the metal surface. The even grey plate tone is produced by leaving a thin film of ink on the smoothly-wiped plate.

In the second state (cat. no. 111), Villon examined various qualities of tone established by intersecting lines: some of the original drypoint has been burnished away and the cross-hatched lines are etched into the plate. The lighter areas are those in which there are fewest lines — the lightest being a small shape at the upper center of the composition, totally devoid of shading. The next lightest areas are those covered only by the diagonal lines which move upward from left to right, then follows a shape created by crossing diagonal lines only; then, areas where horizontal lines are included with the crossing diagonals. Finally,

the darkest areas are the result of overlay of verticals, diagonals and horizontal lines.

In addition, Villon enhances the darkest areas of tone by differential biting of the plate in the acid. Because the artist stopped out the lighter portions of the design with an acid-resistant varnish, the areas intended to be darkest were allowed longer exposure in the etching solvent, were bitten more deeply, and thus retained more ink in the printing process.

In the third state (cat. no. 112) Villon further simplified and abstracted the composition of the second state. Here the last remnants of the initial areas of drypoint have all been burnished away, leaving only the faintest vestiges of the original marks. Further biting of the plate has darkened the upper left and lower right areas of the image. The process is slow, deliberate, systematic, transforming random and seemingly trivial objects into a visually imposing image.

A M

111

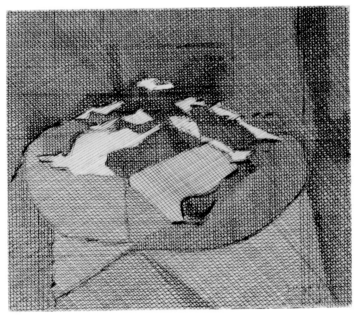

112

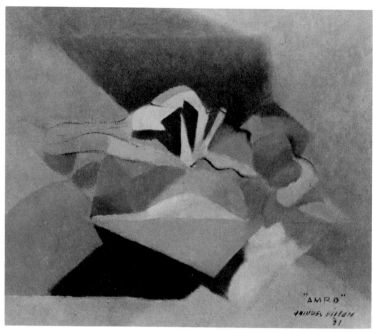

113

113

"Amro" 1931

Oil on canvas

Signed and dated lower right "AMRO Jacques Villon 31"

46 x 55 cm.

PROVENANCE: Jacques Villon

COLLECTION: Centre National d'Art et de Culture Georges Pompidou, Musée Nationale d'Art Moderne, Paris

PUBLISHED: 34, 176, 398, 401, 448, 449, 450

EXHIBITED: 234, 459

The composition of "Amro" may be found in a slightly smaller oil painting of the same year, *Table au papier orange*.[1] As in earlier still lifes such as *Papiers,* 1923 (cat. no. 101) and *Le Tampon noir,* 1926,[2] or later ones like *Nature morte au perroquet,* 1932 (see fig. 127a), the subject derived from material Villon had in his studio, in this case, paper.

Amro is a created word, a baptismal name which became the name of a canvas. Why? Because the canvas, deriving from a mass of papers, is too far removed from its point of departure. It has become a canvas in itself. To distinquish it from other works, to designate it, I have baptised it. As for the name "Amro," I chose it because the arabesque of this word suggests the rhythm of the painting.[3]

Villon "baptized" at least two other paintings with invented, highly private names: *Jilk* and *Phi* (a pendant to *Amro*), a still life with the head of a dead rabbit.[4] The use of the title *Phi,* however, implying familiarity with golden section sequential ratios, leaves room for further speculation about the arbitrariness of the title selected.[5]

D S R

[1] Reproduced in *(27) Cent Tableaux de Jacques Villon* (Paris: Galerie Charpentier, 1961).

[2] *Ibid.*

[3] (397) Bernard Dorival, *Les Etapes de la peinture française contemporaine,* vol. II (Paris: Gallimand, 1944), p. 314.

[4] We are indebted to Hélène Lassalle for this information. See *(77a)* Rouen-Grand Palais, *Villon,* No. 109, p. 106.

[5] In mathematics, Phi is connected with any series formed according to the law that each term is the sum of the two preceding, regardless of whatever the first two terms may be. The ratio of successive terms approximates more and more closely to Phi (the golden ratio) as the sequence increases.

114

L'Architecture 1931

Oil on canvas

Signed and dated lower right "Jacques Villon 31"

55 x 46 cm.

PROVENANCE: Jacques Villon; Louis Carré et Cie, Paris

Private collection, France

PUBLISHED: 27, 32, 34, 39, 114, 132, 142, 153, 180, 236, 365

EXHIBITED: 5, 6, 14, 15, 17, 18, 26, 38, 49, 51, 55, 220

115

Allégresse 1932

Oil on canvas

Signed and dated lower left "Jacques Villon 32"

46 x 38 cm.

PROVENANCE: Jacques Villon; Marcel Guiot, Paris

COLLECTION: Louis Carré et Cie, Paris

PUBLISHED: 27, 29, 152

EXHIBITED: 27, 34, 49, 51, 55, 363

In 1930 or 1931 the normally reticent Jacques Villon, prodded by his friend Albert Gleizes, contributed to *Abstraction-Création, Art non-figuratif,*[1] a movement and later a periodical dedicated to geometric abstraction. For the first issue (1932) he submitted two paintings from the 1920-1923 period, *Figure,* 1921 (cat. no. 80) and an early version of *Noblesse* (fig. 81a).[2] These works were not non-objective, but derived from subjects which can be recognized if carefully compared with the evolving preparatory drawings. For the second issue (and exhibition) of *Abstraction-Création* (1933), Villon submitted two geometrically structured canvases, *Abstraction,* 1932 (fig. 116d) and an untitled painting, 1933 (fig. 117b).[3] These reflect the fresh interest in formal concerns which reawakened in Villon in 1930, when he once more began painting full-time. Two related paintings of that year, *La Modèle* (fig. 114a) and *Figure* (fig. 114b) illustrate his basic working method, which had not changed since the early 1920s insofar as transformation of a subject into geometric terms was concerned. However, a new compositional formula was being developed: rather than conceiving of subject and space as superimposed planes, Villon now began to express both in more linear terms. In *Figure* Villon emphasized contour rather than planar construction; the outline of an arm has become animated, turning into a fluid black line, recalling the linear approach of 1912 (see cat. nos. 42-48). However, space remains behind the subject, serving as a stage, as in the 1920-1923 period.

With *L'Architecture,* 1931 (cat. no. 114), Villon began to assert a compositional formula which would characterize every major canvas from 1931 to 1933. Each painting is divided into two or more concentric rectangles intersected at the center

114a

JACQUES VILLON

La Modèle 1930

Oil on canvas

Location unknown

114b

JACQUES VILLON

Figure 1930

Oil on canvas

Private collection

114

by diagonals drawn from the corners. These concentric rectangles are similar to the proportional device that appeared in a set of squares beside *L'Athlète de Duchamp-Villon,* 1921 (cat. no. 82); although a golden section rectangle is not drawn at the center, closer and closer approximations to the golden ratio result from the addition series, commencing with the dark square just off the center, and progressing to the canvas perimeter. In the series of paintings of these three years, Villon exhibits a greater awareness of intricate mathematical patterns than he had ten years earlier, possibly having used magic squares to generate the linear pattern in catalogue nos. 114 and 115, and probably the *Spira Mirabilis* or equiangular spiral for *L'Espace* (cat. no. 116).[4] Although line was still subservient to figuration one year earlier in the 1930 *Figure* (fig. 114b), in *L'Architecture* Villon magnified and isolated it until the very way that line fits into the space became the subject of the work. For this reason it is justifiable to maintain that the 1931-1933 series of abstractions is as close as Villon ever came to being a non-objective painter, bearing in mind that in these works, idea references that extend beyond mere formal relations are clearly stated both by the title of the work and the movement of the line.

L'Architecture and the slightly smaller *Allégresse,* 1932 (cat. no. 115) use superficially similar linear motifs, but in *L'Architecture* the zigzag lines are based on two isosceles triangles with bases parallel to canvas top and bottom and angles paralleling the corner to corner diagonals; in *Allégresse,* isosceles triangles can only be made by extension, and the bases and angles never parallel the geometric relations of the concentric squares. The result is that *L'Architecture* is stable, and *Allégresse* eccentric. That Villon chose "architecture" for a title, apparently in the spirit of certain human attributes ("nobility," "joy," and "happiness") always reserved in his work for the most abstract paintings and universal emotions, is perhaps another instance of the influence of Raymond Duchamp-Villon, who considered the establishment of a new architecture as the cardinal task of the early twentieth century.[5]

In a second group of paintings, Villon turned his attention from universal emotions or fundamental intellectual principles such as *L'Espace* to more specific visual metaphors where the background structure suggests a theatrical stage and the curving lines recall the movements of actors. One figure is performing in *Comédie*, 1932 (fig. 116a) while two or three figures are suggested in *Dance*, 1932 (fig. 116b) and *Le Théâtre*, 1932 (fig. 116c). The formal and iconographic precedents for these were established years earlier, notably in his merging of actor and stage in a boxed network of intersecting lines in *Pour un portrait de Barré*, 1919 (fig. 52a). Villon first seems to have symbolized a human figure in the form of activated curving lines in *Puteaux: Les Fumées et les arbres en fleur*, 1912 (cat. no. 33). But there, the figure is immersed in a much larger landscape complex of curves and angles and the idea is not as isolated or abstracted as in the 1932 group, where symbolic figures contrast with a background rather than being camouflaged by it.

The curving spiral in *L'Espace* (cat. no. 116) and wandering line of *Abstraction* (fig. 116d) recall Villon's reference to line as "le vol d'une mouche" (the flight of a fly).[6] In *L'Espace* the artist has varied the coloring of the continuous and almost three-dimensional spiral which may be taken for three distinct circular movements sharing the quality of concentricity with the rec-

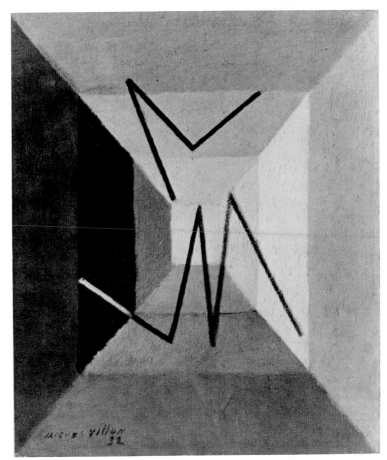

115

tangles. In fact, the spiral involves a complex connection between golden section triangles and equiangular spirals, with care taken that the smallest curve does not degenerate into a circle. The shape is thus freer than one might expect from cursory inspection, but is actually governed by a mathematical rule as rigorous as that which dictates the concentricity of the rectangles. These were originally conceived as pyramids,[7] and may be read as either approaching or receding. Beginning at the top and moving clockwise, the order of color is as logical as the geometry, following the sequence one finds on a color chart illustrating primary and secondary colors: yellow is next to green, which is in turn adjacent to blue. *L'Espace,* 1932, is one of Villon's most abstract realizations of an abstract idea; it contrasts with an earlier engagement of the concept in the 1920 work, *Espaces* (fig. 99b), where the contours of physical objects (most likely globes) are still visible amidst the superimposed planes of space.

Three paintings may be cited which represent a final, yet more lyrical, stage in the development of the *Abstraction-Création* paintings. These are *Voyage,* 1932-1933 (fig. 117a), *Les Fenêtres,* 1932-1933 (cat. no. 117), and an untitled work, 1933 (fig. 117b). These paintings contain the typical background organization, but are unique as a group in that a pair of thick, black orthogonal lines is placed over the middle-sized rectangle. This cross seems to demarcate a subject, most apparent in the untitled work, where a man's head and eye are suggested by ovals and smaller circles which occupy the top portion of the middle of the canvas. Whatever the subject, it is clear that its length and width correspond to the dimensions of the cross, for the vertical reaches upward to the top of the head and downward to the base of the sitter (possibly his

body, a chair, or perhaps a table). *Voyage* probably depicts a ship in water; this seems likely as the end of the arc is articulated above the horizontal line, while the portion below, presumably the submerged hull, is not delineated. *Les Fenêtres* can be read with more certainty. The crossing orthogonals are common to the subject, a window, dividing it into four panes and suggesting that every rectangle in the composition, including the frame of the canvas, is in itself a window. The title has yet another level of meaning which would be known to any cultivated Frenchman, especially one who had participated in the cubist movement. Inescapably, it refers not only to the famous poem "Fenêtres" by Mallarmé, but to Apollinaire's poem with the same title, based not only on Mallarmé, but specifically on Delaunay's 1912 series of paintings having to do with simultaneity, both as a concept characteristic of the modern world, and also in terms of color.

D S R

[1] (43) *Abstraction-Création, art non-figuratif,* I (1932), p. 42; and (44) *Abstraction-Création,* II (1933), p. 47-48.

[2] Reproduced in (43) *Abstraction-Création* (1932), p. 42.

[3] (44) *Abstraction-Création* (1933), p. 48. None of the paintings in this publication appeared with titles.

[4] Until an accurate and detailed biographical study is made of the life of Jacques Villon, it is not possible to state definitively the degree to which he was familiar with mathematical, even arithmetic pattern. The 1930-1933 work, with titles like *Phi,* as well as careful and complex triangulation and spirals argues a pronounced familiarity with elementary formulas dealing not only with golden rectangles, but parabolas, elipses,

pentagrams, hexagrams, gnomons, and other formulas limited by the golden ratio. The literature available to Villon had increased markedly since 1912 and his initial interest in Leonardo (and probably also the theoreticians of neo-Impressionism): D'Arcy Thompson's monumental study *On Growth and Form,* was published in London, 1917. This was surely a source for Matila Ghyka's *Esthétique des proportions dans la nature et dans les arts,* (Paris: Gallimard, 1927), a volume of demonstrable interest to many artists at the end of the 20s. Finally, elementary mathematical concepts of Descartes (equiangular spiral) and Pascal (Pascal's triangle) were part of the curriculum of a well educated French youth at the turn of the century, in part through Henri Poincaré's textbooks. Pascal's triangle, used as a calculator for probability computation, had long been used for games. Its application for solutions to chess problems would probably have been known by all the Duchamp brothers.

[5] See Duchamp-Villon's letter of January 16, 1913 to Walter Pach, in Guggenheim, *Villon, Duchamp-Villon, Duchamp,* n.p.

[6] See cat. no. 33, *Puteaux: Les Fumées et les arbres en fleur.*

[7] See Villon's statement on pyramids in connection with this series in (114) Pierre Courthion, "Décomposition et recomposition de l'espace," *XX Siècle* (Jan. 1952), p. 27-31.

116

L'Espace 1932

Oil on canvas

Signed and dated lower right "Jacques Villon 32"

116 x 89 cm.

PROVENANCE: Jacques Villon

COLLECTION: Louis Carré et Cie, Paris

PUBLISHED: 27, 34, 39, 40, 235, 342, 394

EXHIBITED: 21, 38, 49, 51, 55, 179, 298, 316, 322, 391, 459

117

Les Fenêtres 1932-1933

Oil on canvas

Signed and dated lower left "Jacques Villon 32-33"

46 x 55 cm.

PROVENANCE: Jacques Villon; Louis Carré et Cie, Paris

Private collection, France

PUBLISHED: 27, 34, 40, 342

EXHIBITED: 15, 17, 18, 19, 26, 27, 34, 38, 47, 49, 51, 55, 220

116

116a

JACQUES VILLON

Comédie 1932

Oil on canvas

Private collection

116b
JACQUES VILLON
Dance 1932
Oil on canvas
The Museum of Modern Art, New York

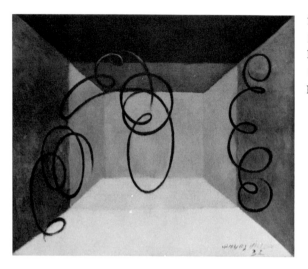

116c
JACQUES VILLON
Le Théâtre 1932
Oil on canvas
Private collection

116d
JACQUES VILLON
Abstraction 1932
Oil on canvas
Philadelphia Musuem of Art, The Louise
and Walter Arensberg Collection

117

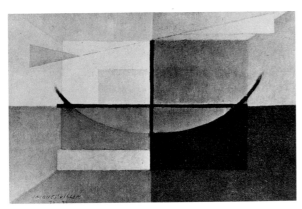

117a

JACQUES VILLON

Voyage 1932-1933

Oil on canvas

Location unknown

Reproduced from *(305) Cent chefs—d'oeuvres peintures de l'École de Paris* (Paris: Galerie Charpentier, 1956)

117b

JACQUES VILLON

Untitled 1933

Oil on canvas

Location unknown

Reproduced from *(44) Abstraction-Création, art non-figuratif* II, 1933 (reprinted by Arno Press, 1968)

118

119

118

Notre Dame de Vie, Mougins 1934

Pencil drawing

Signed and dated lower right "Jacques Villon 34"

18.4 x 26.2 cm.

PROVENANCE: Galerie Marcel Guiot, Paris; John H. Wrenn, Chicago

COLLECTION: The Art Institute of Chicago, The John H. Wrenn Memorial Collection

EXHIBITED: 60

119

Notre Dame de Vie, Mougins 1934

Etching, second state

18.3 x 26 cm.

COLLECTION: Print Department, Boston Public Library

PUBLISHED: AP 263

Although Villon painted several landscapes at the outset of his career,[1] he began to deal with landscape as a major theme only in 1934 when he went on vacation in the south of France. *Notre Dame de Vie* depicts a 17th century monastery near the little village of Mougins, just north of Cannes. In the series of prints to which this motif belongs, the artist devoted himself for the first time since *Puteaux: les Fumées et les arbres en fleur* (cat. no. 33) to a detailed study of the countryside.[2]

Following his usual procedure of working from a drawing to a more complete graphic statement, Villon began this series with a careful pencil drawing of the hill-top cloister bordered by cypress trees. As in *La Petite mendiante* (cat. no. 120), or the Baudelaire drawings (see cat. nos. 70-80), the artist conspicuously marked the *points de repère* which form the basis for the geometric grid of the foreground planes. He also carefully drew the many hatched lines which describe the shadowed areas. In the etched version, Villon tightened up and sharpened the faceted planes of the hills.

Villon also produced two additional etchings of *Notre Dame de Vie*, a close up view of the monastery nestled in the hills (AP 264) and another, less densely hatched view of Mougins (AP 259). Villon's consistency is apparent in the fact that this first deliberate analysis of a landscape scene in more than twenty years was confined to a drawing and etchings: he always felt more comfortable in a well-trusted medium when embarking on new pictorial interests.

MSS

[1] Early single landscapes include:
La Maison de Blainville 1898, reproduced in (40) Vallier, *Villon,* p. 17. (This was Villon's childhood home. Duchamp also painted the family house—see (365a) d'Harnoncourt and McShine, *Duchamp,* cat. nos. 1 and 2.)
L'Ile d'Amour 1899, reproduced in (40) Vallier, *Villon,* p. 20.

[2] Two paintings of Mougins were shown in the (2) Brummer Gallery exhibition, 1928 — #2, *Road at Mougins* and #11, *Mougins.* Unfortunately these paintings have not been located nor is their exact subject matter, beyond that suggested by the titles, known.

120

120

La Petite mendiante 1934

Pencil drawing on paper

Signed and dated lower right "Jacques Villon 34"

24 x 17 cm.

PROVENANCE: B. C. Holland Gallery, Chicago

COLLECTION: Mickey Pallas, Skokie, Illinois

PUBLISHED: *Impressionist and Modern Watercolours and Drawings,* Sotheby and Co. (London, December 3, 1970)

The somber mood of the little girl and her motionless pose amidst active compositional elements recalls other such pictures of young women and girls, such as the 1926 *Louisette* (fig. 120a). *Etude pour La Petite mendiante,* a preparatory study for the 1935 etching *La Petite mendiante* (AP 278) and for the 1936 oil *Jeune fille assise* (fig. 20b), displays an intricate network of points and orthogonals, which Villon used to map out color planes and volumes for the painting. A similar web of lines in *Notre Dame de Vie* (cat. no. 118) activates the surface, functioning as a counterpoint to (if not actually competing with) the sensitive representation of the subject. This re-exploration of early cubist traits, along with reliance on graphic media, characterizes the period following the intense abstract paintings.

JDF

120a

JACQUES VILLON

Louisette 1926

Oil on canvas

Collection of Vincent Tovell, Toronto

120b

JACQUES VILLON

Jeune fille assise 1936

Oil on canvas

Courtesy of Yale University Art Gallery, New Haven

121

Le Petit dessinateur 1935

Ink drawing on tracing paper

Signed and dated lower left "Jacques
Villon 35"

17 x 13.4 cm.

PROVENANCE: Jacques Villon
Private collection, France

PUBLISHED: 195

EXHIBITED: *32, 40, 54, 60*

122

Homme dessinant 1935

Oil on canvas

Signed vertically in lower left

116 x 81 cm.

PROVENANCE: Jacques Villon
Private collection, France

PUBLISHED: 27, 34, 39, 59, 74, 96, 106, 132,
153, 236, 237, 247, 281, 333, 347, 406

EXHIBITED: *13, 15, 26, 27, 34, 38, 43, 45, 46,
47, 49, 51, 60, 198, 220, 459*

121

121a

JACQUES VILLON

Le Petit dessinateur 1935

Etching, AP 267

Print Department, Boston Public Library

In the *Homme dessinant* Villon portrays
himself, measuring his motif with his pencil.
An intense geometrical relationship, based
on a right-angle triangle, is established
between the eyes, the hand, the tool and the
raised arm. The sparkling surface of tiny
regular brushstrokes, the pale blues and
greens of the palette, and the self-portrait
theme are characteristic of Villon's work in
the mid-30s. The only known pencil study
for the oil, *Le Petit dessinateur* — despite
its schematic quality — focuses more on
facial expression than does the painting,
which concentrates on the artist and his
task. This is also true for the etching (fig.
121a), done after the painting the same
year. Neither the etching nor the drawing
has the three vertical bars in the background which assimilate the figure into the
overall design of the painting. The lightly-
indicated table behind the figure in the print
and drawing becomes an undifferentiated
backdrop of green, filling the lower half of
the canvas. The subject of the artist drawing
recurs in the *Le Grand dessinateur* series
(see cat. nos. 123-124), also of 1935, and
the transparent linear rendering of the out-
stretched arm foreshadows the style of the
1942 *Portrait de L'artiste* (cat. no. 140).

J D F

122

123

Portrait de l'artiste 1935

Oil on canvas

Signed and dated lower left "Jacques
Villon 35"

55 x 46 cm.

PROVENANCE: Jacques Villon

Private Collection, New York

PUBLISHED: 40, 342

EXHIBITED: 29, 198, 463

124

Le Grand dessinateur assis 1935

Etching

26.5 x 20 cm.

COLLECTION: Mr. and Mrs. Samuel Sachs II,
'57, Minneapolis

PUBLISHED: AP 266

The *Grand dessinateur* series of 1935 con-
sists of two oils, an etching, and two
drawings.[1] All of these compositions show
the artist in the same attitude, sitting at a
tilted drafting table looking out. His elbows
rest on the arms of a chair; he holds his
pencil casually in two hands. Behind him on
the left (in the paintings and drawing),
Raymond Duchamp-Villon's *Decorative
Basin* stands on a modelling pedestal; in the
middle background the artist has sketched
in a sculptured head, probably another of
Raymond's works; and, on the right, the
heavy wooden table with thick carved legs
— seen in the 1912 *Table servie* (cat. nos.
42-48) — supports Raymond's *Buste de
Baudelaire* (see fig. 70a). What appears to
be a window and curtain creates a backdrop behind the *Baudelaire*. In the drawing
(fig. 123a) the geometricized scaffolding —
most prominent in the head — anticipates
the head of the 1942 *Portraite de l'artiste*
(cat. no. 140) and also relates to the treatment of the arm in the 1935 *Homme dessinant*. This schematization is almost sup-
pressed in the painting and print, but the
artist's veiled expression through half closed
eyes replaces the distorting latticework of
the drawing, perhaps intentionally in order
to maintain the sitter's distance.

In the etching, Villon eliminated still
more details through heavy cross-hatching.
The *Decorative Basin* remains visible, the
Baudelaire becomes barely discernable and
almost no indication of the table or middle
sculpture persists through the black network of lines. The dark eyes in the etching
— unlike the oil and pencil versions — cast
a penetrating glance toward the viewer, but
the mouth is shrouded in darkness. The
drafting table — even more prominent here
than in the drawing and painting — seems
to barricade the sitter from the viewer. This
recalls the 1909 *Portrait de l'artiste* (see fig.
21b), where Villon holds his palette almost
like a shield, and hides his expression in
his beard.

JDF

[1] These are a 1935 painting (Louis Carré et
Cie, Paris) illustrated in (34) Lassaigne,
Villon, pl. XV, and a drawing, shown at
(32) Galerie Louis Carré, Paris, *Dessins de
Jacques Villon*, 1956. Still another oil self-
portrait, *Composition self-portrait*, 1934 (in
the Musée d'Art Moderne, Paris) may be a
preliminary study for this series although
the figure is on a totally different scale

123a

JACQUES VILLON

Etude pour Le Grand dessinateur assis 1934

Drawing

Location unknown

Reproduced from (60) Jean Cassou, Simone
Frigerio, and Peter A. Wick, *Jacques Villon,
Master of Graphic Art (1875-1963)* (Boston:
Museum of Fine Arts, 1964)

123b

JACQUES VILLON

Self Portrait 1935

Oil on canvas

Collection of Vincent Tovell, Toronto

relative to the composition. A third example in oil is in the collection of Vincent Tovell, Toronto (fig. 123b).

2 The *Decorative Basin*, a sculpture fountain basin made for the Salon d'Automne of 1911, grew out of an effort to revitalize French decorative arts.

123

123c

RAYMOND DUCHAMP-VILLON

Decorative Basin 1911

Bronze

Reproduced from (421) Hamilton and Agee, *Duchamp-Villon*

124

125

Intérieur 1936
Oil on canvas
Signed and dated
92 x 63.5 cm.
PROVENANCE: Mrs. J. C. Guggenheimer,
New York
Anonymous loan
EXHIBITED: *164*

125

Intérieur is another example of the re-
examination and synthesis of earlier artistic
interests to which Villon returned in his
figurative painting during the later 1930s.
He reintroduced a divisionist brushstroke,
and although the composition is influenced
by the experiments in planar abstraction
from the early 1920s, Villon now concentrated on intimate artifacts of everyday experience — armchair, hearth, mirror. These
objects allude to the feelings of kinship
and place that had always been part of his
attitude toward genre subjects, recalling
some of the earliest family scenes such as
La Partie d'échecs, 1904 (cat. no. 13), and
La Partie de jacquet, 1903 (fig. 13a).

In *Intérieur*, however, Villon begins a
new approach to this theme of intimacy,
treating large segments of architectural interior space as still life. *Intérieur* provides a
source for numerous later works, such as
a 1950 drawing (fig. 125a) and the lithograph, *Fauteuil*, c. 1950.[1] The motif is also
employed in subsequent paintings such as
Le Grand salon de Bernay, 1945 (cat. no.
143), *Intérieur*, 1954 (cat. no. 160), and
L'Atre, 1955 (fig. 160a).

A M

[1] Reproduced in *Cahiers Art-Documents*, no.
15 (1955), no. 262.

125a
JACQUES VILLON
Intérieur 1950
Drawing
The Museum of Modern Art, New York

126
Poésies de Pierre Corrard 1937
16 black and white etchings
Edited by J. Meynial, Paris
Printed by Leblanc and Troutman
COLLECTION: Harvard College Library,
Department of Printing and Graphic Arts,
Harvard University, Cambridge, Massa-
chusetts

PUBLISHED: AP 387-303

126

Although Villon was highly regarded as a printmaker and illustrator, the fact is that before 1937 he had published few sets of illustrations, apart from his cartoons for Parisian journals.[1] The *Poésies de Pierre Corrard* was the first book of poetry for which he conceived and executed an entire sequence of illustrations. The volume contains seventeen etchings, of which fifteen are directly related to the subjects of poems.

The book is dedicated to the memory of Pierre Corrard, who was killed in the Ardennes in 1914. Corrard's widow had remarried into the Duchamp family, and it was probably she who proposed the project to Villon.[2]

One of the poems in the volume is "L'Art de demain." In eleven stanzas of classical alexandrine verse it dramatically announces the art of the future, of the dawning twentieth century. Villon illustrated this poem with an imaginary art gallery, in which are displayed a number of works, most of them actual, innovative ones from the early years of the century. The most prominent is his brother Raymond Duchamp-Villon's *Le Cheval* (fig. 58a). This is a rare depiction by Villon of this sculpture. His other brother Marcel Duchamp is represented by the

Nude Descending a Staircase No. 2, from 1913. To the right of this work hangs a painting in the mature style of Mondrian. The painting to the far left may be identified as the *Painter and his Model* of 1917 by Matisse; next to it is a painting in the synthetic cubist style of Picasso's harlequins and musicians; to the right of that is an unidentified portrait. The large question mark on the right may be in reference to the second line of the poem, "A cet art de demain, énigmatique encor," ("To this art of tomorrow, still enigmatic.") Despite their subject, both "L'Art de demain" and Villon's illustration are as traditional in style as the rest of the poems and etchings in the book. Villon rarely moved to full abstraction in his illustrative work.[3]

J H

[1] In 1907 Villon had published a portfolio of lithographs, *Impressions dessinées d'après nature,* AP 409-418. In 1921 he contributed 33 plates to *Architectures,* AP 466-499, a collection published by the N.R.F. under the direction of André Mare and Louis Süe which contained a preliminary version of Valery's *Eupalinos ou l'Architecte;* and in

1935 he did a frontispiece, *L'Aventure,* for a *Catalogue des Peintres Graveurs,* AP 271.

[2] Suggested by Lucien Goldschmidt in conversation, winter, 1972.

[3] A rare exception is *A Poèmes rompus* (cat. no. 163), a volume of poetry by Max Jacob, published in 1960.

L'Oiseau empaillé 1938

Oil on canvas

Signed and dated lower left "Jacques Villon 38"

73 x 92 cm.

PROVENANCE: Jacques Villon

COLLECTION: Louis Carré et Cie, Paris

PUBLISHED: 27, 29, 34, 40, 169, 170, 385, 418

EXHIBITED: *15, 17, 18, 22, 26, 27, 34, 38, 49, 51, 55, 56, 220, 243, 277, 459*

127

When painting still life, Villon usually made a selection from objects kept in his studio, ranging from paper and artist's materials to the sculpture of his dead brother, to fruit and flowers. A new item first appeared in 1932 in a drawing[1] and etching, *Nature morte au perroquet* (fig. 127a), where a stuffed bird lies alongside a guitar, accompanied by a detached manikin's arm clutching a book, an empty glove, and other items in provocative arrangement on a table which has a single post for support. By contrast to the 1932 version, in *L'Oiseau empaillé*, 1938, the viewpoint is from above, a favorite vantage point for Villon since *Jeu*, 1919 (see cat. nos. 68-69) and the Baudelaire and Racehorse series (see cat. nos. 70-80; 86-98). The quality of confrontation among the still life objects has also been purged. The table is translated into a simple rectangle at the center of the composition; the post, also centered, is directly below. The forms of the bird and book are hard to recognize, so overwhelming is the interplay of jutting diagonals on the table, surrounded by large geometric shapes. The arm and glove seem to have been eliminated.

The bird is distinguished from the rest by color. The intense reds, oranges and yellows of the bird's feathers are contrasted with cool blues, greens and purples which dominate the background. In addition to careful color differentiation, Villon employed other devices to call attention to the bird: its geometry is smaller and more intricate, and the curve of its beak and head is formed by a distinct equiangular spiral developed from a right angled triangle one point of which touches the canvas center.

Villon gave a description of the mathematical and chromatic method employed in this painting to Yvon Taillander in "Jacques Villon, de la pyramide au carré," *XXe Siècle* (May-June 1959), p. 83-93. He discussed the generation of the forms and determination of the color sequence as if this work were as abstract as *L'Architecture, Allégresse* or *L'Espace* (cat. nos. 114-116) from the 1930-1933 series. While this is the case in construction, a trace of the original conception remains.

D S R

[1] Reproduced in (60) Cassou, Frigerio, and Wick, *Villon*, p. 56.

127a
JACQUES VILLON
Nature morte aux perroquet 1932
Etching, AP 247[1]
Courtesy Museum of Fine Arts, Boston

128

128
Le Joueur de flageolet 1939
Oil on canvas
Signed and dated lower right "Jacques
Villon 39"
162 x 130 cm.
PROVENANCE: Jacques Villon
COLLECTION: Louis Carré et Cie, Paris
PUBLISHED: 27, 34, 40, 52, 234, 236, 342
EXHIBITED: *15, 34, 38, 49, 51, 55,* 220, 253,
320, 420, 447, 459

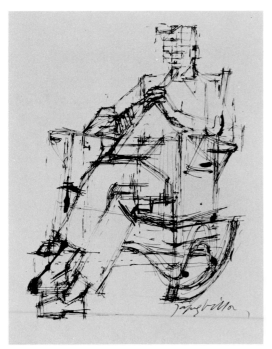

128a

JACQUES VILLON

Le Jouer de flageolet 1937-1938

Drawing

Collection of Irving M. Sobin, Boston

128b

JACQUES VILLON

Le Jouer de flageolet 1938

Etching, AP 314

Print Department, Boston Public Library

Le Joueur de flageolet is developed from a 1937 or 1938 drawing (fig. 128a), also the source for the 1938 etching (fig. 128b). The subject is Vincent Tovell, of Toronto, who lived *'en famille'* with the Villons during the summers of 1937 and 1938. Mr. Tovell and one other art student, Beatrice Stein from New York,[1] are the only people who received regular lessons in painting from Villon, who tended to avoid the term "student" for these relationships. *Joueur de flageolet* depicts Mr. Tovell, then in his late teens, playing a recorder.[2]

The composition of the painting, although it retains important figurative elements, is a geometric grid based on the golden section. The vertical division just to the left of the figure's head is located on the golden mean of the width of the canvas. The long side of the rectangle divided by short side provides two of the horizonal movements within the painting, and yet another is supplied by the golden section of the long side. By expanding this system of proportion, and by using diagonal elements between the points where verticals and horizontals intersect, a complex structure is created, into which characteristics of the subject are fitted. By a process of selec-

tion and reduction, a kind of dialogue between individual and formal demands, the final fusion of subject and design is achieved.

A M

[1] The diagrams that Villon drew in the sketch book of Beatrice Stein, now in the possession of a New York private collector, provide further evidence that the artist was well acquainted with the theories of Ghyka, and possibly also with the work of the American Jay Hambidge. Cleve Gray also confirms that Villon referred to the studies of Hambidge, whose principal literature is: *Diagonal,* periodical, edited by Hambidge; New York, 1919-1920; *Dynamic Symmetry in the Greek Vase,* New York, 1923; *Dynamic Symmetry in Composition,* New York, 1923. (See cat. no. 115, footnote 4 for Matila Ghyka.)

[2] Letter from Mr. Tovell to Mr. David Rubin, August 23, 1974. The American painter Cleve Gray was also very close to Villon, especially in 1944-1945, receiving advice and criticism, but as a friend and younger colleague, not the same as "élève." Villon was very traditional in his use of the term "élève," acknowledging only Mr. Tovell and Miss Stein in this sense.

129
La Lutte 1939
Etching and drypoint
28.2 x 25.2 cm.
COLLECTION: The Museum of Modern Art,
New York, Lent anonymously
PUBLISHED: AP 329

129

The drypoint *La Lutte* (AP 329) is part of a series executed by Villon that year, which also includes two paintings, *Les Lutteurs,* and *La Lutte, le chaos* (fig. 129a). The subject of the print, two wrestlers, goes back to a drawing of 1913 and recalls the theme of figures in movement and tension, which first enters Villon's oeuvre in *Les Haleurs* (cat. no. 20).

La Lutte is also clearly related to two similar subjects with which Villon worked: *Le Jeu de boxe,* 1937 (AP 302), an illustration for the book *Poésies de Pierre Corrard* (cat. no. 126) and another etching of 1939, *L'Effort* (AP 328, fig. 129b), which won the gold medal in the *Peintres-Graveurs* exhibition of 1940.

The print exhibits Villon's continuing interest in developing his imagery through linear syntax, relating the major movements to the shape of the plate. A colored lithograph of 1957, also called *La Lutte* (not in AP), again shows Villon's method of redeveloping a theme that had entered his work many years previously.

A M

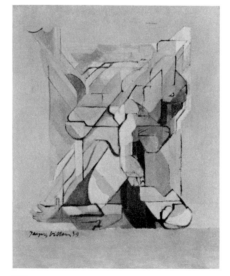

129a
JACQUES VILLON
La Lutte, le chaos 1939
Oil on canvas
Collection of Haakon Onstad, Munkedal,
Sweden

129b
JACQUES VILLON
L'Effort 1939
Etching, AP 328
Print Department, Boston Public Library

130

130
Les Trois ordres: le château, l'église, la campagne 1939

Etching

28.4 x 18.8 cm.

COLLECTION: Print Department, Boston Public Library

PUBLISHED: AP 325

131
Les Trois ordres 1940

Oil on canvas

Signed and dated lower left "Jacques Villon 40"

46 x 38 cm.

PROVENANCE: Palais Galliera, Paris; Galerie Couturier, Paris

COLLECTION: Mrs. Frances W. Kelly, Cambridge, Massachusetts

PUBLISHED: Sales catalogue, Paris: Palais Galliera, May 30, 1967

During the "false war" in 1939-1940, Villon spent several months in seclusion at Beaugency, a small town on the Loire, making a group of etchings of the main architectural monuments there. One etching, *Les Trois ordres* (cat. no. 130), has particular significance as the basis for a major 1944 painting of the same title (fig. 130a). In addition, between the etching and the painting Villon made a little known oil sketch, shown here for the first time (cat. no. 131). This must have been completed soon after Villon's return to Puteaux from Beaugency in 1940. Both paintings conform to the composition of the etching, following the areas of light and shade, stressing the broad diagonal band of light in the foreground which leads back to the simple Romanesque church. The darkest shadows, resembling ivy growing up the square tower, have also been transferred from the print onto canvas.

A comparison of the two paintings is essential for understanding Villon's handling of color in the 1940s. The pale, translucent tones of the preparatory sketch are consistent with Villon's painting from about 1940-1942 (see cat. nos. 134, 139, 140). However, in the 1944 version Villon shifted to the brilliant colors which become characteristic of his intensified landscape palette throughout the 1940s and 1950s.

Several months after the liberation of Paris *Les Trois ordres*, 1944 and its companion piece, *Le Pont de Beaugency* (fig. 130b) of the same year, were exhibited at the gallery of Louis Carré in Paris. This show marked the beginning of a great rise in Villon's popularity. *Les Trois ordres: le château, l'église, la campagne* depicts the physical monuments of the town and countryside, and the artist had made these symbolize the *ancien régime* orders of nobility, clergy and *tiers état*. Villon sought calm and stability in the face of chaos, and created it by representing faithfully an old town on the banks of the Loire which escaped the damage suffered by much of the region (fig. 130c). The national feeling that *Les Trois ordres* and *Le Pont de Beaugency* evoked may, in part, explain their success at the Carré exhibition. Villon's sense of order and discipline, combined with blazing color and a subtle evocation of eternal values and traditional beliefs have an enduring appeal that made particular impact when the paintings were exhibited in Paris in 1944 and again in New York in 1949.

M S S

130b

JACQUES VILLON

Le Pont de Beaugency 1944

Oil on canvas

Collection of Mr. and Mrs. Paul Mellon

130a

JACQUES VILLON

**Les Trois ordres: le château, l'église, la
campagne** 1944

Oil on canvas

Collection of Mr. and Mrs. Paul Mellon

130c
Photograph of Beaugency

1950s

Reproduced from Georges Alepée, *Loiret*
(in the series "Les Documents de France"),
Paris, n.d.

131

132

Letter to a friend September 16, 1940

Ink on paper

Private Collection, New York

PUBLISHED: 185

133

Potager à la Brunié 1941

Oil on canvas

Signed and dated lower right "Jacques Villon 41"

65 x 92 cm.

PROVENANCE: Jacques Villon; Louis Carré Gallery, New York

COLLECTION: The Cleveland Museum of Art, Purchase, Leonard C. Hanna Jr., Bequest

PUBLISHED: 27, 28, 34, 40, 115, 185; *Handbook of the Cleveland Museum of Art,* Cleveland: The Cleveland Museum of Art, 1966 and 1969

EXHIBITED: *10, 13, 15, 26, 27, 34, 38, 45, 46, 47, 49, 55, 62, 220, 459*

Villon spent the turbulent summer and fall of 1940 at La Brunié, a farm in the Tarn Valley owned by M. and Mme Marc Vène.[1] Here he made sketches of the farm, among which are drawings of all four sides of the vegetable garden, or *potager,* sketched in a letter to his friend Francis Steegmuller, the husband of his pupil Beatrice Stein. After he returned to Puteaux, Villon spent two years (1940-1942) transferring these quick *plein-air* drawings onto canvas, producing his first important series of landscape paintings.

Among the La Brunié paintings, *Le Potager aux citrouilles* (cat. no. 134), is the most striking. It depicts the pumpkin patch on the east side of the garden. Villon divided the foreground and sky into regular horizontal bands, as if he wanted to measure the size of the garden and the space outside its confines. As the ground planes recede towards the horizon, they mirror the vanishing bands of the sky. The silhouetted trees which mark the end of the garden are used as were the cypresses of *Notre Dame de Vie,* 1934 (see cat. nos. 118, 119), but their angularity also suggests an urban skyline. This effect is more pronounced in other paintings of this series, especially in the *Potager à la Brunié* (cat. no. 133) where the tall poplar trees resemble buildings.[2]

In most of his landscapes Villon used similar compositional devices — the balanced geometric division of the canvas, with particular emphasis on the deep foreground; and the strict, linear delineation and faceting of the forms, especially apparent in the prismatic network of the trees. The clarity and lucidity of *Le Potager aux citrouilles* also characterizes the majority of his later landscape paintings.

Although Villon's spontaneous drawings were the source for the composition of the *potager* paintings, his choice of delicate and translucent tones of peach, green, pink, yellow and blue was intended to "reinforce and enhance the linear structure."[3] Many commentators, notably Jerome Mellquist, have noted the new lyricism and incandescence of Villon's luminous colors in this period.[4] Yet in the early forties Villon still worked out his palette on the Rosenstiehl color wheel, as revised in 1934 by Julie Beaudeneau (see cat. nos. 99, 100, footnote[1]). At La Brunié he never painted directly from nature.

These farm paintings also include representations of workers hoeing in the vegetable garden (fig. 133a). His interest in farm labor subsequently became an important theme in Villon's work.

M S S

132

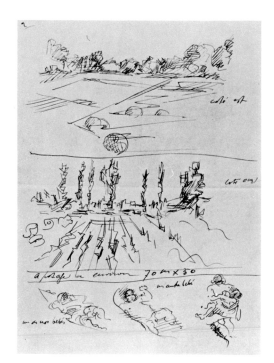

[1] Mme Vène (Anne-Françoise Mare) was the daughter of André Mare and Villon's godchild.

[2] Jerome Mellquist has identified these trees as poplars. (238) Jerome Mellquist, "Jacques Villon ou le feu de l'esprit," *Synthèses,* XI (April-May, 1956), p. 136. Apparently the configuration of the garden at La Brunié reminded Villon of a typical Norman vegetable garden, with trees on all four sides. *(43) Jacques Villon. L'Oeuvre gravé (1891-1958),* Bibliothèque Nationale (Paris, 1959), p. 63.

[3] (185) Edward B. Henning, "Two New Modern Paintings," *The Bulletin of the Cleveland Museum of Art,* 52 (January, 1965), p. 11.

[4] (233) Jerome Mellquist, "The Master of Puteaux and Others," *Apollo,* LXXIV (June, 1961), p. 199-200. (235) Mellquist, "Jacques Villon," p. 10. (238) Mellquist, "Feu de l'esprit," p. 1366.

133a

JACQUES VILLON

Potager à la Brunié 1941

Oil on canvas

Private collection, New York

134

Le Potager aux citrouilles 1942

Oil on canvas

Signed and dated lower right "Jacques Villon 42"

50 x 65 cm.

PROVENANCE: Jacques Villon; Mme Louis Carré, Paris; E. V. Thaw and Co., New York; Frank B. Hubachek, Chicago

COLLECTION: Loan from the Alsdorf Foundation, Chicago

PUBLISHED: 27, 29, 34, 40, 57, 153, 193, 342, 377

EXHIBITED: *34, 38, 49, 51, 55*

134

133

140

140

Portrait de l'artiste 1942

Oil on canvas

Signed and dated lower right "Jacques Villon 42"

92 x 65 cm.

PROVENANCE: Jacques Villon; Louis Carré Gallery, New York

Private collection, New York

PUBLISHED: 27, 29, 33, 34, 39, 40, 86, 106, 128, 227, 263, 281, 313, 342, 344

EXHIBITED: *7, 10, 13, 15, 29, 49, 198, 322*

This self-portrait may be most remarkable for its resonant color and its pronounced geometric schematization. The style is consistent with that of other works of the period, including the landscapes of the *Potager* series (see cat. nos. 132-134) and the earlier version of *Les Trois ordres* (cat. no. 131). Having constructed his typical series of concentric rectangles cornered on diagonals, Villon interrupted these rectangles with minor variations to eliminate what might otherwise have become an overbearing symmetry. This rich abstract pattern gives stability to the composition and acts as both structural and symbolic foil for the soft, asymmetrical human forms. The head is rendered with a volumetrically segmented surface which systematically exploits transitions from light to shadow, following the direction established by the larger geometry of the whole canvas. The figure itself casts a shadow, and the artist's right hand, resting at the base of the outermost rectangle, seems to hold a tool. Unlike many of Villon's other self-portraits, this work is less impassive and projects a searching quality, and a high degree of emotional intensity.

J D F

135

136

138

137

135
Colin-Maillard 1941
Drawing, India ink on white paper
Signed lower right "Jacques Villon"
17.6 x 11 cm.
PROVENANCE: Jacques Villon
COLLECTION: Louis Carré et Cie, Paris
PUBLISHED: 40, 342

136
Colin-Maillard 1941
Drawing, India ink on white paper
Signed and dated lower right "Jacques
Villon 41"
17.6 x 11 cm.
PROVENANCE: Jacques Villon
COLLECTION: Louis Carré et Cie, Paris
PUBLISHED: 40, 342

137
Colin-Maillard 1941
Drawing, India ink on white paper
Signed lower right "Jacques Villon"
18 x 9 cm.
PROVENANCE: Jacques Villon
COLLECTION: Louis Carré et Cie, Paris
PUBLISHED: 40, 342

138
Colin-Maillard 1941
Drawing, India ink on white paper
Signed and dated lower right "Jacques
Villon 41"
18 x 9 cm.
PROVENANCE: Jacques Villon
COLLECTION: Louis Carré et Cie, Paris
PUBLISHED: 40, 342

139
Colin-Maillard 1942

Oil on canvas

Signed and dated lower right "Jacques
Villon 42"

81 x 65 cm.

PROVENANCE: Jacques Villon; Louis Carré
Gallery, New York

COLLECTION: Charles Zadok, Greenwich,
Connecticut

PUBLISHED: 26, 27

EXHIBITED: 7, 20, 49, 322

139

The title, *Colin-Maillard,* or blind man's
buff, recalls the ancient game especially as
it was represented in eighteenth-century
French painting. In Villon's version, the
setting is abstract — the receding series of
concentric rectangles divided by diagonals
to the corners derives from the format the
artist had perfected in the early 1930s, with
Architecture, Fenêtres, and *L'Espace* (see
cat. nos. 114-117). As in his 1942 self-portrait
(cat. no. 140), Villon used the geometric
structure as an armature into which he integrated a figurative subject.

However, the long-robed female figures
of *Colin-Maillard* do not appear to play
blind man's buff or even to interact. Instead, Villon has presented three treatments
of the same figure, developed from four
preparatory sketches (cat. nos. 135-138)
showing nearly identical figures in varying
degrees of light and shade. The sketches
demonstrate Villon's mature drawing
method. For the first figure, in brightest light,
he delineated the areas of light, isolating
them from the rapid strokes representing
shade. The three following sketches show
the same woman in progressively deeper
shadows. With each addition of hatching or
dots, new areas emerge while the brightest
spots remain highlighted.[1] The result ani-
mates the figure so that she appears to turn.

In the painting the figures correspond to
three degrees of lighting of the sketches, the
darkest at left and lightest at right. One
has the impression that the viewer is the one
who plays blind man's buff, searching for
the elusive figure as she slips in and out of
the geometric dimensions of light.

J H

1 (40) Vallier, *Villon,* p. 72.

141

141

Notre Dame die Vie, Mougins 1944
Oil on canvas
Signed lower right "Jacques Villon"
73 x 100 cm.
COLLECTION: Mme Robert Philippe, Paris
PUBLISHED: 27, 40, 153, 333, 342
EXHIBITED: *10, 15, 49, 55*
(not in exhibition)

In many of his landscapes of southern France, Villon characteristically worked out the compositions in his drawings and prints — plotting the geometric divisions and the areas of light and dark — and then transferred his arrangements onto canvas, often as much as ten years later.[1] This view of the monastery on the plateau near the ancient Roman town of Mougins remains faithful to the format of the 1934-1935 etchings of this region (cat. nos. 118, 119), although the architecture is more distinguishable. In addition, Villon has expanded the faceted foreground hills into pyramidal forms, replacing the small triangular areas of hatching in the etchings.

The origin of these large pyramidal shapes in the foreground can actually be traced further back in Villon's oeuvre to a crucial early work, *Les Soldats en marche* of 1913 (cat. no. 53). According to the artist,[2] the faceted planes in *Les Soldats en marche* describe the marching soldiers of his pre-World War I reserve unit. The equally movemented triangles in *Notre Dame de Vie, Mougins* may possibly be interpreted as the French and American troops who marched from Toulon to Menton in the late summer of 1944 to liberate the Côte d'Azur. If so, this painting would represent a very significant, yet hardly surprising return, both formally and thematically, to a work of great import for Villon's career.

M S S

[1] Jean Revol calls this Villon's process of "interior assimilation." (294) Jean Revol, "Braque et Villon (fin)," *La Nouvelle Revue Française* IX, 105 (September 1961), p. 525.

[2] (23) Jacques Villon, "Un travail solitaire dans un chemin privé," *Arts, Lettres, Spectacles,* April 26-May 2, 1961, p. 1.

142

142

Globe céleste, le ciel 1944

Etching

26 x 21 cm.

COLLECTION: The Museum of Modern Art,
New York, Purchase

PUBLISHED: AP 347

Villon's fascination with the globe extended
throughout much of his life. It appeared in
many different forms and contexts. A
photograph of Villon's studio reveals that
he owned two globes.[1] One shows the surface of the earth in relief; the other is en-
circled with armilary rings marking the
longitudinal and latitudinal movements of
the sphere.

The terms *"globe terrestre"* and *"globe
céleste"* were first used in a drawing of 1920.
The subject was a simple rotary machine,
identical to the one which served as the
dynamo in both Villon's *Atelier* series (cat.
nos. 58-62) and Raymond Duchamp-Villon's *Le Cheval* (fig. 58a). Villon had done
several studies of this machine in 1913 and
1914. In 1920 Villon used the machine,
which consisted of a smaller wheel set inside
a larger one, as an analogy to the Ptolemaic
system of the celestial globe. This ancient
astronomical theory assumed that the Earth
was the central body around which the sun
and planets revolved. Villon may also have
intended to relate the mechanical forces of
the machine to those of the universe.

The globe in *Globe celéste, le ciel,* closely
resembles the spherical model with its longitudinal and latitudinal armilaries seen in

the photograph of the artist's studio. Although the 1944 version is a more conventional depiction of the globe, it is not without symbolic overtones. The globe has a
strong anthropomorphic quality. A large
head, with crossing rings suggesting a face,
seems to loom over a disproportionately
small base. A further reference to the figure
of Atlas is not improbable.

New freedom is seen here in Villon's
etching technique, typical of his drawing in
later years. The background grid, familiar
in his work of the thirties, dissolves in several places leaving dazzling light areas, set
off by only a few lines. A new synthesis is
present in his use of constructive and free-
flowing line. The lines of the grid are looser,
and infused with some of the same energy
as those which describe the object.

The same globe can be seen in a painting
of 1925, *Celestial Globes* (fig. 42a). Here the
globes are merged with the body of the
horse in a sculpture by Raymond Duchamp-
Villon entitled *Cheval et chavalier* (second
state), 1914, study for the *Cheval* of the
same year. The hemispherical haunches of
the horse, which resembled mechanical
gears in the sculpture, were transformed by
Villon into spheres. A phonograph horn is

142a

JACQUES VILLON

Celestial Globes 1925

Oil on canvas

Collection of Lee A. Ault and Co.,
New York

142b

JACQUES VILLON

Terre et ciel 1947

Oil on canvas

Collection of Ragnar Moltzau, Oslo

also shown, and the horse is now riderless. These changes suggest that this work, too, was intended as a memorial to his brother; the term "celestial globe" associates with after-life or heaven, and the riderless horse may symbolize death. The phonograph horn refers to music, a constant interest among the Duchamp family. In still earlier work, musical instruments are attributes of members of the family. *Instruments de musique,* 1912 (Art Institute of Chicago), and *Fillette au piano,* 1911 (cat. no. 34) are examples.

Terre et ciel (fig. 142b) is one of the more abstract versions in the globe series and relates closely in composition not only to *Ciel et terre,* 1948 (fig. 142c) but to *Boire à la chimère* (fig. 142d), the culminating painting insofar as complexity of idea is concerned. All three are composed of strong diagonal forms which intersect to create two distinct X-shaped configurations. Foreground and background are divided into geometric planes. All have a strong sense of architectural form, reminiscent of the stacked planar abstractions of the early twenties; however, because of the aggressive, intersecting diagonals, they remain linked with the compositional formula de-

veloped in the early thirties for the *Abstraction-Création* paintings.

The most significant difference between the 1948 globe paintings and *Boire à la chimère* (fig. 142d) is that the two overlapping spheres have reappeared above the X-forms which summarize the bases of the globes, as seen in the studio photograph. The absence of all but a hint of the globes in *Boire à la chimère* must be the basis of the illusion referred to in the title. It is typical for Villon to transform a subject in many ways over a long period of time, developing and changing its potential expressive and symbolic meaning. An engraving, *Les Deux vases,* 1950 (not in AP), is based on *Boire à la chimère,* and two 1951 prints, *Les Lampes* and *L'Univers* (neither in AP), relate to the two globes of *Ciel et terre.*

S G

[1] (430) Wilhelm Maywald, *Portrait + Atelier* (Zurich: Die Arche, 1958), n.p.

142c
JACQUES VILLON
Ciel et terre 1948
Oil on canvas
Louis Carré et Cie, Paris

142d
JACQUES VILLON
Boire à la chimère 1947
Oil on canvas
Collection of Mr. and Mrs. Paul Mellon

143

143a

JACQUES VILLON

Le Salon de Bernay 1939

Oil on canvas board

Galeria Alvarez, Porto, Portugal

143

Le Grand salon de Bernay 1945

Oil on canvas

Signed lower left "Jacques Villon"

73 x 92 cm.

PROVENANCE: Jacques Villon; Louis Carré et Cie, Paris; Svensk-Franska Konstgalleriet, Stockholm; A.-B. Marabou, Sundbyberg, Sweden

Private collection, Switzerland

PUBLISHED: 33, 114, 299, 339, 342, 343

EXHIBITED: 19, 45, 47, 76, 205, 211, 224, 244, 279

(not in exhibition)

Le Grand salon de Bernay depicts the salon in the home of the wife of Villon's long-time friend and colleague, André Mare, located in Bernay (Eure), where Villon had often visited (see cat. no. 132-134) and where he went for a prolonged visit at the outbreak of World War II. The motif was established in a study signed and dated 1939 (fig. 143a), drawn over in ink.[1]

The complex 1945 painting, originating in a simple interior view, provides a convenient means of exploring the geometry at the base of Villon's method in this period, when he was especially concerned with combining figuration with construction. The grid substructure of the painting was developed through successive measurements of the canvas shape by means of essential geometric elements and the Golden Section ratio, in this case simplified to its whole number equivalent, the "Fibonaci series."[2]

The vertical and horizontal axes and the main diagonals formed the basis of the grid (fig. A). The golden section proportion, applied to both the vertical and horizontal sides of the rectangle, supplied further divisions and intervals to the structure (fig. B), making more diagonals possible. Further

Diagrams by Alvin Martin

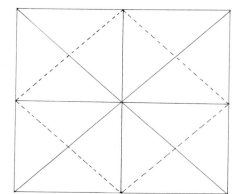

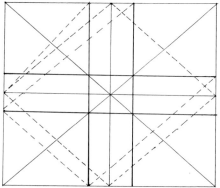

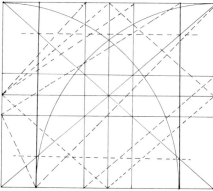

A. The rectangle is divided by main verticals, horizontals, and diagonals. The broken line indicates other potential diagonals.

B. The darker verticals and horizontals are located by the golden section to their points of intersection with the edges of the rectangle. More potential diagonal divisions are indicated by the broken line.

C. Two darker verticals are located by dividing the longer side of the rectangle by the shorter, as indicated by the curved lines. Again, more potential divisions are suggested. By continuing the process of locating divisions by such applications of geometry, an infinite number of design possibilities may be established.

vertical divisions were found by dividing the long side of the rectangle by its short side (fig. C). By subsequent selection and application of the verticals, horizontals, and diagonals (governed by geometric logic and the golden section), the basic abstract elements of the composition were established. This is not to say that Villon's mode of design or expression was completely subservient to system. Each motif made its own expressive demands. Villon said:

In composing a painting I always begin with a proportion which I then plot. My starting point is in nature, but I don't feel the need in sticking to nature. My painting's got to be my own creation. But instead of relying on chances, I make sure that I have something certain, a proportion on which I can base myself. Then I move a step further. I divide the canvas and once this is done the canvas begins to take shape. Sometimes I leave to the very end quite visible all these lines of subdivision which may be called the regulating plot. In this way I can rely on their lead as I move along.[3] . . . In the Middle Ages they used to recite a prayer before starting work on a painting. Much of the same way, I lean on the golden section to get my initial assurance.[4]

Villon's interest in geometry, proportion, and the golden section began before 1912 and developed steadily over the years. In the mid-1940s, at the time Cleve Gray became the artist's friend (and for a time his disciple) Villon advised the young American painter to buy the books of Matila Ghyka and Jay Hambidge, even before the treatises on color of Rosenstiehl and Rood. (See cat. nos. 99, 100, footnote 1; also cat. nos. 114-117, footnote 4). Subsequently, Villon contributed introductory essays to two books on geometry in art: Lucien Schwob's *Réalité en art,* Lausanne, 1955; and Charles Bouleau's *La Géometrie secrète des peintres,* Paris, 1960.

A M

[1] Villon frequently drew in ink over his oil studies. The practice seems to have become common from the early forties; but as he sometimes worked over earlier studies lying about the studio, it is difficult to establish a precise date for the origin of this trait.

[2] The golden section, also known as the golden mean, or the mean and extreme proportion, is a ratio that has fascinated mathematicians and estheticians at least since Pythagoras and Euclid. Most simply stated, it is a ratio of a part to a whole, formulated so that the smaller part is to the larger part as the larger part is to the whole. This ratio is expressed mathematically as $\frac{\sqrt{5}}{2-1}$. The Fibonaci series is a sequence in which the sum of the previous two units equals the successive number — 2:3:5:8:13, etc. As the sequence grows, the ratios more and more closely approach the golden section. The literature on both the golden section and the Fibonaci series is vast.

[3] (40) Vallier, *Villon,* p. 114.

[4] *Ibid.,* p. 115.

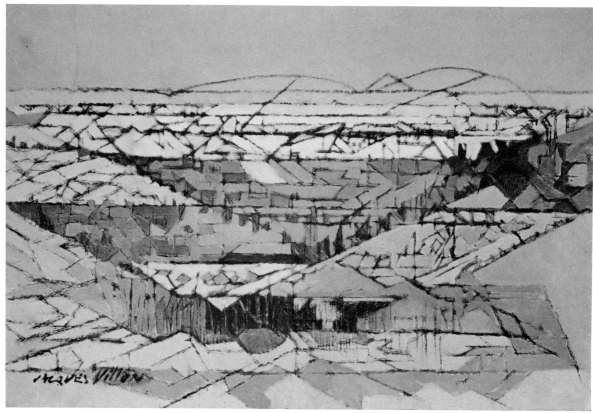

144

144

Les Fonds de St. Paul 1945

Oil on canvas

Signed lower left "Jacques Villon"

60 x 92 cm.

PROVENANCE: Jacques Villon; Louis Carré et Cie, Paris

COLLECTION: Genia Zadok, Greenwich, Connecticut

PUBLISHED: 34, 86, 147, 232, 288, 305, 333, 397

EXHIBITED: *8, 9, 10, 13, 20, 21, 322*

145

Les Grands fonds 1945

Oil on canvas

Signed lower right "Jacques Villon" and dated on the back "45"

46 x 65 cm.

PROVENANCE: Jacques Villon

Private collection, France

PUBLISHED: 27, 29, 33, 34, 40, 96, 153, 155, 235, 263, 342, 396, 432

EXHIBITED: *8, 9, 10, 13, 15, 26, 27, 34, 38, 49, 55, 220*

Les Fonds de St. Paul (cat. no 144) is one of several views of the plateaued vistas of southern France that Villon conceived while staying at La Brunié and executed later in Puteaux. Another beautiful example, *Entre Toulouse et Albi* (fig. 144a), closely resembles *Les Fonds de St. Paul* but lacks the calligraphic indications of the hills on the horizon. The sweeping grandeur of this great panorama is dramatically expressed in one of Villon's most celebrated works, *Les Grands fonds* (cat. no. 145). Here Villon has stripped away the small geometric units that describe the topography of the St. Paul landscape, leaving only the enormous structural triangles and areas of light and dark visible under the network of lines in *Les Fonds de St. Paul.* These are what Villon called the "keystone" of the landscape.[1] The title, *Les Grands fonds,* reiterates Villon's progression from representation to abstraction, between his 1941 perception of the scene and its final depiction in 1945. *Les Grands fonds* means both the "landed property" which he saw, and the "organic essences" which he revealed.

These paintings represent the most powerful statement of Villon's desire to come to terms with the land and to describe its fields, hills, and valleys — as well as to express its hidden structural format. Villon has visualized the great space of the region as unending, yet governed by the inherent balance and rhythm of Nature. As in *Les Trois ordres* (cat. nos. 130, 131), Villon reacted to the external turmoil of the 1940s by turning to the eternal, indestructible qualities of the land. He himself said, "Le paysage a un movement . . . le paysage suggère l'éternité."[2]

M S S

[1] (4) Villon's statement to Walter Pach, "Thus is Cubism Cultivated," *Art News,* XLVIII (May 1, 1949), p. 51.

[2] (43) Bibliothèque Nationale, *Villon,* p. 56.

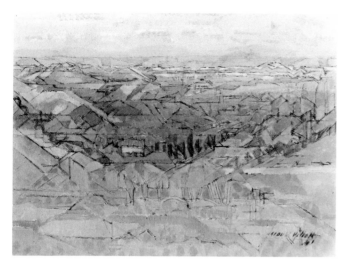

144a

JACQUES VILLON

Entre Toulouse et Albi 1941

Oil on canvas

Musée National d'Art Moderne, Paris

145

146

Cantique spirituel 1945
by Racine
5 black and white etchings
Edited by Raoul Mortier, Paris
Printed by Leblanc

COLLECTION: Harvard College Library,
Department of Printing and Graphic Arts,
Harvard University, Cambridge, Massachusetts; Gift of Philip Hofer

PUBLISHED: AP 349-353

The crucifix, the fourth etching for Racine's *Cantique spirituel* (AP 349-353), is the most monumental of the group. The roughly outlined forms of Christ's body are luminous against a background of vertical hatching. A figure, perhaps Mary, emerges from the shadows at the base of the cross. The economy, even severity, of Villon's touch lend this print great dignity and restraint.

The prints for *Cantique spirituel* are the only known instances of explicitly religious themes in Villon's work. He was not a practicing Catholic and may even have shared mildly the anticlerical feelings of his brothers. However, Villon chose the devout text himself, perhaps in a spirit of thanksgiving for the liberation of France.[1]

Villon's interest in Racine and his theater prompted him to take the fifteenth-century bust of Racine by Caffieri at the Théâtre Français as the model for the frontispiece of *Cantique spirituel*. Villon felt responsible, as an illustrator, to be faithful to the spirit of a text. In a 1946 interview he said, "I think that the illustrator should not give a translation of the text, his task is, above all, to recreate the atmosphere."[2]

J H

[1] Suggested by Francis Steegmuller; confirmed by Cleve Gray.

[2] (60) René Barotte, "Jacques Villon, illustrateur," *Le Livre et ses amis,* 8 (1946), p. 22.

146

147

147
L'Orgeuil 1947

Oil on canvas

Signed lower left "Jacques Villon"

73 x 54 cm.

PROVENANCE: Jacques Villon; Louis Carré et Cie, Paris; Saidenberg Gallery, New York

Private collection, Providence, Rhode Island

PUBLISHED: 34, 40, 227, 342

EXHIBITED: 8, 9, 15, 26, 220, 281, 346

L'Orqueil is one of a number of finished works from a series Villon projected in 1947 on the theme of the Seven Deadly Sins. Others are a drawing and etching Colère, 1952 (fig. 147a) (not in AP) and an etching and painting Paresse.

L'Orgueil is composed primarily of interacting triangles. Once again, the composition of the image is determined by a complex grid constructed through the use of the golden section. Visible on the surface are traces of the marks left by the strings Villon sometimes stretched across the canvas as initial guides in establishing the proportional system.

The prideful subject of the composition is a human figure, his bulk carried anxiously by the narrow vertices that suggest his feet; his arms swinging dramatically in several directions, his small head thrown back with an expression of hauteur enhanced by overdrawing in ink. The pose recalls the final version of Rodin's Balzac.

A M

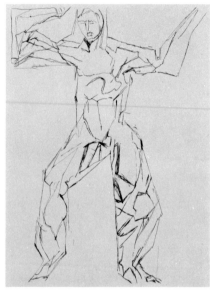

147a

JACQUES VILLON

Colère 1952

Etching, not in AP

Courtesy Museum of Fine Arts, Boston

Le Grain ne meurt 1947

Oil on canvas

Signed lower left "Jacques Villon"

63 x 140 cm.

PROVENANCE: Jacques Villon; Louis Carré Gallery, New York

The Phillips Collection, Washington, D.C.

PUBLISHED: 33, 34, 40, 235, 263, 342

EXHIBITED: 10, 13, 20, 29, 198, 221, 281

In 1946 Villon began a series of harvest scenes, a project which continued until 1950. The series includes a large number of oils and graphic works developed from quick sketches done at La Brunié in 1940 (fig. 148a). *Le Grain ne meurt,* one of the most complex paintings of this group, synthesizes Villon's long-standing fascination with machinery and his more recently manifested interest in a traditional theme in French art so familiar in the work of Le Nain and Millet, and more recently Gleizes — men relating to the land through agriculture.[1] Despite inspiration from a specific locale, this painting is a celebration of human involvement with the land, rather than a representation of any particular time or place. *Le Grain ne meurt* and related paintings such as *Du Blé à la paille* (fig. 148b) also embody Villon's particular concern for the timeless and eternal harvest ritual.[2] According to Walter Pach, *Le Grain ne meurt* refers to a verse in the New Testament:[3]

Except a corn of wheat fall onto the ground and die, it abideth alone; but if it die, it bringeth forth much fruit. (JOHN 11:24)

However, Villon may have been more immediately inspired by the André Gide novel "Si le grain ne meurt."[4]

The narrow horizontal format repeats the shape of the Jockey drawings of the early 1920s (cat. nos. 86-98). Strong diagonals and large planes of vivid color create energetic movement, even restlessness, with choppy lines separating the colors. In addition, areas of small brush strokes catch the light and enhance the visual stimulation. Villon used an extraordinary amount of black in this painting, as a separate color and as a wash over other colors.

Du blé a la paille contains the same formal vocabulary, with an energetic diagonal emphasis created by the straining motion of the laborers.

M S S

[4] *(198) Jacques Villon-Lyonel Feininger* (Boston: Institute of Contemporary Art, 1949), p. 10.

[2] Michele Sanouillet reminded us that Villon's real name, Duchamp, means "field" and smacks "of the soil and evokes generations of hard working middle-class villagers and anonymous laborers living

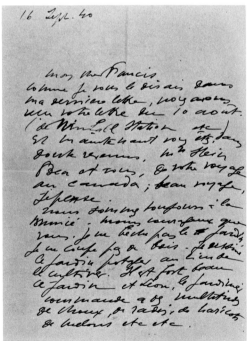

148a

JACQUES VILLON

Letter to a Friend (verso), June 16, 1940

Private collection, New York

close to the land." "Marcel Duchamp and the French Intellectual Tradition," chapter in (395a) d'Harnoncourt and McShine, *Duchamp*, p. 48.

3 (4) Pach and Villon, "Thus is Cubism Cultivated," p. 35. Note that the caption for *Le Grain ne meurt* has been reversed with another reproduction, p. 24.

4 Francis Steegmuller kindly suggested the Gide title as a possible source for Villon.

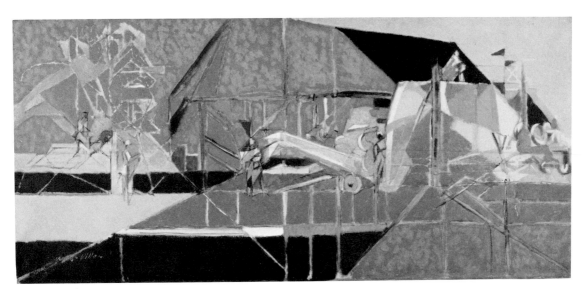

148

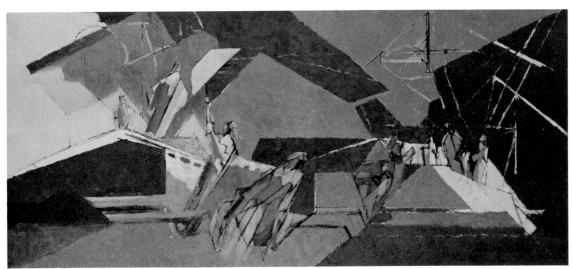

148b

JACQUES VILLON

Du Blé à la paille 1946

Oil on canvas

Collection of Mr. and Mrs. Paul Mellon

149

149
Jardin en fête 1948
Oil on canvas
Signed lower left "Jacques Villon" and
dated on the back "48"
54 x 73 cm.
PROVENANCE: Jacques Villon
COLLECTION: Louis Carré et Cie, Paris
PUBLISHED: 27, 29, 32, 34, 153, 211, 359
EXHIBITED: *13, 15, 17, 19, 21, 27, 34, 38, 45,
46, 47, 49, 51, 55, 220, 322, 249*

150
Le Long du parc 1955
Oil on canvas
Signed and dated lower right "Jacques
Villon 55"
65 x 81 cm.
PROVENANCE: Jacques Villon
COLLECTION: Louis Carré et Cie, Paris
PUBLISHED: 27, 29, 40, 102, 103, 153, 196,
240, 342, 414, catalogue to exhibition no.
47 (not in exhibition)
EXHIBITED: *34, 38, 49, 51, 55, 313, 322, 361,
391, 419, 459*

151
Parc 1955
Oil on canvas
Signed and dated lower right "Jacques
Villon 55"
81 x 100 cm.
PROVENANCE: Jacques Villon
COLLECTION: Louis Carré et Cie, Paris
PUBLISHED: 40, 229, 342
EXHIBITED: *38, 304*

152
Le Long du bois 1958
Oil on canvas
Signed and dated lower left "Jacques
Villon 58"
114 x 146 cm.
PROVENANCE: Jacques Villon; Louis Carré
et Cie, Paris
COLLECTION: Musée d'Art moderne de la
ville de Paris
PUBLISHED: 27
EXHIBITED: *49, 55, 459, 492*

151

The park series spans a ten-year period and
includes at least eight major paintings.
Unlike some of Villon's landscapes series,
which progress chronologically from a
detailed treatment of a scene to a much
simplified version, this group is characterized by two different modes which Villon
used interchangeably between 1948 and
1958.

The first mode is exemplified by *L'Entrée
du parc* (fig. 152a) and *Le Long du bois*
(cat. no. 152). Although the former seems
more representational than the latter, done
ten years later, both depict the lush verdure
of trees and bushes in full foliage. The other
paintings reproduced here (cat. nos. 149-
151) demonstrate the alternate handling of
the same scene: all the leaves have been
stripped away, exposing the bare trunks
of the saplings. Although this abstracting
process might be interpreted as indicating
a change in the seasons, the title *Jardin en
fête* and the splendid color suggests that
this reduction of foliage was intended to
reveal an essential aspect of the park often
hidden under the full verdure. With these
contrasting modes, Villon was able to show
both external details and internal structures
from the same scene, as he did earlier in his

treatment of the panoramic landscape of
southern France (see cat. nos. 144, 145).

The three earliest works of the park series
exhibit a striking compositional connection with the earlier *potager* paintings (see
cat. nos. 133, 134) in their receding foreground, flat horizon and silhouetted trees.
However, Villon also introduced in *Le Long
du parc* and *Jardin en fête* a tripartite color
division of the background, a device previously absent from his landscape paintings,
but consonant with the quest for symmetry
in design and clarity of color relationships
which permeates most of his oeuvre.

These four different versions of the same
scene, as well as the other variation here
reproduced (fig. 152a), indicate that Villon
was more concerned with conveying the
concept of park than with representing the
individual details of any specific site.

M S S

150

152

152a

JACQUES VILLON

L'Entrée du parc 1948

Oil on canvas

Louis Carré et Cie, Paris

153

La Grande faucheuse aux chevaux 1950

Oil on canvas

Signed lower right "Jacques Villon"

97 x 146 cm.

PROVENANCE: Louis Carré et Cie, Paris and New York; Mr. and Mrs. Harry Lynde Bradley, Milwaukee

COLLECTION: Milwaukee Art Center Collection, Gift of Mr. and Mrs. Harry Lynde Bradley

PUBLISHED: 27, 32, 34, 70, 97, 153, 280, 316

EXHIBITED: 20, 49, 207, 233, 353, 413, 471a, 480, 499

In *La Grande faucheuse aux chevaux* Villon returned once again to horses, which he earlier depicted in the sport of racing and now represents as powerful beasts of burden. Whereas *Le Grain ne meurt* (cat. no. 142) emphasized farm laborers and their machinery, this mowing scene celebrates the traditional role of the horse in agriculture.

Villon did not often use the diagonal plane in his landscapes,[1] as he generally preferred a symmetrical composition. Nor did he usually monumentalize individual animated elements within a landscape. In this painting he set the horses, the dominant features in the foreground, on a diagonal course in order to stress the rapid movement of the mowers across the field. The blades of the machine, described as long bars over the horses' heads, also express the speed of the animals' labor. The sense of periodic recurrence of the harvest is communicated by Villon's multiple image of horses moving through the fields, recalling the artist's statement to Dora Vallier: *"Je veux exprimer la synthèse du mouvement par la continuité."*[2]

Villon executed at least seven sketched, painted, and etched versions of this event, representing the horses from behind (fig. 153a) as well as in front. In each variation he conveyed the dynamism and significance which he found in the harvest events. *La Grande faucheuse aux chevaux* won the grand prize at the 1950 Carnegie International exhibition at Pittsburgh and marked Villon's rise to international fame.

M S S

[1] The few previous examples include:
L'Usine, 1935, etching, 20.9 x 26.9 cm.
L'Usine au cannet, 1945, oil on canvas, 65 x 92 cm.

[2] (40) Vallier, *Villon*, p. 77.

153

153a

La Faucheuse aux chevaux (de dos) 1949

Oil on canvas

Courtesy of Margit Chanin, Ltd., New York

155

155a

JACQUES VILLON

Un Philosophe 1951

Oil on canvas

Collection of Haakon Onstad,
Munkedal, Sweden

155

Marcel Duchamp 1951

Oil on canvas

Signed and dated lower left "Jacques
Villon 51"

146 x 114 cm.

PROVENANCE: Jacques Villon; Louis Carré
et Cie, Paris

COLLECTION: Sonja Henie-Niels Onstad
Foundations, Norway

PUBLISHED: 27, 28, 91, 99, 111, 198, 300,
307, 367, 416

EXHIBITED: 20, 45, 49, 225, 322, 388, 394, 398
406, 407, 410, 412, 414, 416, 418, 425, 428,
431, 470, 484

155b

JACQUES VILLON

Marcel Duchamp 1953

Drawing

Private collection, Boston

In 1951 and 1953 Villon did a series of
portraits of his brother, Marcel Duchamp.
Although Duchamp had been living per-
manently in New York since 1942, he continued to see Villon on his frequent trips to
France. A special event that may have
brought the brothers together around this
time was a family show in New York in 1952
Duchamp Frères et Soeur at the Rose Fried
Gallery.

In this group of portraits of Marcel there
are at least five oil paintings, four of which
were done in 1951.[1] In 1953 Villon did
another series consisting of a sketch, an
etching, and a painting.[2]

Un Philosophe, 1951 (fig. 155a) is one of
the most representational and individual of
the paintings, and may be the first. While the
others of both years are broken into cubist
planes, only *Un Philosophe* is executed in
curved lines. The sixty-four-year-old
Duchamp seen in three-quarters profile is
seated in a large arm chair, stretched diagonally across the canvas. He has a self-
absorbed expression; his head rests gently
against his hand, and his legs, crossed and
extending outward, are wrapped in a
blanket. The position and expression remain the same throughout the series.

The other 1951 versions of *Marcel
Duchamp* have much in common. The figure
and chair, no longer totally distinct from
each other, are fragmented into geometric
planes and set in an abstract space. Among
this group, *Marcel Duchamp* (cat. no. 155)
is the simplest and most tightly organized.

The ambiguous space in which *Marcel
Duchamp* is set relates to Villon's abstract
paintings of the early 1930s, constructed by
placing smaller rectangles inside larger ones
and connecting corners with diagonals. This
proportional device, with many variations,
had become standard for a figure or still life.

In *Marcel Duchamp* (cat. no. 155), however, compared to the self-portrait of 1942
(cat. no. 140), there is more interaction between the figure and the surrounding space.
The large off-center figure diagonally inter-
sects the fairly symmetrical rectangular
background construction. Color plays a key
role in the organization of the work. Where
the figure overlaps a background plane, as
in the case of the head, it takes on the
dominant color of that plane. This allows
the continuity of both the irregular form of
the figure and the more symmetrical setting
to be maintained without one significantly
dominating the other.

The brilliant colors of this work, three
warm, three cool, and all of the same relative intensity, are typical of much of Villon's
later paintings, especially the landscapes.
The distinct and finely-patterned brushstroke, reminiscent of pointillism, provides
contrast with the harsh fragmentation of
form. In exploiting contrasting colors, symmetry and asymmetry, soft texture with
hard lines, Villon has harmonized opposing
forces. Their dynamic balance served to
express the complex personality of his sitter.

In the drawing, etching, and painting
of 1953, Villon emphasizes the structural
solidity of the body to a greater extent. For
example in the drawing (fig. 155b), the left
shoulder is reduced to a powerful wedge
shape which relates to the architectural
massiveness of the chair in which Duchamp
sits.[3]

S G

[1] Other versions of 1951: *Mon frère Marcel;
Portrait de mon Frère; Mon Frère; Un
Philosophe*

[2] Works of 1953: *Marcel Duchamp*, drawing;
Marcel Duchamp, etching; *Portrait de Rose
Sélavy*, oil on canvas

[3] The chair is the same as the one which
appears in the *Petit dessinateur* series (cat.
nos. 123-124).

154
La Signature 1951
Etching and drypoint
20.7 x 16.7 cm.

COLLECTION: The Museum of Modern Art,
New York, Gift of Hubert de Givenchy
Not listed in AP

This etching belongs to a series of self-
portraits which includes a drawing, *Portrait
de l'artiste of 1949;*[1] and five oil paintings:
Figure d'homme, 1949 (Galerie Louis Carré,
Paris); *L'Usurier,* 1949 (Henie-Onstad
Collection); *Le Matois,* 1949 (Carnegie
Institute, Pittsburgh); *Le Finaud,* 1949; and
Le Scribe, 1949 (Musée d'Art Moderne,
Paris). The self-deprecatory titles of *Le
Finaud, L'Usurier,* and *Le Matois* (meaning
the sly fox, the usurer and the slick cus-
tomer) are in accord with the period during
which the artist had been developing a
sequence based on the *Seven Deadly Sins*
(cat. no. 147). Although the painting
entitled *Le Scribe* (fig. 154a) is the most
depersonalized and abstract of the series,
Villon has depicted the hands and the paper
in much the same way in all the versions.
La Signature (cat. no. 154) is the clue that
suggests the genesis of the titles of the other
self-portraits. With his relationship with the
Galerie Louis Carré and sudden rise to fame
at the end of the war, Villon's works were
finally in demand; not only did he need to
sign editions of prints, but drawings and
paintings that had long been in his studio
as well. At least one of his friends, Gleizes,
reproached him for allowing himself to be
promoted to fame. His equivocal feelings
about receiving recognition at last are
humorously, yet intensely explored in this
group of works.

J D F

[1] (32) Exhibited Carré, *Dessins.*

154

154a

JACQUES VILLON
Le Scribe 1949
Oil on canvas
Musée National d'Art Moderne, Paris

156

156

La Cage et l'oiseau 1952

Oil on canvas

Signed and dated lower right "Jacques Villon 52"

46 x 55 cm.

PROVENANCE: Jacques Villon; Louis Carré et Cie, Paris

Private collection, Paris

PUBLISHED: 27, 40, 342

EXHIBITED: 22, 26, 27, 34, 49, 247, 254, 459

A bird in a cage was a subject often used by Villon in the 1950s. Although he had treated the theme of the bird in earlier periods, first in *L'Oiseau*, 1921 (AP 207, fig. 156a), and subsequently in *Nature morte au perroquet*, 1932 (AP 247) and *L'Oiseau empaillé,* 1938 (cat. no. 127), in the 1950s Villon changed the theme by adding a cage, with thin wire bars. Various integrations of bird and cage in harmonious arrangements of vivid color, shape and line constitute some of his most abstract compositions of this period. In *La Cage et l'oiseau* (cat. no. 156), the feathers are reduced to simple geometric shapes, spread out and separated by the horizontal and vertical parallel lines signifying the cage. In the 1921 etching (fig. 156b), they were clustered three-dimensionally, creating an illusionistic space. In a 1955 version (fig. 156c), the wires are seen from above, and the space is not illusionistic although the linear pattern deliberately alludes to a spider web as a metaphor for the cage. In *La Cage et l'oiseau* series, Villon has delighted in contrasting forms and surface textures: the lines of the cage are played off against the dabbing and dotting of paint across the entire picture surface. A 1952 version of *La Cage et l'oiseau* (fig. 156a),

employs a pattern of dots reminiscent of the treatment in the 1921 etching *L'Oiseau* and *Composition en jaune et bleu ou galop,* 1921 (cat. no. 97a).

D S R

156a
JACQUES VILLON
La Cage et l'oiseau 1952
Oil on canvas
Galerie Couturier, Paris

156b
JACQUES VILLON
L'Oiseau 1921
Etching, AP 207
R. S. Johnson-International Gallery,
Chicago

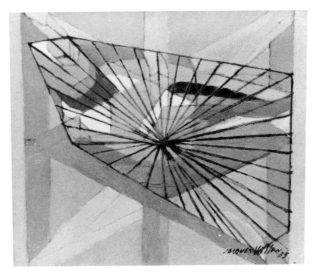

156c
JACQUES VILLON
La Cage et l'oiseau 1955
Oil on canvas
Collection of Ragnar Moltzau, Oslo

157

La Ferme normande 1953

Oil on canvas

Signed and dated lower left "Jacques Villon 53"

89 x 146 cm.

PROVENANCE: Jacques Villon

COLLECTION: Louis Carré et Cie, Paris

PUBLISHED: 27, 40, 342

EXHIBITED: 34, 38, 45, 46, 47, 49, 51, 55, 273, 285, 293, 299, 322, 349

158

Le Pigeonnier normand 1953

Oil on canvas

Signed and dated lower left "Jacques Villon 53"

97 x 146 cm.

PROVENANCE: Jacques Villon; Louis Carré et Cie, Paris; Private collection; Galerie Charpentier, Paris

Private collection, New York

PUBLISHED: 27, 29, 88, 113, 139; Sales catalogue, Paris: Palais Galliera, June 6, 1956

EXHIBITED: 34, 49, 55, 263, 322, 344, 359, 417, 459

A large group of paintings of a dovecote, or *pigeonnier*, in a Norman farmyard is another manifestation of Villon's continued attraction to rural scenes, which began at La Brunié during World War II. In developing the curiously irregular shape of the dovecote as the main motif for this 1952-1954 series, Villon paralleled Cézanne, who painted a similar subject c. 1894-1896 (fig. 157a).

The vitality of these paintings, among the boldest of all Villon's landscapes, results from the juxtaposition of large blocks of background color against the organic lines of the farm buildings. These vary from the long, sweeping lines of *La Ferme normande* (cat. no. 157) to the short, choppy strokes in *Le Pigeonnier normand* Villon was perhaps increasing linear activity to the maximum degree before it would necessarily lose relationship with the rest of the composition. The strong blocks of color, conceived, as Villon once explained to an interviewer, out of a "desire for sobriety of expression,"[1] are sufficiently assertive to counterbalance the explosive effect of the lines and to maintain the calm order characteristic of all Villon's landscapes.

Another device essential to the unity of these compositions is the horizontal black rectangle below the dovecote. Villon used this bar in one of the first paintings of the group, a small oil sketch entitled *La Ferme au pigeonnier* (fig. 157b), and retained it throughout the series as the central point of focus, a stabilizer for bolder colors and lines.

The culmination of these paintings recalls Villon's treatment of *Les Fonds de St. Paul* and *Entre Toulouse et Albi* (see cat. nos. 144-145; fig. 144a). Having animated the lines to the point where they almost overwhelm the composition, Villon then reduced them to regular, geometric, linear patterns, to produce *Rhythme campagnard* (fig. 158a). This abstract painting presents all the essential devices of the *Pigeonnier* paintings distilled from the method used to construct each of these vital works. The large triangles in the upper half of *Rhythme campagnard*, though absent from the *Pigeonnier* paintings (cat. nos. 157-158), derive from a related work of 1953, *Le Four à pain* (fig. 158b). The evocative title of *Rhythme campagnard* is reminiscent of *Les Grand fonds* (cat. no. 145) and represents another example of Villon's prowess at condensation and synthesis in the expression of the flow and rhythm of life.

M S S

[1] Unpublished interview with Francis Steegmuller.

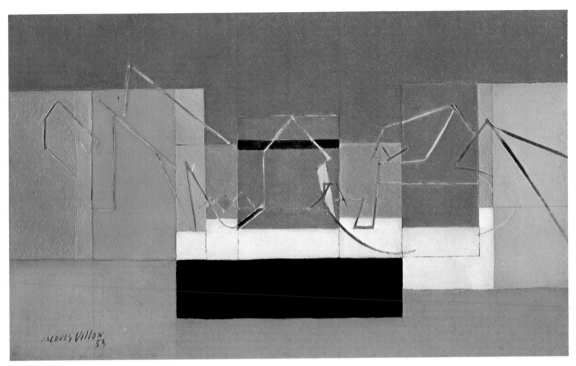

157

157a

PAUL CEZANNE

Pigeon Tower at Montbriand 1894-1896

Oil on canvas

The Cleveland Museum of Art
The James W. Corrigan Memorial

157b

JACQUES VILLON

La Ferme au pigeonnier 1953

Oil on canvas

Private collection, New York

158

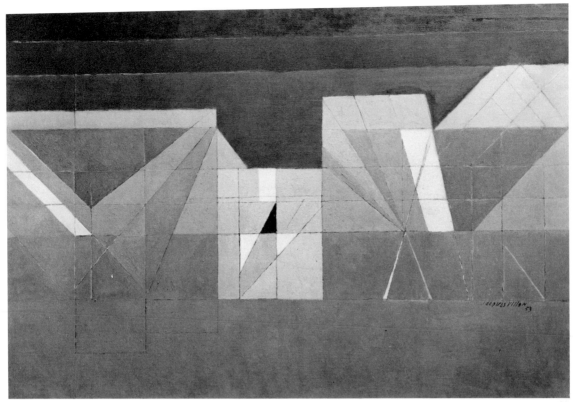

158a

JACQUES VILLON

Rythme campagnard 1953

Oil on canvas

Collection of Dr. Jan Österlöf, Stockholm

158b

JACQUES VILLON

Le Four à pain 1953

Oil on canvas

Collection of Henning Throne-Holst,
Stockholm

159

159

Villacoublay 1954

Oil on canvas

Signed and dated lower right "Jacques
Villon 54"

89 x 146 cm.

PROVENANCE: Jacques Villon; Louis Carré
et Cie, Paris; Galerie Bonnier, Geneva

COLLECTION: Bengt Nylen, Geneva

EXHIBITED: *45, 46, 47, 76, 298, 391*

Like so many of the Right Bank cubists,
Villon was fascinated by aviation. His first
drawings of airplanes probably date from
1912,[1] the year of the Paris aviation meet
that also inspired Delaunay, de la Fresnaye,
Picasso and indeed caused "two out of every
three collections of poems published in 1912
to contain a reference to aviators or the
conquest of the stars."[2] However, Villon
waited until 1937 to develop a major project
based on aviation, working with Gleizes
and Delaunay on murals for the *Pavillion
de l'air* at the Exposition Universelle. The
Villon murals were never completed, and
Villon and Gleizes conceived the idea of
adapting and integrating their designs for a
sloping wall mural in the auditorium of
the Ecole des Arts et Métiers. Four Villon
panels dealing with the physical conquest of
space[3] would alternate with four panels by
Gleizes reflecting man's dream of space (fig.
159a-159b). Villon and Gleizes worked
intermittently on this project until 1942,
when it became clear that the mural would
not be commissioned.[4]

 Villacoublay (cat. no. 159) and two other
French airports, Orly and Le Bourget, provided titles for a new group of works dealing with flight. In this series the airplanes

are based on toy models.[5] The same basic
format is employed in *L'Escadrille*, 1954,
Encore plus haut, 1954, and Orly, 1954.[6]
By outlining the airplanes with black overdrawing, Villon transformed the wings and
wheels into forms resembling the limbs of
insects. Indeed, the connection between
these two flying forms was made by the
artist in a 1953 work entitled *L'Insecte*. This
painting, like *Le Depart*, 1953, and *Vers le
Ciel*, 1954 (fig. 159c), focuses on an individual airplane about to take off and is
preliminary to the 1954 work, *Air France*.

D S R

[1] We are indebted to Hélène Lassalle for this
information. *(77a)* Rouen-Grand Palais,
Villon, p. 124, no. 149.

[2] Georges Duhamel *Lumières sur ma vie*, vol.
II,*Le Temps de la Recherche* (Paris, 1947),
p. 14.

[3] At least one of Villon's designs (fig. 159a)
was based on a 1912 drawing made at the
Paris Aviation Meeting.

[4] The Gleizes-Villon project, like *Villacoublay*, was chosen in 1963 by the Mobilier
National to be translated into a tapestry at
the Gobelins studio.

159a

JACQUES VILLON

Autour des premiers circuits d'aviation

1937

Gouache

Courtesy Lucien Goldschmidt Inc.

159b

JACQUES VILLON

Les Ballons 1938

Gouache

Courtesy Lucien Goldschmidt Inc.

5 Villon mentioned using toy airplanes as models for these paintings in an interview with Dora Vallier. (40) Vallier, *Villon,* p. 116.

6 Reproduced in (40) Vallier, *Villon,* p. 98, 99. *Orly, L'Insecte,* and *Air France* are reproduced in *(49)* Galerie Charpentier, *Cent Tableaux.*

159c

JACQUES VILLON

Vers le ciel 1954

Oil on canvas

Collection of Ragnar Moltzau, Oslo

160

Intérieur 1954

Oil on canvas

Signed and dated lower right "Jacques Villon 54"

81 x 65 cm.

PROVENANCE: Jacques Villon; Louis Carré et Cie, Paris; Leon Duesburg, Verviers

COLLECTION: Sonja Henie-Niels Onstad Foundations, Norway

PUBLISHED: 27, 40, 155, 342, 387

EXHIBITED: 49

160

In *Intérieur*, 1954 (cat. no. 160) Villon continued to develop the theme of interior space treated as still life, previously used in *Intérieur*, 1936 (cat. no. 125) and *Le Grand salon de Bernay*, 1945 (cat. no. 143). Once again adopting his motif from observation of a familiar locale, he depicts the corner of a table, a portion of the ceiling from which hangs a chandelier, and a mantle with a mirror above.

Here Villon continued to construct his composition from a structural grid based on Golden Section proportions. However, the linear aspect of the grid in *Intérieur* is more assertive than in many of the artist's previous interior paintings. The lines are emphasized as surface pattern rather than as vestigial elements of observation, as in earlier works such as *Joueur de flageolet*, 1939 (cat. no. 128) and *Le Grand salon de Bernay*, 1945 (cat. no. 143). This linear quality developed in the landscape series that includes *Jardin en fête*, 1948 (see. cat. nos. 149-152) and the still life series, *La Cage et l'oiseau*, 1952 (cat. no. 156), can also be seen in the two closely related interiors, *L'Âtre*, 1954 and *L'Atre*, 1955.

A M

160a

JACQUES VILLON

L'Âtre 1955

Oil on canvas

Private collection: France

161

161
Passage de la visitation 1956
by André Frénaud
1 black and white etching, frontispiece
Edited by G.L.M., Paris
Printed by Leblanc
COLLECTION: Harvard College Library,
Department of Printing and Graphic Arts,
Harvard University, Cambridge,
Massachusetts

In *Passage de la visitation* a figure is described by outline; while hatching lines give geometric structure to the composition, represent areas of space, determine the value areas of the composition, and almost conceal a familiar motif.

The print is more closely related to Villon's own oeuvre than to the Frénaud poems in the book. Its source is found precisely in the drawings, prints and painting that make up *L'Équilibriste* (see cat. nos. 54-57) of 1913-14. It was not unusual in Villon's later years for him to take up early themes in his illustrations. For example, the bust of Baudelaire, a subject developed extensively in the early 1920s, is the subject of his illustrations in *Poésies de mots inconnus,* published by Iliazd in 1949, and in *La Soif du jonc* by Tiggie Ghika, published in 1955.

André Frénaud was a young poet whom Villon knew. Before *Passage de la visitation,* Villon had already illustrated two earlier volumes of his works, *Mystères de Paris,* 1945, and *Poèmes de Brandebourg,* 1947.

J H

162

162

Les Yeux futiles 1956

Color aquatint

15.2 x 13.1 cm.

COLLECTION: The Museum of Fine Arts, Boston, Gift of Mr. and Mrs. Peter A. Wick

Les Yeux futiles was made as an illustration for a volume of poetry by Paul Eluard, *Un Poème dans chaque livre,* published in Paris by Louis Broder. Four preliminary states and a trial proof show the steps in the laborious and exacting process of color aquatint. *Les Yeux futiles* was probably printed by Le Courrière, one of the best printers to use the sugar-lift method by which the grainy effect of the background is achieved.[1]

The subject of a skeleton with a chain around its neck, and a cow or ox, is very strange for Villon, who gave little place in his oeuvre to the fantastic and the un-natural. Since Eluard had died four years before the publication of *Un Poème dans chaque livre,* Villon's print may be a comment on the temporality of life. Mortality is certainly the subject of a related print which Villon executed in the same year, as a frontispiece for a book of *Epitaphes grecques* compiled by Jean Cocteau (fig. 162a). This black and white etching shows a Greek grave with a skeleton, an overturned vase, and a stele inscribed, "I am dead but I remain with you."

Villon and Eluard must have had more than a casual acquaintance in their later years, for shortly after the War Villon professed admiration for Eluard and particularly for his activity in the Resistance.[2] In 1948 Eluard was co-author with René-Jean of *Jacques Villon ou l'art glorieux,* a book of reproductions of his works accompanied by poetic texts. The last illustration of the book is a drawing by Villon of a death's head, which may comment on the trauma of war.

The title of *Les Yeux futiles* is certainly derived from the name of a book of poetry that Eluard published in 1936, *Les Yeux fertiles.* This is a collection of love poetry in which the image of the eyes occurs frequently, as in the following example from the poem "L'Entente":

Multiple tes yeux divers et confondus
Font fleurir les miroirs
Les couvrent de rosée de givre de pollen
Les miroirs spontanés où les aubes voyagent
Où les horizons s'associent

(Multiple your eyes diverse and confused
Make the mirrors flower
Cover them with dew with frost with pollen
The spontaneous mirrors where dawns travel
Where the horizons meet)

In the print we find not only the vacant eyes of the skeleton, but also a single large, disembodied eye staring out of the background to the left of the skeleton's shoulder. This eye is most noticeable in the fourth state. It may be a reference to Odilon Redon's use of the single, staring eye in his mystical works.[3] In Villon's uncharacteristically pessimistic interpretation, the once fertile eyes have become empty, mirroring the vanity of human existence.[4]

J H

[1] Information given by Mr. Peter Wick during a meeting of the Villon seminar, October 11, 1972.

[2] Letter from Francis Steegmuller to Jane Hancock, July 30, 1974.

[3] Works such as the sketch, *Eye with Poppy,* 1892; and the lithographs "The Eye, a strange Balloon, moves toward the infinite," 1882; and "There was perhaps a preliminary vision tested in the flower," 1883

[4] According to (77a) Rouen — Grand Palais, *Villon,* p. 129, the correct title for this print is *Les Yeux fertiles.*

163

163

À Poèmes rompus 1960

by Max Jacob

5 color soft-ground etchings, 1 black and
white etching (cover)

Edited by Louis Broder, Paris

Printed by Leblanc

COLLECTION: Harvard College Library,
Department of Printing and Graphic Arts,
Harvard University,
Cambridge, Massachusetts

162a

JACQUES VILLON

Illustration from Jean Cocteau's *Épitaphes
grecques* (frontispiece)

Harvard College Library, Department of
Printing and Graphic Arts, Harvard
University, Cambridge, Massachusetts

The frontispiece of *À Poèmes rompus*, like
four other color etchings that follow it, is a
sharp departure from Villon's usual practice
in book illustration: no identifiable subjects may be observed. Not only are the
plates without apparent reference, but at
this late date in Villon's life he seemed willing to abandon the geometric framework
that had, since the cubist years, organized
his pictorial space. For this group he introduced an unstructured space in which complex shapes, tenuously attached to one
another, are distributed freely, giving equal
weight to all areas of the surface.

The superposition of several plates representing different states of the print, and
the combinations of different values of the
same colors, provide rich effects of brilliant,
shifting, and transparent tones. Their shapes
are reinforced by the drawing, faintly visible on the gray background.

It was typical of Villon to explore a new
formal configuration in graphic media,
before attempting it in painting. It is impossible to say whether he would eventually
have adopted this new, ambiguous space in
painting, for he died only three years after
the publication of *À Poèmes rompus,* and
his last paintings remain in the tradition of
geometric composition.

J H

165

165a
JACQUES VILLON
Les Environs de Rouen 1960
Oil on canvas
Courtesy Galerie Louis Carré

164

164

La Seine au val de la Haye 1959

Oil on canvas

Signed and dated lower right "Jacques Villon 59"

97 x 162 cm.

PROVENANCE: Jacques Villon

COLLECTION: Louis Carré et Cie, Paris

PUBLISHED: 27, 28, 153, 309, 327, 366, 433

EXHIBITED: 45, 46, 47, 49, 51, 55, 377, 380, 419, 459

165

Les Grues près de Rouen 1960

Oil on canvas

Signed and dated lower left "Jacques Villon 60"

60 x 92 cm.

PROVENANCE: Jacques Villon

COLLECTION: Louis Carré et Cie, Paris

PUBLISHED: 27

EXHIBITED: 49, 76

Villon's last landscape series depicts cranes loading cargo boats in the Seine near Rouen. In most of the earlier landscapes which included machines, such as *Le Grain ne meurt* (cat. no. 148), humans play an important, if secondary, role. In the purely industrial landscape of the Crane group, however, the physical presence of humans has been completely eliminated.

Silhouetted like trees against the sky, the cranes recall the first sustained interest in landscape, the *Mougins* series of 1934-1935 (cat. nos. 118-119). But the expansive foreground of the shore and jagged background of the Crane pictures more closely relate to the *Potager* series (cat. nos. 132-134). Villon used overdrawings with pen and ink to further define the cranes, a technique he seemed to have developed in the early forties (see cat. no. 143; f. n. 1).

It is touching that Villon should have returned at the end of his life to paint the region of his birth. These paintings also show Villon adding new elements to his previous landscape formulae, still striving for new forms of visual expression. The large irregular planes of color in *Les Grues près de Rouen* (cat. no. 165) differ markedly from the regulated blocks of the Norman dovecote series (see cat. nos. 157-158). Also, the small dabs of paint, a readaptation of neo-impressionist brush technique originating in the mid thirties (see cat. nos. 122 and 125), used effectively in landscape in *Le Grain ne meurt,* have been developed into large areas of textured color. Areas of grey have been generously used to suggest the atmospheric conditions of the river near Rouen. Finally, the depiction of the same scene (compare cat. no. 164 to 165; 165a) from two such contrasting distances is rare in Villon's previous landscapes. Still another departure from his usual procedure is that Villon produced no etchings of this subject prior to these paintings. The only known previous approach to the *Cranes* subject is a much earlier drawing, in a New York private collection, which Villon obviously drew while standing on a boat while it was being loaded.

M S S

BOOKS ILLUSTRATED WITH ORIGINAL PRINTS BY JACQUES VILLON

Architectures
Edited by Louis Süe and André Mare.
Paris: Nouvelle Revue Française, 1921.
34 etchings
AP 466-499

Poésies
by Pierre Corrard. Paris: J. Meynial, 1937.
16 etchings
AP 287-303

Courants d'Air Sur le Chemin de Ma Vie
by Jean Crotti.
13 etchings after drawings by the author
AP 539-551

Les Mystères de Paris
by André Frénaud. Paris: Edition du Seuil,
1945.
frontispiece, drypoint
AP 342

Cantique Spirituel
by Racine. Paris: Raoul Mortier, 1945.
5 etchings
AP 349-353

Poèmes de Brandebourg
by André Frénaud. Paris: Editions
Gallimard, 1947.
6 color etchings
AP 367-372

Du Cubisme
by Albert Gleizes and Jean Metzinger.
Paris: Compagnie Française des Arts
Graphiques, 1947.
1 etching
AP 207

À la Gloire de la Main
Zurich: Edition du Groupe Graphis, 1949.
1 etching
AP 378

Poésie de Mots Inconnus
edited by Iliazd. Paris, 1949.
1 etching

**Jacques Villon, Catalogue Raisonné de Son
Oeuvre Graphique**
Jacqueline Auberty and Charles Pérusseaux.
Paris: Paul Proute, 1950.
frontispiece, drypoint

Humour Poétique
Edited by Georges Charbonnier. Paris:
La Nef, 1951.
frontispiece, color lithograph

La Soif du Jonc
by Tiggie Ghika. Trad. Jacques Dupin.
Paris: Cahiers d'Art, 1955.
3 drypoints

Miennes
by Tristan Tzara. Paris: Imprimerie
Caractères, 1955.
7 etchings

Les Bucoliques
by Virgil. Trad. Paul Valéry. Paris: Scripta
et Picta, 1955.
23 lithographs, 1 drypoint

Laus Veneris
by Algernon Charles Swinburne. Paris:
Manuel Bruker, 1956.
10 etchings

A Immoler
by Pierre-André Benoit. Alès: Louis Broder,
1956.
1 drypoint

Un Poème dans Chaque Livre
by Paul Eluard. Paris: Louis Broder, 1956.
1 color etching

Epitaphes Grecques
selected by Francis Garnung, preface by
Jean Cocteau. Paris: Société des
Impénitants, 1956.
frontispiece, drypoint

Passage de la Visitation
by André Frénaud. Paris: GLM, 1956.
frontispiece, etching

Oeuvre Poétique
by Robert Ganzo. Paris: Marcel Sautier,
1957.
8 color and black and white etchings.

Galets Abandonnés Sur la Plage
by Pierre de Massot. Alès: Louis Broder,
1958.
1 etching

Dents de Lait, Dents de Loup
by Henri Pichette. Paris: Pierre de Tartas,
1959.
13 etchings

Ajournement
by André DuBouchet. Paris: Iliazd, 1959.
7 etchings

A Poèmes Rompus
by Max Jacob. Paris: Louis Broder, 1960.
6 color etchings, 1 engraving

Jacques Villon
by Lionello Venturi. Paris: Louis Carré,
1962.
8 color lithographs

Les Travaux et les Jours
by Hesiod. Trad. Cocteau. Paris: Tériade,
1962.
24 etchings in color and black and white.

Le Grand Testament
by François Villon. Paris: Henri Jonquières,
1963.
18 color lithographs

TAPESTRIES

Personnages
1951, atelier of La Baume-Dürrbach
Cartoon 1950, 200 x 290 cm.

Taureau et Gemeaux
1953, atelier of La Baume-Dürrbach
Cartoon 1937, 220 x 385 cm.

Zodiaque
1953, atelier of La Baume-Dürrbach
Cartoon 1937, 230 x 392 cm.

Le Colombier
1959, Aubusson, 160 x 186 cm.

Le Pigeonnier Normand
1962, atelier Gobelins, 201 x 283 cm.

Le Val de la Haye
1963, atelier Gobelins, 197 x 292 cm.

Villacoublay
1963, atelier Gobelins, 203 x 324 cm.

Legende de la Ciel, (with Gleizes)
1963, atelier Gobelins, size unknown

STAINED GLASS WINDOWS

Cathédrale de Metz, Chapelle du Saint Sacrement

1957
Five windows, ten meters high. Executed in the Jacques Simon atelier in Rheims by Charles Marq and Brigitte Simon.
La Crucifixion, Les Noces de Cana, La Cène, Le Rocher d'Horeb, L'Agneau pascal.

Chapelle du Moulin de Vauboyen, Bièvres
1962
La Crucifixion

Église de Bouchevilliers, Eure
1963
Panel of the central window. Charles Marq, painter-glassmaker
La Chute d'Icare.

ONE-MAN EXHIBITIONS

1922

1 December 16 to January 10, 1923, New York, GALLERIES OF THE SOCIETE ANONYME, *Villon,* preface by Walter Pach, 20 paintings

1928

2 March 26 to April 12, New York, BRUMMER GALLERY, *Villon,* preface by Walter Pach, 35 works (paintings, drawings, prints)

3 April 20 to November 20, Paris, GALERIE BERNHEIM-JEUNE, *Exposition des états des gravures en couleurs de Jacques Villon,* aquatints after the works of modern masters

1930

4 October 20 to November 20, New York, BRUMMER GALLERY, *Villon,* texts by Jean-Daniel Maublanc and Robert Valançay, 43 paintings

1933

5 November 28 to December 23, Chicago, THE ARTS CLUB, *Exhibition of Paintings and Etchings by Jacques Villon,* preface by Walter Pach, 21 paintings, 10 prints

1934

6 January 8 to 27, New York, MARIE HARRIMAN GALLERY, *Jacques Villon,* 24 paintings

1944

7 December 12 to 31, Paris, GALERIE LOUIS CARRE, *Jacques Villon,* preface by René-Jean, 39 paintings

1948

8 January 23 to February 15, Paris, GALERIE LOUIS CARRE, *Jacques Villon: 1945-1946-1947,* 29 paintings

9 April to May, Copenhagen, STATENS MUSEUM FOR KUNST, *Jacques Villon Retrospektiv Udstilling,* 32 paintings

1949

10 April 26 to May 14, New York, LOUIS CARRE GALLERY, *Villon,* preface by Jerome Mellquist, 17 paintings

1950

11 Washington, D.C., PHILLIPS GALLERY, *Jacques Villon*

12 May, Paris, LA HUNE, *Jacques Villon. Oeuvre gravé 1891-1950,* 150 prints

13 June to October, Venice, XXᵉ BIENNALE DI VENEZIA, SALLE XLIX, *Jacques Villon,* preface by Lionello Venturi, 24 paintings

14 December, Beaune, GALERIE DE BEAUNE, *Quelques Tableaux de Jacques Villon, Prix Carnegie 1950,* 8 paintings

1951

15 February 5 to March 25, Paris, MUSEE NATIONAL D'ART MODERNE, *Jacques Villon,* preface by Jean Cassou, 85 paintings

16 February 20 to March 17, Paris, GALERIE LOUIS CARRE, *Jacques Villon, gravures de 1899 à 1950,* 60 prints

1952

17 January 26 to February 14, Liège, ASSOCIATION POUR LE PROGRES INTELLECTUEL ET DE LA WALLONIE, *Villon,* preface by Frank Elgar, 37 paintings

18 April, London, THE LEFEVRE GALLERY, *Villon,* preface by Jerome Mellquist, 32 paintings

19 May, Stockholm, SVENSK-FRANSKA KONSTGALLERIET (GOSTA OLSON), *Retrospektiv Utstallning Jacques Villon,* 42 paintings, 26 prints and drawings

20 December 19 to January 10, 1953, Chicago, THE ARTS CLUB, *Jacques Villon,* 26 paintings, 8 drawings

1953

21 January 19 to February 14, New York, ROSE FRIED GALLERY, *Villon,* 11 paintings

22 September to October, Turin, PALAZZO BELLE ARTI, IIIᵉ Exposition Peintres d'Aujourd'hui, France-Italie, *Jacques Villon,* preface by Jerome Mellquist, 22 paintings

23 September 9 to November 15, New York, MUSEUM OF MODERN ART, *Jacques Villon: His Graphic Art,* preface by William S. Lieberman, 96 prints

1954

24 March 4 to April 10, Paris, GALERIE LOUIS CARRE, *Jacques Villon oeuvre gravé,* preface by Jean Adhémar, 59 prints

1955

25 April 1 to 30, New York, LUCIEN GOLD-SCHMIDT, INC., *Jacques Villon,* preface by William S. Lieberman, 15 paintings, 34 prints, 4 book illustrations

26 April 3 to 30, Albi, MUSEE TOULOUSE-LAUTREC, *Exposition Jacques Villon,* text by Edouard Julien and André Chastel, 46 paintings

27 May 13 to June 12, Paris, GALERIE LOUIS CARRE, *Jacques Villon, Peintures,* 27 paintings

28 June 26 to July 31, Geneva, MUSEE RATH, *L'Oeuvre gravé de Jacques Villon,* text by Jerome Mellquist, 280 prints

9 October 31 to November 19, New York, GRACE BORGENICHT GALLERY, *Jacques Villon (in honor of his 80th birthday)*, 24 paintings, 8 drawings

0 October to April, 1956, Vancouver, THE VANCOUVER ART GALLERY, *Jacques Villon: His Graphic Art*, 96 prints

1 November 27 to December 4, Stockholm, KONSTHALLEN, *Jacques Villon, Ur Oscar Sterns Samling*, prefaces by Sven Lövgren and Jan Runnqvist, 122 works

1956

2 March 16 to April 28, Paris, GALERIE LOUIS CARRE, *Dessins de Jacques Villon*, preface by Pierre Mazars, 52 drawings

3 April 14 to May 5, Nice, GALERIE H. MATARASSO, *Jacques Villon. Peintures, dessins, oeuvres graphiques*, 77 works

4 June to October, Venice, XXVIIIe BIENNALE DI VENEZIA, Section Française, *Jacques Villon*, preface by Raymond Cogniat, 38 paintings (Villon won the grand prize for painting)

1957

5 February 11 to March 2, New York, DEITSCH GALLERY, *Villon: Prints and Drawings*

6 March 1 to April 5, Paris, GALERIE LOUIS CARRE, *Jacques Villon. Gravures*, 43 prints

7 June 28 to September 30, Menton, QUATRIEME BIENNALE, *Hommage à Jacques Villon*, 3 paintings, 10 prints

8 November 2 to December 1, Paris, GRAND PALAIS DES CHAMPS-ELYSEES, *Salon d'Automne: Hommage à Jacques Villon*, preface by Paule-Marie Grand, 52 paintings

9 December to January, 1958, Oslo, NASJONAL GALLERIET, *Jacques Villon Grafiske Arbeider*, preface by Jan Askeland, 56 prints

1958

0 March 14 to 31, Athens, INSTITUT FRANÇAIS, *Jacques Villon: Gravures, dessins, aquarelles*, preface by Paule-Marie Grand, 40 prints, 20 drawings and watercolors

1959

1 January 14 to 31, Paris, GALERIE DE VARENNE, *L'Oeuvre religieuse de Jacques Villon*, preface by l'Abbé Maurice Morel, 16 drawings, 4 gouaches

2 January 24 to March 8, Worcester, Massachusetts, WORCESTER ART MUSEUM, *Prints by Jacques Villon*, 69 prints

43 May 22 to September 20, Paris, BIBLIOTHEQUE NATIONALE, *Jacques Villon, l'oeuvre gravé (1891-1958)*, preface by Julien Cain, text by Jean Vallery-Radot and Jean Adhémar, 155 prints

44 to June 12, Paris, BERES, *Jacques Villon*

45 November 14 to January 3, 1960, Oslo, KUNSTNERNES HUS, *Jacques Villon*, preface by Alf-Jorgen Aas and Henning Gran, 80 paintings

1960

46 January 15 to February 7, Bergen, BERGENS KUNSTFORENING, *Jacques Villon, Maleri*, preface by P. Remfeldt, 62 paintings

47 March, Stockholm, MODERNA MUSEET, *Jacques Villon, Maleri och Grafik 1902-1959*, text by Carl Nordenfalk and K. G. Hulten, 94 paintings, 58 prints

48 November 1 to 26, New York, DEITSCH GALLERY, *Jacques Villon*

1961

49 April 27 to June 22, Paris, GALERIE CHARPENTIER, *Cent tableaux de Jacques Villon*, foreword by Raymond Nacenta, preface by Jean Tardieu, 219 works

50 July 2 to August 13, Minneapolis, WALKER ART CENTER, *Jacques Villon*, 50 prints and drawings

51 September to December, São Paulo, MUSEU DE ARTE MODERNA, VI BIENAL DE SAO PAULO, *Jacques Villon*, 33 paintings, 22 prints

1962

52 July 7 to September 30, Le Havre, MUSEE MAISON DE LA CULTURE, *L'Oeuvre gravé de Jacques Villon, cinquante années de gravure, 1900-1950*, 102 works

53 November 23, Paris, HOTEL DRUOUT, *Jacques Villon*, preface by Charles Perussaux, 148 prints

1963

54 January to February, Paris, GALERIE LOUIS CARRE, *La Figure dans l'oeuvre graphique de Jacques Villon*, 42 prints, 15 drawings and watercolors

55 February 9 to March 17, Zurich, KUNST-HAUS, *Jacques Villon*, foreword by Eduard Huttinger, preface by Dora Vallier, 81 paintings, 23 drawings, 33 prints

56 October, Asnières, SALLE DES FETES, *Salon d'Asnières 1963, Hommage à Jacques Villon*

57 December 9 to January 4, 1964, London, ZWEMMER GALLERY, *Jacques Villon*

1964

58 January 25 to February 17, Rouen, GALERIE MENUISEMENT, *Hommage à Jacques Villon*, preface by René Gouast

59 February, New York, HELENE C. SEIFER-HELD GALLERY, *Jacques Villon, Master Printmaker*, introduction by Francis Steegmuller, 102 prints

60 February 20 to April 19, Boston, MUSEUM OF FINE ARTS, *Jacques Villon, Master of Graphic Art (1875-1963)*, texts by Jean Cassou, Simone Frigerio, and Peter A. Wick, 189 works. Also Chicago, THE ART INSTITUTE OF CHICAGO

61 March 6 to April 4, Paris, BIBLIOTHEQUE NATIONALE, Société des Peintres-Gravures français, *Hommage à Jacques Villon*, 28 prints

62 March 24 to April 18, New York, E. V. THAW AND CO., *Jacques Villon, Paintings 1909-1960*, preface by William S. Lieberman, 15 paintings

63 April 1 to 25, New York, LUCIEN GOLD-SCHMIDT, INC., *Jacques Villon, Master Drawings and Watercolors 1908-1956*, 39 drawings and watercolors

1965

64 March 16 to April 7, Paris, LE NOUVEL ESSOR, *Villon avant le Cubisme*, preface by Bernard Anglade, 48 works

1966

65 January 29 to March 13, Reims, MUSEE DE REIMS, *Jacques Villon, oeuvre gravé*, 250 works

66 April 15 to May 22, Cologne, KÖLNISCHER KUNSTVEREIN, *Jacques Villon, Blick auf des graphische Oeuvre*, preface by Jean Cassou, 64 prints

67 May 10 to June 11, Paris, LE NOUVEL ESSOR, *Hommage à Jacques Villon: Gravures de 1891 à 1945*, 64 works

68 1966 to 1967, New York, LUCIEN GOLD-SCHMIDT, INC., *Jacques Villon, Drawings and Watercolors*, 32 drawings and watercolors

1967

69 February 10 to March 10, Providence, Rhode Island, MUSEUM OF ART, RHODE ISLAND SCHOOL OF DESIGN, *Jacques Villon, Drawings and Watercolors*

70 April 12, Paris, HOTEL DRUOUT, *Jacques Villon*, 118 prints

71 April 27 to May 13, Rouen, GALERIE MENUISEMENT, *Jacques Villon. 30 gravures originales*

72 May 16 to June 18, Santa Barbara, California, SANTA BARBARA MUSEUM OF ART, *Jacques Villon, Drawings and Watercolors* 32 works

73 June 13 to September 30, Geneva, GALERIE GERALD CRAMER, *Jacques Villon, gravures originales 1891-1962*, 23 prints

74 November to December, Chicago, INTERNATIONAL GALLERIES, *Master of Graphic Art, Jacques Villon, 1875-1963*, preface by Jean Cassou, text by S. E. Johnson, 66 prints

1970

75 October 22 to November 19, New York, LUCIEN GOLDSCHMIDT, INC., *Jacques Villon: A Collection of Graphic Work 1896-1913 in Rare or Unique Impressions*, introduction by Riva Castleman, 120 prints

1973

76 March to April, Geneva, GALERIE BONNIER, *Jacques Villon: Vingt-deux peintures 1939-1961*, 22 paintings

77 October to November, Boston, BOSTON UNIVERSITY SCHOOL OF FINE AND APPLIED ARTS GALLERY, *Jacques Villon*, 80 prints

1975

77a June to December, Rouen, MUSEE DES BEAUX-ARTS, and Paris, GRAND PALAIS, *Jacques Villon*, 155 works

GROUP EXHIBITIONS

1901

78 April 22 to June 30, Paris, GRAND PALAIS, *Société Nationale des Beaux-Arts*, 2 prints

1902

79 April 20 to June 30, Paris, GRAND PALAIS, *Société Nationale des Beaux-Arts*, 1 watercolor, 2 prints

1903

80 April 16 to June 30, Paris, GRAND PALAIS, *Société Nationale des Beaux-Arts*, 1 painting, 2 prints

81 October 31 to December 6, Paris, PETIT PALAIS, *Salon d'Automne (first exhibition)*, 2 paintings, 3 watercolors, 3 prints

1904

82 April 17 to June 30, Paris, GRAND PALAIS, *Société Nationale des Beaux-Arts*, 3 prints, 1 drawing

83 October 15 to November 15, Paris, PETIT PALAIS, *Salon d'Automne*, 3 paintings, 4 prints, 2 drawings

1905

84 Rouen, GALERIE LEGRIP, *Raymond Duchamp-Villon et Jacques Villon*, preface by Georges Dubosc, 53 prints and drawings

85 April 15 to June 30, Paris, GRAND PALAIS, *Société Nationale des Beaux-Arts*, 2 prints

86 October 18 to November 25, Paris, GRAND PALAIS, *Salon d'Automne*, 5 paintings, 1 drawing, 3 prints

1906

87 April 15 to June 30, Paris, GRAND PALAIS, *Société Nationale des Beaux-Arts*, 2 prints

88 October 6 to November 15, Paris, GRAND PALAIS, *Salon d'Automne*, 1 painting, 4 drawings, 1 print

1907

89 April 14 to June 30, Paris, GRAND PALAIS, *Société Nationale des Beaux-Arts*, 4 prints

90 October 1 to 22, Paris, GRAND PALAIS, *Salon d'Automne*, 1 painting, 2 prints

1908

91 April 15 to June 30, Paris, GRAND PALAIS, *Société Nationale des Beaux-Arts*, 1 print

92 October 1 to November 8, Paris, GRAND PALAIS, *Salon d'Automne*, 1 painting

1909

93 April 15 to June 30, Paris, GRAND PALAIS, *Société Nationale des Beaux-Arts*, 3 prints

94 October 1 to November 8, Paris, GRAND PALAIS, *Salon d'Automne*, 4 paintings, 1 drawing, 2 prints

95 December 20 to January 20, 1910, Rouen, SALLE BOIELDIEU, *Exposition de Peinture Moderne* (1st exhibition of the Société Normande de Peinture Moderne), preface by Elie Faure, 3 works

1910

96 October 1 to November 8, Paris, GRAND PALAIS, *Salon d'Automne*, 2 prints

1911

97 May 6 to June, Rouen, *Deuxième exposition de la Société Normande de la Peinture Moderne*, 10 prints, 2 watercolors

98 October 1 to November 8, Paris, GRAND PALAIS, *Salon d'Automne*, 2 paintings, 1 drawing, 2 prints

99 November 20 to December 16, Paris, GALERIE D'ART ANCIEN ET D'ART CONTEMPORAIN, *Exposition d'art contemporain* (Société Normande de Peinture Moderne, second exhibition), preface by René Blum, 1 coffee set, 1 print

1912

100 June 15 to July 15, Rouen, *Troisième exposition de la Société Normande de Peinture Moderne, Salon de Juin*, prefaces by Elie Faure and Maurice Raynal, 7 prints

101 October 1 to November 8, Paris, GRAND PALAIS, *Salon d'Automne*, (Maison Cubiste), 1 painting, 1 coffee set

102 October 10 to 31, Paris, GALERIE LA BOETIE, *Salon de la "Section d'Or,"* preface by René Blum, 4 paintings

1913

103 February 17 to March 15, New York, ARMORY OF THE 69TH REGIMENT, *International Exhibition of Modern Art (The Armory Show)*, 9 paintings. Also Chicago, THE ART INSTITUTE OF CHICAGO; March 24 to April 15; and Boston, COPLEY SOCIETY OF BOSTON; April 28 to May 18

104 November 15 to January 5, 1914, Paris, GRAND PALAIS, *Salon d'Automne*, 2 paintings, 3 prints

1914

105 February to March, Prague, S.V.U. MANES, *Moderni Umeni*, preface by Alexandre Mercereau, 3 paintings, 5 prints

106 March 1 to April 30, Paris, CHAMP DE MARS, *30th Salon des Indépendants*, 3 paintings

107 April 6 to May 3, Paris, GALERIE ANDRE GROULT, *Sculptures de R. Duchamp-Villon; dessins, aquarelles d'Albert Gleizes; gravures de Jacques Villon; dessins de Jean Metzinger*, preface by André Salmon, 6 prints, 2 drawings

108 May (?), Prague, S.V.U. MANES, *Group of Avant-Garde Artists*

109 May 9 to November 2, Brussels, PALAIS DU CINQUETENAIRE, *Exposition générale des Beaux-Arts, Salon Triennal*, 3 works

110 May 16 to June 7, Brussels, GALERIE GEORGES GIROUX, *Salon des Artistes Indépendants de Paris*, 3 paintings

111 June to July, Berlin, GALERIE DER STURM, *Gleizes, Metzinger, Duchamp-Villon, Villon*

1915

112 to January 2, New York, CARROLL GALLERIES, *First Exhibition of Works by Contemporary French Artists*, preface by Frederick James Gregg, 6 prints, 1 drawing

113 March 8 to April 23, New York, CARROLL GALLERIES, *Third Exhibition of Contemporary French Art*, 6 paintings

1916

114 Oslo, *Christiania Exhibition*

115 April 3 to 29, New York, BOURGEOIS GALLERIES, *Exhibition of Modern Art*, 1 painting

116 May 17 to June 15, Philadelphia, MCCLEES GALLERIES, *Advanced Modern Art*, 1 painting

117 November to December, Oslo, KUNST-NERFORBUNDET, *Den Franske Utstillung,* foreword by Jean Cocteau, prefaces by Guillaume Apollinaire and André Salmon

1917
118 April 10 to May 6, New York, GRAND CENTRAL PALACE, The Society of Independent Artists, *First Annual Exhibition*

1919
119 April 29 to May 24, New York, ARDEN GALLERY, *Evolution of French Art,* organized by Marius de Zayas

1920
120 January 28 to February 29, Paris, *31st Salon des Indépendants*

121 March, Paris, GALLERIE LA BOETIE, *Exposition de la "Section d'Or,"* 2 paintings. Also Rotterdam, The Hague, Arnhem, and Amsterdam, STEDELIJK MUSEUM, October 23 to November 7; Anvers and Brussels, December 4 to 17, and Rome, CASA D'ARTE ITALIANA, April, 1921

122 April 30 to June 15, New York, GALLERIES OF THE SOCIETE ANONYME, *First Exhibition of the Société Anonyme*

123 December 15 to February 1, 1921, New York, GALLERIES OF THE SOCIETE ANONYME, *Sixth Exhibition of the Société Anonyme*

1921
124 January, Berlin, GALLERIE DER STURM, *Albert Gleizes, Jacques Villon, Louis Marcoussis (93rd Exhibition)*

125 November 3 to December 5, Worcester, Massachusetts, WORCESTER ART MUSEUM, *Paintings by Members of the Société Anonyme (Eighteenth Exhibition of the Société Anonyme)*

1922
126 Paris, GALERIE DE L'EFFORT MODERNE

127 April 24 to May 8, New York, MAC-DOWELL CLUB, *Exhibition of the Collection of the Société Anonyme (Nineteenth Exhibition of the Société Anonyme)*

128 May 13 to 28, Paris, GALERIE POVOLOZKY (GALERIE DE LA CIBLE), *Jacques Villon et Louis Latapie,* text by Alexandre Mercereau

129 September 19 to October 22, Chicago, THE ART INSTITUTE OF CHICAGO, *The Arthur Jerome Eddy Collection of Modern Paintings*

1923
130 February 5, New York, GALLERIES OF THE SOCIETE ANONYME, *22nd Exhibition of the Société Anonyme*

131 April 4 to May 12, Poughkeepsie, New York, VASSAR COLLEGE, *26th Exhibition of the Société Anonyme*

132 August 31 to September 9, Detroit, STATE FAIR PARK, *Exhibition B* (Société Anonyme)

1925
133 January 12 to 31, Paris, GALERIE VAVIN-RASPAIL, *Salon de la "Section d'Or,"* preface by Guillaume Dalbert, 2 paintings, 3 prints

134 November 30 to December, Paris, SALLES DU SYNDICAT DES NEGOCIANTS EN OBJETS D'ART, *L'Art d'aujourd'hui (L'Art plastique non-imitatif)*

1926
135 February 20 to March 21, Paris, GRAND PALAIS, *Trente ans d'art indépendant, 1884-1914: Exposition rétrospective de la Société des Artistes indépendants*

136 November 19 to January 9, 1927, Brooklyn, New York, BROOKLYN MUSEUM, *International Exhibition of Modern Art,* assembled by the Société Anonyme, introduction by Katherine S. Dreier, 5 works. Also New York, ANDERSON GALLERIES, January 25 to February 5, 1927; Buffalo, New York, ALBRIGHT ART GALLERY, February 25 to March 20; and The Grange, Toronto, TORONTO MUSEUM OF ART, April

1927
137 Paris, GALERIE ARMAND DROUANT, *Pour la défense du Franc*

138 February 5, New York, AMERICAN ART GALLERIES, *Paintings and Sculpture—The Renowned Collection of Modern and Ultra-Modern Art Formed by the Late John Quinn*

1928
139 February 10 to March 24, New York, ARTS COUNCIL GALLERY, *The Barbizon*

1930
140 Paris, COURS-LA-REINE, *VIIIe Salon des Tuileries 1930,* 3 paintings

141 Tokyo, *Exhibition in French Art*

142 March 17 to April 5, Paris, BIBLIOTHEQUE NATIONALE (SALLE MORTREUIL), *Société des Peintres-Graveurs Français, XVIIe exposition,* 5 prints, 1 drawing

143 October 7 to November 8, New York, RAND SCHOOL OF SOCIAL SCIENCE, *58th Exhibition of the Société Anonyme*

144 January 1 to February 10, New York, NEW SCHOOL FOR SOCIAL RESEARCH, (opening of the New School)

145 January 5 to March 16, New York, RAND SCHOOL OF SOCIAL SCIENCE, *62nd Exhibition of the Société Anonyme*

1934
146 June 8 to July 8, San Francisco, THE CALIFORNIA PALACE OF THE LEGION OF HONOR, *Exhibition of French Painting from the Fifteenth Century to the Present Day,* 1 painting

1935
147 April 8 to May 27, Paris, BIBLIOTHEQUE NATIONALE (SALLE MORTREUIL), *exposition de la Société des Peintres-Graveurs Français, XXIIe,* 4 prints

148 1935 to 1937, American Federation of Arts, *Circulating Exhibition of Contemporary American and European Painting*

1936
149 March 2 to April 19, New York, MUSEUM OF MODERN ART, *Cubism and Abstract Art,* text by Alfred H. Barr, Jr., 2 paintings. Also San Francisco, SAN FRANCISCO MUSEUM OF ART, July 27 to August 24; Cincinnati, CINCINNATI ART MUSEUM, October 19 to November 16; Minneapolis, MINNEAPOLIS INSTITUTE OF ARTS, November 29 to December 27; 1937, Cleveland, CLEVELAND MUSEUM OF ART, January 7 to February 7; Baltimore, BALTIMORE MUSEUM OF ART, February 17 to March 17; Providence, MUSEUM OF ART, RHODE ISLAND SCHOOL OF DESIGN, March 24 to April 21; and Grand Rapids, Michigan, GRAND RAPIDS ART GALLERY, April 29 to May 26

150 September to July, 1937, traveling exhibition organized by the College Art Association, *New Forms of Art*

151 November 23 to December 5, New York, DELPHIC STUDIOS, *73rd Exhibition of the Société Anonyme*

1937
152 Paris, *Exposition internationale de Paris* (Villon won two gold medals for painting and engraving)

153 March 1 to 20, Paris, BIBLIOTHEQUE NATIONALE (SALLE MAZARINE), *XXIVe Exposition de la Société des Peintres-Graveurs Français,* 4 prints

154 June to October, Paris, PETIT PALAIS, *Les Maîtres de l'art indépendant 1895-1937,* 3 paintings

155 July 30 to October 31, Paris, MUSEE DU JEU DE PAUME, *Origines et développement de l'art international indépendant,* 1 painting

1938
156 June, Paris, GALERIE MARCEL GUIOT

157 June 4 to July 3, Paris, PAVILLON DES ARTS GRAPHIQUES ET PLASTIQUES, *XVe Salon des Tuileries 1938,* 3 paintings, 3 prints

1939

158 New York, NEW YORK WORLD'S FAIR, Palais de la France, Section des Beaux-Arts, *L'Art français contemporain,* preface by Georges Huisman, 1 painting, 1 print

159 New York, MUSEUM OF MODERN ART, *Art in Our Time,* preface by A. Conger Goodyear, text by Alfred H. Barr, Jr., 1 aquatint

160 January 10 to 30, Springfield, Massachusetts, SPRINGFIELD MUSEUM OF ART

161 June 15 to 28, Paris, GALERIE CHARPENTIER, *Salon des Réalités Nouvelles*

162 July to August, Paris, CONSERVATOIRE NATIONAL DES ARTS ET METIERS, *L'Affiche en couleurs de Chéret a nos jours,* 4 posters

163 November 9 to December 17, Springfield, Massachusetts, GEORGE VINCENT SMITH ART GALLERY, *Some New Forms of Beauty, 1909-1936, A Selection of the Collection of the Société Anonyme,* (Anniversary Exhibition), catalogue by George Walter, 3 paintings

1940

164 April, Chicago, THE ARTS CLUB

1942

165 New York, ART OF THIS CENTURY, *Art of This Century: Objects, Drawings, Photographs, Paintings, Sculpture, Collages, 1910-1942,* edited by Peggy Guggenheim

166 January 13 to February 23, New Haven, YALE UNIVERSITY ART GALLERY, *Exhibition Inaugurating the Collection of the Société Anonyme*

167 March, Middletown, Connecticut, WESLEYAN UNIVERSITY

168 March 7 to 20, Paris, GALERIE DE FRANCE, *Peintures de Jacques Villon de 1909 à 1941 et sculptures de Raymond Duchamp-Villon,* preface by René-Jean, 52 paintings

1943

169 January 4 to 31, Zanesville, Ohio, ZANESVILLE ART INSTITUTE, *Twentieth Century Paintings Lent by the Columbus Gallery of Fine Arts*

170 March to May, New Haven, Yale University, SAYBROOK COLLEGE

1944

171 February 19 to March 18, New York, MORTIMER BRANDT GALLERY, *Color and Space in Modern Art since 1900,* prefaces by Robert Lebel and Walter Pach

172 December 6 to 31, Buffalo, New York, ALBRIGHT ART GALLERY, *French Paintings of the Twentieth Century (1900-1939),* sponsored by the French Embassy, 1 painting. Also Cincinnati, CINCINNATI ART MUSEUM, January 18 to February 18, 1945; St. Louis, CITY ART MUSEUM, March 8 to April 16

1945

173 Paris, GALERIE CHARPENTIER, *Paysages d'eau douce,* 1 painting

174 February 25 to March 25, New Haven, YALE UNIVERSITY ART GALLERY, *Duchamp, Duchamp-Villon, Villon,* preface by George Heard Hamilton, 4 paintings. Also Williamsburg, Virginia, COLLEGE OF WILLIAM AND MARY, November; San Francisco, CALIFORNIA SCHOOL OF FINE ARTS, December to January, 1946; Meadville, Pennsylvania, ALLEGHENY COLLEGE, May; St. Paul, ST. PAUL GALLERY AND SCHOOL OF ART, September; Northfield, Minnesota, CARLTON COLLEGE, October; Orono, Maine, UNIVERSITY OF MAINE, January, 1947

175 May 25 to June 30, Paris, GALERIE DE FRANCE, *Le Cubisme, 1911-1918,* preface by Bernard Dorival, 3 paintings

1946

176 Paris, GALERIE CHARPENTIER, *Cent chefs-d'oeuvre des peintres de l'École de Paris*

177 New York, MUSEUM OF MODERN ART, *Paintings from New York Private Collections*

178 July to August, Vienna, STAATLICHES KUNSTGEWERBEMUSEUM, *Salon d'Automne*

179 July 19 to August 18, Paris, PALAIS DES BEAUX-ARTS DE LA VILLE DE PARIS, *Ier Salon des Réalités Nouvelles*

180 September to March, 1947, Baden-Baden, Berlin, Vienna, *Exposition d'art français contemporain,* introduction by Jean Cassou, 1 painting

181 October 16 to November 6, New York, JACQUES SELIGMANN AND CO., INC., *1910-1912: The Climactic Years in Cubism,* 2 paintings

1947

182 Paris, *Retrospective au Salon d'Automne*

183 Paris, *XXIVe Salon des Tuileries*

184 Brussels, GALERIE GIROUX, *Art Vivant dans les collections Belges*

185 Switzerland, *Quelques oeuvres des collections de la Ville de Paris*

186 January 25 to March 2, New York, WHITNEY MUSEUM, *Painting in France 1939-1946,* foreword by Juliana Force, text by Bernard Dorival, 1 painting

187 March 18 to May 3, London, THE LONDON GALLERY, *The Cubist Spirit in its Time,* foreword by Robert Melville, 1 drawing

1948

188 April to June, Paris, GALERIE BERNHEIM-JEUNE, *Exposition de la femme 1800-1930,* preface by Gérard Bauer

189 June 6, Venice, *XXIV Biennale di Venezia,* 1 painting, 1 print

190 June 10 to July 11, Paris, MUSEE DES BEAUX-ARTS DE LA VILLE DE PARIS, *Salon des Tuileries XXVe Exposition,* 2 paintings, 1 print

191 August, Norfolk, Connecticut, NORFOLK MUSIC SCHOOL

192 September 24 to November 1, Paris, MUSEE DES BEAUX-ARTS DE LA VILLE DE PARIS, *Salon d'Automne 1948,* 1 painting, 4 prints, 1 book illustration

1949

193 Lugano, VILLA CIANI, *Exposition internationale de gravure* (Villon won the Grand Prize for engraving)

194 February 3 to March 9, Providence, MUSEUM OF ART, RHODE ISLAND SCHOOL OF DESIGN, *Isms in Art Since 1800,* 1 painting, 8 drawings

195 June 4 to September 30, Boston, INSTITUTE OF CONTEMPORARY ART, *Société Anonyme Collection*

196 September 30 to November 6, Paris, MUSEE DES BEAUX-ARTS DE LA VILLE DE PARIS, *Salon d'Automne 1949,* 2 paintings, 2 prints

197 October to November, Stockholm, NATIONALMUSEUM, *Fransk Konst 1938-1948,* preface by Jean Cassou, 3 paintings

198 October 7 to November 20, Boston, INSTITUTE OF CONTEMPORARY ART, *Jacques Villon-Lyonel Feininger,* foreword by James S. Plant, texts by Jacques Villon, George Heard Hamilton, Thomas B. Hess, and Frederick S. Wight, 25 paintings, 8 drawings and watercolors, 11 prints. Also Washington, D.C., PHILLIPS GALLERY, December to January, 1950; and Wilmington, Delaware, DELAWARE ART CENTER, 1950

199 October 20 to December 18, Chicago, THE ART INSTITUTE OF CHICAGO, *20th Century Art from the Louise and Walter Arensberg Collection,* text by Katherine Kuh and Daniel Catton Rich, 3 paintings

1950

200 Paris, GALERIE CHARPENTIER, *XXVe Salon des Tuileries 1950,* preface by Jean Cassou, 2 paintings

01 Brussels, PALAIS DES BEAUX-ARTS, *Cercle Royal Artistique et Littéraire de Gand*

02 April to May, London, THE LEICESTER GALLERIES, *In Paris Now*

03 May to June, Berlin, *Französische Malerei und Plastik, 1938-1948,* Preface by Jean Mougin, text by Jean Cassou, 1 painting

04 June 16 to July 17, Paris GRAND PALAIS, *Salon d'Automne 1950,* 2 paintings

05 September 2 to October 10, Copenhagen, CHARLOTTENBORG, *Levende Farver-Fransk Konst,* preface by Havaard Rostrup, 12 paintings

06 October 5 to 23, Saginaw, Michigan, SAGINAW MUSEUM, *Collection of the Société Anonyme*

07 October 19 to December 21, Pittsburgh, CARNEGIE INSTITUTE, *The Pittsburgh International Exhibition of Paintings,* 1 painting (Villon won the Carnegie First Prize)

08 October 22 to November 5, Verviers, LA SOCIETE ROYALE DES BEAUX-ARTS, *La Peintre sous le signe d'Apollinaire,* 3 paintings. Also Gand, LE CERCLE ROYAL ARTISTIQUE ET LITTERAIRE, November 11 to 26; and Brussels, PALAIS DES BEAUX-ARTS, December

09 October 24 to November 18, New York, LOUIS CARRE GALLERY, *The Artist in the Machine Age,* 4 paintings

10 November 8 to 26, Paris, BIBLIOTHEQUE NATIONALE (GALERIE MAZARINE), *Société des Peintres-Graveurs français, XXXVIe exposition,* texts by Ed Goerg, Pierre Dubreuil, Marcel Roche, Jean Adhémar, 2 prints

11 December 16 to January 12, 1951, Paris, GALERIE BERNHEIM-JEUNE, *Rythmes et couleurs*

1951

12 Paris, GALERIE CHARPENTIER, *Plaisir de France,* foreword by Jean-Louis Vaudoyer, 2 paintings

13 Paris, GALERIE CHARPENTIER, *XXVIe Salon des Tuileries 1951,* preface by Robert Rey, 1 painting

14 New York, LOUIS CARRE GALLERY, *Selected Paintings from its Permanent Collection*

15 January 2 to February 3, New York, SIDNEY JANIS GALLERY, *1913: Climax in 20th Century Art,* 1 painting

16 January 4 to February 18, Pittsburgh, CARNEGIE INSTITUTE, *French Contemporary Prints*

217 February to March, Malmö, MALMÖ MUSEUM, *Utställning Fransk Konst,* 5 paintings

218 February 2 to March 4, Paris, MUSEE D'ART MODERNE DE LA VILLE DE PARIS, *Les peintres témoins de leur temps; I. Le Travail,* 1 painting

219 February 9 to 28, Paris, GALERIE MARCEL GUIOT, *Villon, Gromaire, Vieillard, gravures originales,* 15 prints

220 May 5 to June 3, Berne, KUNSTHALLE, *Jacques Villon-Louis Moilliet,* prefaces by Arnold Rüdlinger, text by Jerome Mellquist and Hans Bloesch, 53 paintings

221 June 1 to October 1, Chapel Hill, North Carolina, University of North Carolina, PERSON HALL ART GALLERY

222 July, London, THE LEFEVRE GALLERY, *The School of Paris,* 2 paintings

223 July 14 to September 9, Knocke, Le Zoute, Albert Plage, Belgium, GRANDE SALLE DES EXPOSITIONS DE "LA RESERVE," *75 Oeuvres du demi-siècle,* 1 painting

224 October, Turin, PALAZZO BELLE ARTI, *Peintres d'aujourd'hui, France-Italie*

225 November 6 to 25, Paris, GRAND PALAIS, *Salon d'Automne 1951,* 1 painting

1952

226 Paris, GALERIE CHARPENTIER, *XXVIIe Salon des Tuileries 1952,* preface by Raymond Cogniat, 1 painting

227 Dijon, MUSEE DE DIJON, *La Gravure française contemporaine,* foreword by Pierre Quarre, preface by Jean Adhémar, 3 prints

228 January, Andover, Massachusetts, ABBOT ACADEMY

229 February 25 to March, New York, ROSE FRIED GALLERY, *Duchamp Frères et Soeur oeuvres d'art,* preface by Walter Pach, 3 paintings

230 February 28 to April 13, Pittsburgh, CARNEGIE INSTITUTE, *The Howald Collection from the Columbus Gallery of Fine Arts*

231 March, New London, Connecticut, LYMAN ALLYN MUSEUM, *Annual Exhibition*

232 March to April, Paris, MUSEE DES ARTS DECORATIFS, *Cinquante ans de peinture française dans les collections particulières de Cézanne à Matisse,* 3 paintings

233 April 6 to 27, Dallas, MUSEUM OF FINE ARTS, *Some Businessmen Collect Contemporary Art,* foreword by E. De Golyer, introduction by Stanley Marcus

234 April 18 to July 14, Amsterdam and Brussels, *100 Chefs-d'oeuvre du Musée d'Art Moderne*

235 May to June, Paris, MUSEE NATIONAL D'ART MODERNE, *L'Oeuvre du XXe Siècle,* foreword by James Johnson Sweeney, preface by Jean Cassou, 1 painting

236 May 22 to September 14, Tokyo, Osaka, Nagoya, Fukuoka, and Kyoto, *The First International Art Exhibition,* Japan, organized by the Mainichi Newspapers, 2 paintings

237 June 14, Venice, *XXVI Biennale di Venezia,* 18 prints

238 June 20 to September 14, Lausanne, MUSEE CANTONAL DES BEAUX-ARTS, *Rythmes et couleurs,* preface by Guy Weelen, 4 paintings

239 July 15 to August 17, London, THE TATE GALLERY, *XXth Century Masterpieces,* introduction by James Johnson Sweeney, 1 painting

240 September to June, 1954, New York, MUSEUM OF MODERN ART, *Musical Themes*

241 September, Stockholm, SVENSK-FRANSKA KONSTGALLERIET, Collection of Oscar Stern, preface by Otte Skold, 5 paintings, 5 prints

242 September 5 to 28, Bloomfield Hills, Michigan, THE MUSEUM OF CRANBROOK ACADEMY OF ART, *Light and the Painter*

243 September 11 to October 12, Berlin, HOCHSHULE FÜR BILDENDE KÜNSTE *Werke Franzoesischer Meister der Gegenwart,* prefaces by Maurice Jardot and Adolf Jannasch, 5 paintings

244 October 11 to November 2, Stockholm, MALMÖ MUSEUM AND SVENSK-FRANSKA KONSTGALLERIET, *Klee, Laurens, Léger, Picasso, Rouault, Villon,* 12 paintings, 15 prints

245 October 16 to December 14, Pittsburgh, CARNEGIE INSTITUTE, *The 1952 Pittsburgh International Exhibition of Contemporary Painting,* foreword by Gordon Washburn, 1 painting

246 October 25 to November 16, Stockholm, SVENSK-FRANSKA KONSTGALLERIET, *Den Unga Kubismen,* 2 paintings

247 October 31 to November 21, Paris, GRAND PALAIS DES CHAMPS-ELYSEES, *Salon d'Automne 1952,* 1 painting

248 December 15 to February 1, 1953, New Haven, YALE UNIVERSITY ART GALLERY, *In Memory of Katherine S. Dreier 1877-1952: Her Own Collection of Modern Art,* 3 paintings

1953

249 France, traveling exhibition, organized by le Service Educatif de la Direction des Musées de France, *De Bonnard à Picasso: Cinquante ans de peinture française,* catalogue by Bernard Dorival, prefaces by Georges Salles and Jean Cassou, 1 painting

250 Paris, PETIT-PALAIS, *Un Siècle d'art français, 1850-1950,* preface by André Chanason, 2 paintings

251 January 30 to March, Paris, MUSEE D'ART MODERNE DE LA VILLE DE PARIS, *Les Peintres témoins de leur temps: III. Le Dimanche,* 1 painting

252 January 30 to April 9, Paris, MUSEE NATIONAL D'ART MODERNE, *Le Cubisme (1907-1914),* preface by Jean Cassou, 6 paintings

253 January to September, Australia, traveling exhibition, *French Painting Today*

254 March, Halmstad, HALLANDS MUSEUM, *Fransk Konst,* 13 paintings. Also Göteborg, Sweden, KONSTHALLEN, April 11 to May 3

255 March 6 to 30, Paris, MUSEE GALLIERA, *Célèbres et révélations de la peinture contemporaine,* 2 works

256 April, Stockholm, SVENSK-FRANSK KONST-GALLERIET, *Fransk Konst*

257 April 24 to June 28, Minneapolis, WALKER ART CENTER, *The Classic Tradition in Contemporary Art,* 1 painting

258 May, Paris, *Salon de Mai 1953*

259 May 20 to October 30, Tokyo, Osaka, Fukuoka, Seseno, Nagoya, and Takamatsu, *The Second International Art Exhibition, Japan,* organized by the Mainichi Newspapers, 1 painting

260 June 23 to October 4, New York, MUSEUM OF MODERN ART, *Museum Collections: New Acquisitions*

261 July 4 to October 4, Albi, MUSEE TOULOUSE-LAUTREC, *Peintures contemporaines,* preface by Edouard Julien

262 September to December, Israel, Association des Musées d'Israël, *Un Demi-Siècle de peinture française*

263 November 4 to 29, Paris, GRAND PALAIS DES CHAMPS-ELYSEES, *Salon d'Automne 1953, Cinquantenaire,* 1 painting

264 November to December, Stockholm, SVENSK-FRANSKA KONSTGALLERIET, *Jubileumsutstallning, Svensk-Franska Konstgalleriet 1918-1953,* 11 paintings

265 December to January, 1954, Paris, MUSEE NATIONAL D'ART MODERNE, *De Corot à nos jours au Musée du Havre,* prefaces by Jean Vergnet-Ruiz and Bernard Dorival, 1 painting

1954

266 Paris, GALERIE CHARPENTIER, *Plaisirs de la campagne,* 2 paintings

267 Paris, PETIT-PALAIS, *Collection Girardin,* preface by André Chamson, 1 painting

268 Paris, GALERIE MARCEL GUOIT, *Estampes originales des XIXe et XXe siècles,* 22 prints

269 Philadelphia, PHILADELPHIA MUSEUM OF ART, *The Louise and Walter Arensburg Collection,* 3 paintings

270 Rio de Janeiro, MUSEU DE ARTE, *O Cubismo*

271 Aix-en-Provence, MUSEE GRANET, *Salon des Tuileries*

272 Amsterdam, STEDELIJK MUSEUM, *Exposition Collection Dotremont.* Also Eindhoven, STEDELIJK VAN ABBE-MUSEUM

273 Milan, *3rd Triennale*

274 April, Rouen, MUSEE DES BEAUX-ARTS, *Les Grandes étapes de l'art moderne,* preface by Jean Cassou, 3 paintings

275 June 27 to July 31, Ostende, KURSAAL, *Tendances actuelles de l'art français,* preface by Bernard Dorival, 1 painting

276 June to October, Paris, MUSEE NATIONAL D'ART MODERNE, *Le Dessin de Toulouse-Lautrec au Cubistes,* catalogue by Bernard Dorival, preface by Jean Cassou, 10 drawings

277 July 10 to September 20, Rotterdam, MUSEUM BOYMANS-VAN BEUNINGEN, *Vier Euwen Stilleven in Frankrijk,* text by Charles Sterling, 2 paintings

278 July 25 to August 16, Conches, *L'Eure et ses peintres,* 1 painting

279 September, Stockholm, LILJEVALCHS KONSTHALL, *Cézanne Till Picasso,* texts by Kjeil Hagglof and Ragnar Hoppe, 21 paintings

280 October 19 to January 23, 1955, New York, MUSEUM OF MODERN ART, *XXVth Anniversary Exhibition: Paintings*

281 October 22 to November 7, Nantes, MUSEE DES BEAUX-ARTS, *Recontre d'octobre: Aspects de la peinture d'aujourd'hui,* preface by Raymond Cogniat, 2 paintings

282 November 5 to 30, Paris, GRAND PALAIS DES CHAMPS-ELYSEES, *Salon d'Automne 1954,* 3 works

1955

283 Saarbrucken, Germany, SAARLAND-MUSEUM, *Kunst 1955*

284 Oslo, KUNSTFORENING, *Fransk og Italiensk Natidskunst*

285 January 15 to February 28, Paris, MUSEE GALLIERA, *Regards sur la peinture contemporaine,* text by André Chamson, 2 paintings

286 February 6 to March 4, Sarasota, Florida, THE JOHN AND MABLE RINGLING MUSEUM OF ART, *Directors Choice*

287 March 18 to April 8, Paris, BIBLIOTHEQUE NATIONALE (GALERIE MANSART), *Société des Peintres-Graveurs français, XLe exposition,* text by Bersier, 3 prints

288 March to May, Marseille, MUSEE CANTINI, *Premières étapes de la peinture moderne,* preface by Jean Cassou, 3 paintings

289 April 24 to May 30, St.-Etienne, MUSEE D'ART ET D'INDUSTRIE, *Nature-Morte de Géricault à nos jours,* catalogue by Maurice Allemand, 2 paintings

290 April 30 to May 15, Rouen, MUSEE DES BEAUX-ARTS, *Art 1955,* text by Hubert Guillet, 1 painting

291 Spring, Madrid, Barcelona, Valencia, Saragossa, and Bilbao, *Tendencias Recientes de la Pintura Francesa, 1945-1955,* preface by Jacques Lassaigne, 5 paintings

292 Spring, Jerusalem, NATIONAL MUSEUM, *Ayala and Sam Zacks Collection of Twentieth Century French Art,* 1 painting, 1 drawing. Also Tel Aviv, TEL AVIV MUSEUM; Ein Harod, MISHKAN FOR ART; and Haifa, MUNICIPAL MUSEUM OF MODERN ART

293 May 7 to 30, Paris, MUSEE D'ART MODERNE DE LA VILLE DE PARIS, *XIe Salon de Mai*

294 May to June, Vienna, GALERIE WÜRTHLE, *Léger, Gromaire, Villon, Kupka,* 5 paintings, 13 prints

295 May 31 to September 5, New York, MUSEUM OF MODERN ART, *Paintings from Private Collections,* preface by Alfred H. Barr, Jr., 1 painting

296 June 3 to July 3, Paris, MUSEE DES TRAVAUX PUBLICS, *Salon des Tuileries et Société des Artistes-Décorateurs,* 1 painting

297 June 17 to July 10, San Francisco, SAN FRANCISCO MUSEUM OF ART, *Art in the 20th Century* (United Nations Exhibition of Modern Art), foreword by E. Morris Cox, 1 painting

298 June 24 to September 26, Lausanne, MUSEE CANTONAL DES BEAUX-ARTS, *Le Mouvement dans l'art contemporain,* preface by Guy Weelen, 5 paintings

299 July 15 to September 18, Cassel, MUSEUM FRIDERICIANUM, *Documenta, Kunst des XX Jahrhunderts,* foreword by Heinz Lenke, preface by Werner Haftmann, 4 paintings

00 July 16 to August 7, Antwerp, STEDELIJKE FEETZAAL MEIR, *Laboureur-Villon*, text by J. Wilms, 56 prints

01 October 3 to November 4, Chicago, THE ARTS CLUB, *An Exhibition of Cubism on the Occasion of the Fortieth Anniversary of the Arts Club of Chicago*

02 October 7 to November 21, 1956, New York, MUSEUM OF MODERN ART, *Exhibition #324*

03 October 13 to December 18, Pittsburgh, CARNEGIE INSTITUTE, *The 1955 Pittsburgh International Exhibition of Contemporary Painting*, foreword by Gordon Bailey Washburn, 1 painting

04 November 5 to 30, Paris, GRAND PALAIS DES CHAMPS-ELYSEES, *Salon d'Automne 1955*, 1 painting

1956

05 Paris, GALERIE CHARPENTIER, *Cent chefs-d'oeuvre des peintures de l'École de Paris*, 1 painting

06 France, traveling exhibition, *Cinquante chefs-d'oeuvre du Musée National d'Art moderne*, preface by Jean Cassou, 2 paintings

07 Munich, HAUS DER KUNST, *Austellung*

08 Helsinki, ATENEUM, *Fransk Konst, Moltzau Samling*

09 Copenhagen, NY CARLSBERG GLYPTOTEK, *Fra Renoir til Villon, Moltzau Samling*

10 Stockholm, NATIONALMUSEUM, *Art Moderne, Moltzau Collection*

11 January 3 to February 4, New York, SIDNEY JANIS GALLERY, *Cubism 1910-1912*, 1 painting

12 April 26 to June 10, Newark, New Jersey, THE NEWARK MUSEUM, *Abstract Art, 1910 to Today*

13 May 5 to 27, Paris, MUSEE D'ART MODERNE DE LA VILLE DE PARIS, *XIIe Salon de Mai*

14 May 19 to June 17, Cincinnati, THE CONTEMPORARY ARTS CENTER, CINCINNATI ART MUSEUM, *Modern Art in Evolution 1900-1956*, introduction by Allon T. Schoener, 1 painting

15 August to October, Basel, GALERIE BEYELER, *Maîtres de l'art moderne*, 1 painting

16 August 19 to October 2, Berlin, AKADEMIE DER KUNSTE, *120 Meisterwerke des Musée d'Art Moderne Paris*, text by H. Scharoun, Jean Cassou, and Th. Werner, 4 paintings

17 August 29 to September 9, Sacramento, California, CALIFORNIA STATE FAIR AND EXPOSITION

318 October 5 to November 4, Toronto, ART GALLERY OF TORONTO, *A Selection from the Ayala and Sam Zacks Collection, Nineteenth and Twentieth Century Painting and Drawings*, 2 paintings. Also Ottawa, NATIONAL GALLERY OF CANADA, November 15 to December; Winnipeg, WINNIPEG ART GALLERY, December 15 to January 19, 1957; Minneapolis, WALKER ART CENTER, February 7 to March 17; Vancouver, THE VANCOUVER ART GALLERY, April 4 to May 1; San Francisco, SAN FRANCISCO MUSEUM OF ART, May 20 to June 30; Santa Barbara, SANTA BARBARA MUSEUM OF ART, July 16 to September 1; Pasadena, PASADENA ART MUSEUM, September 15 to October 15; Kingston, Canada, QUEENS UNIVERSITY, November 8 to December 9; and Montreal, MONTREAL MUSEUM OF FINE ARTS, December 30 to February 1, 1958

1957

319 Paris, GALERIE CHARPENTIER, *École de Paris 1957*, 1 painting

320 Paris, GALERIE CHARPENTIER, *Cent chefs-d'oeuvre de l'art français 1750-1950*

321 St. Etienne, MUSEE D'ART ET D'INDUSTRIE, *L'Art abstrait, les premières générations: 1910-1939*, catalogue by Maurice Allemand, 1 painting

322 January 8 to February 17, New York, THE SOLOMON R. GUGGENHEIM MUSEUM, *Jacques Villon, Raymond Duchamp-Villon, Marcel Duchamp*, preface by James Johnson Sweeney, 27 paintings. Also Houston, MUSEUM OF FINE ARTS, March 8 to April 8

323 February 9 to March 31, Zurich, KUNSTHAUS, *Sammlung Ragnar Moltzau, Oslo*, preface by René Wehril, 13 paintings

324 March 23 to April, Paris, MUSEE NATIONAL D'ART MODERNE, *Depuis Bonnard*, preface by Jean Cassou, 4 paintings

325 March to May, Paris, MUSEE GALLIERA, *Les Peintres témoins de leur temps: VI, Le Sport*, 1 painting

326 April 9 to May 4, New York, KNOEDLER AND CO., *Modern Painting, Drawing and Sculpture*, catalogue by Charles Scott Chetham, 2 paintings. Also Cambridge, Massachusetts, FOGG ART MUSEUM, May 16 to September 15

327 April 13 to May 18, London, R.B.A. GALLERIES, *An Exhibition of Paintings from the Musée d'Art Moderne Paris*, foreword by Philip James, introduction by Jean Cassou, 3 paintings

328 April 19 to June 11, The Hague, GEMEENTEMUSEUM'S-GRAVENHAGE, *Collectie Ragnar Moltzau, Oslo*, foreword by L. J. F. Wijsenbeek, 13 paintings

329 June 24 to July 21, Marseilles, MUSEE CANTINI, *50 Chefs-d'oeuvre contemporains de Bonnard à N. de Stäel*

330 July 16 to September 1, Salisbury, Rhodesia, THE RHODES NATIONAL GALLERY, *Rembrandt to Picasso*

331 September 27 to November 3, Detroit, THE DETROIT INSTITUTE OF ARTS, *Collecting Modern Art: Paintings, Sculpture and Drawings from the Collection of Mr. and Mrs. Harry Lewis Winston*, 1 print. Also Richmond, THE VIRGINIA MUSEUM OF ART, December 13 to January 5, 1958; San Francisco, THE SAN FRANCISCO MUSEUM OF ART, January 23 to March 13; and Milwaukee, THE MILWAUKEE ART INSTITUTE, April 11 to May 12

332 October to November, Basel, GALERIE BEYELER, *Maîtres de l'art moderne*, 2 paintings

333 October 2 to November 17, Boston, INSTITUTE OF CONTEMPORARY ART, *Paintings from the Musée National d'Art Moderne*, foreword by Bernard Dorival, 1 painting. Also Columbus, THE COLUMBUS GALLERY OF FINE ARTS, December 1 to January 1, 1958; Pittsburgh, CARNEGIE INSTITUTE, January 10 to February 9; and Minneapolis, WALKER ART CENTER, March 1 to April 15

334 October 4 to November 3, Hartford, Connecticut, WADSWORTH ATHENEUM, *Connecticut Collects*, 1 painting

335 October 5 to November 3, Stockholm, SVENSK-FRANSKA KONSTGALLERIET, *11 Mästare i Fransk Konst*

336 October 10 to November 17, Boston, MUSEUM OF FINE ARTS, *European Masters of Our Time*, introduction by Perry T. Rathbone, 2 paintings

337 December 14 to January 15, 1958, Paris, GALERIE EUROPE, *Maîtres Modernes*, 3 paintings

1958

338 Reims, Bar-Le-Duc, Brive-La-Gaillarde, *Dessins contemporains*

339 Edinburgh, ROYAL SCOTTISH ACADEMY, *Moltzau Collection*

340 New York, NEW ART CENTER GALLERY, *Graphic Art of the 20th Century*, 8 prints

341 January to March, Zagreb, Belgrade, *Savremeno francusko slikarstvo*

342 January 26 to March 30, Cologne, WALLROF-RICHARTZ-MUSEUM, *The Solomon R. Guggenheim Museum, Eine Auswahl*, introduction by Otto H. Forster, 1 painting

343 February 17 to March 17, Amherst, Massachusetts, MEAD ARTS BUILDING, AMHERST COLLEGE, *The 1913 Armory Show in Retrospect,* 1 painting

344 April 17 to July 21, Brussels, PALAIS INTERNATIONAL DES BEAUX-ARTS, *50 ans d'Art Moderne,* foreword by Marquis de la Boessière-Thiennes, preface by Emile Lanqui, 2 paintings

345 April 23 to June 1, Paris, MUSEE DES ARTS DECORATIFS, PALAIS DU LOUVRE, PAVILLON DE MARSAN, *Collection Solomon R. Guggenheim, New York,* introduction by James Johnson Sweeney, catalogue by François Mathey, 1 painting

346 April 27 to June 1, Lincoln, Massachusetts, DECORDOVA AND DANA MUSEUM, *A Decade in Review*

347 June 27 to November 11, Paris, MUSEE NATIONAL D'ART MODERNE, *De l'Impressionnisme à nos jours. Aquarelles, Pastels, Gouaches,* 4 watercolors, 1 gouache

348 June to July, Metz, MUSEE CENTRAL, *Evolution de la peinture en France de 1905 à 1914,* 1 painting

349 July 5 to September 21, Rouen, MUSEE DES BEAUX-ARTS, *Paysages de France de l'impressionnisme à nos jours,* prefaces by Bernard Tissot and Hubert Guillet, 7 paintings

350 October 3 to November 2, London, THE TATE GALLERY, *From Cézanne to Picasso, The Moltzau Collection,* introduction by David Baxandall, 3 paintings

351 November 2 to December 1, Paris, GRAND PALAIS DES CHAMPS-ELYSEES, *Salon d'Automne 1958,* 2 paintings

352 November 6 to December 6, Paris, BIBLIOTHEQUE NATIONALE (GALERIE MANSART), *Société des Peintres-Graveurs français, 42e Exposition,* text by Jean Vallery-Radot and Pierre Dubreuil, 4 prints

353 December 5 to February 8, 1959, Pittsburgh, CARNEGIE INSTITUTE, *1896-1955 Retrospective Exhibition of Paintings from Previous Internationals,* foreword by Gordon Bailey Washburn, text by Leon Anthony Arkus, 1 painting

1959

354 Montauban, VILLENEUVE-SUR-LOT, *Exposition de dessins*

355 January 19 to 31, New York, NEW ARTS CENTER, *Matisse, Villon*

356 March to May, Paris, MUSEE GALLIERA, *Les Peintres témoins de leur temps: VIII, L'Age mécanique,* 1 painting, 1 drawing

357 April 9 to 26, Hartford, Connecticut, WADSWORTH ATHENAEUM, *Paintings by Artists of the Société Anonyme*

358 April 30 to May 31, Warsaw, MUZEUM NARODOWE, *Malarstwo Francuskie od Gauguina do Dnia Dzisiljszego,* 1 painting

359 May 1 to 18, Paris, FOIRE DE PARIS, PLACE DE LA PORTE DE VERSAILLES, *Troisième foire des antiquaires*

360 May 2, Paris, traveling exhibition, *Le Dessin français de Signac aux Abstraits,* preface by Germaine Cart, introduction by Bernard Dorival, 2 drawings

361 May 5 to June 7, Chartres, CHAMBRE DE COMMERCE, *Aspects de la peinture française depuis Cézanne*

362 May 9 to 31, Paris, MUSEE D'ART MODERNE DE LA VILLE DE PARIS, *XVe Salon de Mai,* 1 painting, 1 print

363 June 23 to July 11, Paris XXe SIECLE REVUE, *Signe et matière*

364 July 9, Paris, MUSEE NATIONAL D'ART MODERNE, *L'École de Paris dans les collections belges,* text by Jean Cassou and Maurice Berard, 1 painting

365 July 11 to October 11, Cassel, MUSEUM FRIDERICIANUM (HESSISCHES LANDESMUSEUM), *II, Documenta: Kunst nach 1945,* introduction by Werner Haftmann, 2 paintings, 3 illustrated books

366 September 3 to November 15, Hamburg, KUNSTHALLE, *Französische Zeichnungen des XX. Jahrhunderts,* 13 drawings

367 October 2 to 25, Paris, MUSEE D'ART MODERNE DE LA VILLE DE PARIS, *Première Biennale de Paris,* 1 painting

368 October 3 to 31, Paris, GALERIE DU BATEAU-LAVOIR, *Dessins de jeunesse de maîtres du XXe siècle*

369 October 8 to 31, Vienna, KUNSTLERHAUS, *80 Maler der Ecole de Paris 1900-1959,* 1 painting. Also Linz, NEUE GALERIE DER STADT, November 20 to January 17, 1960

370 October 21, New York, THE SOLOMON R. GUGGENHEIM MUSEUM, *Inaugural Selection,* 2 paintings

371 October 30 to November 30, Paris, GRAND PALAIS DES CHAMPS-ELYSEES, *Salon d'Automne 1959,* 1 work

372 November 20 to December 19, Paris, GALERIE MADAME MARCEL GUIOT, *De Watteau à Picasso: Le Charme dans le dessin français,* text by Claude Roger-Marx, 2 drawings

373 December 7 to 31, Paris, BIBLIOTHEQUE NATIONALE (GALERIE MANSART), *Société des Peintres-Graveurs français, 43e exposition,* text by Pierre Dubreuil and Bersier, 2 prints

374 December 12 to January 31, 1960, Allentown, Pennsylvania, ALLENTOWN ART MUSEUM, *Four Centuries of Still Life,* 1 print

1960

375 Paris, GALERIE CHARPENTIER, *Cent tableaux de collections privées de Bonnard à de Stäel,* 2 paintings

376 March 6 to April 3, Berkeley, UNIVERSITY OF CALIFORNIA DEPARTMENT OF ART, *Art from Ingres to Pollock: Painting and Sculpture since Neoclassicism,* text by Herschel B. Chipp, 1 painting

377 May 8 to 29, Paris MUSEE D'ART MODERNE DE LA VILLE DE PARIS, *XVIe Salon de Mai,* 1 painting, 1 print

378 May 25 to June 25, Chicago, INTERNATIONAL GALLERIES, *Contemporary French Masters 1960,* 1 painting

379 May to July, Pontoise, MUSEE DE PONTOISE, *Exposition d'art moderne*

380 June 11 to July 24, Zurich, KUNSTHAUS, *Salon de Mai, Paris 1960,* preface by Gaston Diehl, 1 painting

381 June to December, Quimper, Rennes, Bourges, and Dijon, *Le Dessin français de Signac aux Abstraits*

382 July to September, Nice, PALAIS DE LA MEDITERRANEE, *Peintres à Nice et sur la Côte d'Azur 1860-1960*

383 July 20, Venice, *XXX Biennale Internazionale d'Arte,* 1 painting

384 Autumn, Paris, MUSEE GALLIERA, *Dix ans de Biennale de Menton*

385 October 18 to November 27, San Francisco, THE SAN FRANCISCO MUSEUM OF ART, *25th Anniversary Exhibition*

386 November 4 to December 4, Paris, GRAND PALAIS DES CHAMPS-ELYSEES, *Salon d'Automne*

387 November 4 to January 23, 1961, Paris, MUSEE NATIONAL D'ART MODERNE, *The Sources of the XXth Century, The Arts in Europe from 1884-1914,* 2 paintings

388 November 12 to January 1, 1961, Oslo, KUNSTNERNES HUS, *Sonja Henie, Niels Onstad; Samlingen,* introduction by Henning Gran, 10 paintings

389 November 27 to October 15, Zurich, KUNSTHAUS, *Thompson Collection,* 1 painting

390 November 29 to December 24, Paris, GALERIE MADAME MARCEL GUIOT, *'Elles.' Evocations feminines de Watteau à Villon,* text by Claude Roger-Marx, 1 drawing

1961

1 Nice, PALAIS DE LA MEDITERRANEE, *Dix peintres français autour de Jacques Villon*

2 Oslo, KUNSTINDUSTRIMUSEET, *Moltzau Collection*

3 Moscow, *Exposition française de Moscou*

4 January 14 to February 12, Copenhagen, LUISIANA ART MUSEUM, *Henie-Onstad Collection*

5 January 28 to March 5, Marseille, MUSEE CANTINI, *L'Estampe française contemporaine*, preface by Jean Adhémar, 4 prints

6 February 7 to April 16, New York, THE SOLOMON R. GUGGENHEIM MUSEUM, *Paintings from the Arensberg and Gallatin Collections of the Philadelphia Museum of Art*, 2 paintings

7 February 17 to April 9, The Hague, HAAGS GEMEENTEMUSEUM, *Collectie Thompson uit Pittsburgh*, 1 painting

8 February 18 to March 19, Gothenburg, GÖTEBORG KONSTMUSEUM, *Henie-Onstad Collection*

9 March to May, Paris, MUSEE GALLIERA, *Les Peintres témoins de leur temps: X, Richesses de la France*, 1 painting

10 April 7 to 30, Stockholm, MODERNA MUSEET, *Henie-Onstad Collection*

11 May 4 to July 16, Boston, MUSEUM OF FINE ARTS, *The Artist and the Book 1860-1960*, 4 illustrated books

12 May 7 to 28, Paris, MUSEE D'ART MODERNE DE LA VILLE DE PARIS, *XVIIᵉ Salon de Mai*

13 May 12 to July 2, Hambourg, KUNSTHALLE, *Henie-Onstad Collection*

14 May to August, New York, THE SOLOMON R. GUGGENHEIM MUSEUM, *One Hundred Paintings from the G. David Thompson Collection*, 1 painting

15 June 7 to July 7, Amsterdam, STEDELIJK MUSEUM, *Zeventiende Salon de Mai*

16 August 13 to September 17, Essen, MUSEUM FOLKWANG, *Henie-Onstad Collection*

17 October 7 to December 11, Stuttgart, KUNSTVEREIN, *Henie-Onstad Collection*

18 November 3 to 25, New York, M. KNOEDLER AND CO., *Cincinnati Collects*, 1 painting

19 November 3 to January 15, 1962, Tokyo, TOKYO NATIONAL MUSEUM, *Exposition d'art français au Japon 1840-1940*, prefaces by Jean Daridan and Bernard Dorival, 6 prints. Also Kyoto, MUNICIPAL MUSEUM, January 26 to March 15, 1962

410 November 24 to January 1, 1962, Frankfurt, FRANKFURTER KUNSTVEREIN, *Henie-Onstad Collection*

1962

411 Paris, GALERIE CHARPENTIER, *Chefs-d'oeuvre de collections françaises (dix-neuvième-vingtième siècle)*, 1 painting

412 January 20 to February 18, Basel, KUNSTHALLE, *Henie-Onstad Collection*

413 February 1 to March 4, Milwaukee, MILWAUKEE ART CENTER, *The Collection of Mr. and Mrs. Harry Lynde Bradley*

414 March 2 to April 8, London, TATE GALLERY, Arts Council of Great Britain, *Sonja Henie, Neils Onstad Collection*, foreword by Gabriel White, introduction by Lars Gyllensten, 10 paintings. Also Edinburgh, ROYAL SCOTTISH ACADEMY, August 18 to September 16; and Liverpool, WALKER ART GALLERY, September 22 to October 28

415 April 11 to 25, New York, WILDENSTEIN GALLERIES, *Modern French Painting*, 1 painting. Also Waltham, Massachusetts, ROSE ART MUSEUM, BRANDEIS UNIVERSITY, May 10 to June 13

416 April 27 to May 27, Paris, MUSEE D'ART MODERNE DE LA VILLE DE PARIS, *Collection Sonja Henie/Niels Onstad*, 10 paintings

417 May 16 to June 24, Paris, GALERIE MAX KAGANOVITCH, *Oeuvres choisies du XXᵉ siècle*

418 June 14 to July 29, Vienna, KÜNSTLERHAUS, *Henie-Onstad Collection*

419 June 16 to October 7, Venice, CA PESARO, XXXIᵒ Biennale Internazionale d'Arte, *I Grandi Premi della Biennale 1948-1960*, 3 paintings

420 July 1 to September 30, Tours, MUSEE DES BEAUX-ARTS, *Neuf peintres autour de Jacques Villon*

421 September 12 to December 9, Cologne, WALLRAF-RICHARTZ-MUSEUM, *Europäische Kunst 1912*, 1 painting

422 September 21 to November 4, Vienna, MUSEUM DES 20. JAHRHUNDERTS, *Kunst von 1900 bis Heute*, foreword by Werner Haftmann, 1 painting

423 October, Paris, GALERIE LOUIS CARRE, *Exhibition Duchamp-Villon, Jacques Villon, Kupka, Léger, Robert Delaunay, Raoul Dufy, Gromaire, Borès, Gilioli*

424 October 20 to November 20, Mexico, *Dessins français*. Also Stockholm, August to December, 1963

425 November 22 to January 6, 1963, The Hague, GEMEENTEMUSEUM, *Henie-Onstad Collection*

426 December 14 to January 6, 1963, Buffalo, New York, ALBRIGHT-KNOX ART GALLERY, *Gifts to the Albright-Knox Art Gallery from A. Conger Goodyear*, 1 painting

1963

427 Montreal, MUSEE DE MONTREAL, *Peinture française contemporaine*, prefaces by Evan H. Turner and Jacques Lassaigne, 1 painting

428 January 25 to February 24, Geneva, MUSEE D'ART ET HISTOIRE, *Henie-Onstad Collection*

429 February 17 to March 31, Utica, New York, MUNSON-WILLIAMS-PROCTOR INSTITUTE, *Armory Show 1913-1963, 50th Anniversary Exhibition*, introduction by Milton W. Brown, 5 paintings. Also New York, ARMORY OF THE 69TH REGIMENT, April 6 to 28

430 March 30 to May 12, Munich, HAUS DER KUNST, *Französische Malerei der Gegenwart*, preface by Raymond Cogniat, 3 paintings

431 May 10 to June 23, Bergens, KUNSTFORENING, *Henie-Onstad Collection*

432 June 8 to September 15, Strasbourg, CHATEAU DES ROHAN, *La Grande aventure de l'art du XXᵉ siècle*, 2 paintings

433 June 19 to August 31, Grenoble, MUSEE DE PEINTURE ET DE SCULPTURE, *Albert Gleizes et tempête dans les Salons, 1910-1914*, preface by G. Kueny, 1 painting, 4 prints, 5 drawings

434 September 20 to October 27, Chicago, THE ART INSTITUTE OF CHICAGO, *Chicago Collectors*, 1 painting

435 October 4 to November 17, Rotterdam, MUSEUM BOYMANS-VAN BEUNINGEN, *Franse Landschappen van Cézanne tot Heden*, 1 painting

436 October 23 to November 24, Paris, GRAND PALAIS DES CHAMPS-ELYSEES, *Salon d'Automne 1963, Hommage à Paris*, 1 painting

437 November 6 to January 5, 1964, New York, THE SOLOMON R. GUGGENHEIM MUSEUM, *20th Century Master Drawings*, text by E. Rauh and S. Simon, 1 drawing. Also Minneapolis, UNIVERSITY OF MINNESOTA, February 3 to March 15, 1964; Cambridge, Massachusetts, FOGG ART MUESUM, April 6 to May 24

438 December 26 to February 16, 1964, Stockholm, MODERNA MUSEET, *Onskmuseet . . . Notre Musee ideal tel qu'il devrait etre*, text by Gerard Bonnier and K. G. Hulten, 2 paintings

1964

439 January to April, Copenhagen, LUISIANA MUSEUM, *Dessins du Musée d'Art Moderne*

440 March 1 to April 15, Lawrence, Kansas, MUSEUM OF ART, THE UNIVERSITY OF KANSAS, *The Organizers of the Armory Show*, 1 print

441 March 27 to May 11, 1969, New York, MUSEUM OF MODERN ART, *Painting and Sculpture from the Museum Collection*

442 October 6 to November 15, Baltimore, THE BALTIMORE MUSEUM OF ART, *1914 An Exhibition of Paintings, Drawings and Sculpture (In Celebration of the 50th Anniversary of the Baltimore Museum of Art)*, foreword by Charles Parkhurst, texts by George Boas, Henri Peyre, Lincoln F. Johnson, Jr., 1 painting, 1 print

443 October 28 to December 5, New York, LEONARD HUTTON GALLERIES, *Albert Gleizes and the Section D'Or*, texts by William A. Camfield and Daniel Robbins, 2 paintings, 2 drawings

444 1964 to 1965, Portland, Oregon, PORTLAND ART MUSEUM, *The Pleasure of the Eye—The Collection of Caroline and Erwin Swann*, 1 drawing. Also New York, GALLERY OF MODERN ART; Seattle, SEATTLE ART MUSEUM; Salt Lake City, ART CENTER; Colorado Springs, FINE ARTS CENTER; Kansas City, Missouri, WILLIAM ROCKWELL NELSON GALLERY OF ART; Ann Arbor, UNIVERSITY OF MICHIGAN MUSEUM OF ART; and Dayton, Ohio, ART INSTITUTE OF OHIO

1965

445 Poughkeepsie, New York, VASSAR COLLEGE ART GALLERY, *An Exhibition of Modern Art in Honor of Agnes Rindge Claflin*

446 February 1 to 27, New York, LUCIEN GOLDSCHMIDT, INC., *French Master Drawings of the 20th Century*, 2 drawings

447 March 1 to April 30, Lisbon, FONDATION CALOUSTE GULBENKIAN, *Un siècle de peinture française: 1850-1950*, preface by Germaine Bazin, 2 paintings

448 April 3 to May 4, Lille, PALAIS DES BEAUX-ARTS, *Apollinaire et le Cubisme*, 1 drawing, 2 prints

449 Spring to Summer, Cambridge, Massachusetts, Harvard University, CARPENTER CENTER FOR THE VISUAL ARTS, *Proportion: A Measure of Order*, text by Eduard F. Sekler

450 September 5 to October 17, Heidelberg, HEIDELBERGER KUNSTVEREIN, *Internationale Druckgraphik des 20. Jahrhunderts aus Heidelberger Privatbesitz*, texts by Georg Poensgen and Adolph Gangel, 4 prints

451 September 24, St. Denis, MUSEE MUNICIPAL D'ART ET D'HISTOIRE, *Les peintres et la nature en France dupuis l'impressionnisme*, 2 paintings

452 October 16 to January 6, 1966, Paris, BIBLIOTHEQUE NATIONALE, *Les Plus belles gravures du monde occidental 1410-1914*, texts by E. Dennery, Jean Adhémar, P. Halm, K. G. Boon, W. Wegner, W. Koschatzky, 1 print

1966

453 New York, *Seven Decades, 1896-1965*

454 Cleveland, CLEVELAND MUSEUM OF ART, *Fifty Years of Modern Art: 1916-1966*, text by Edward B. Henning, 1 painting

455 May 13 to September 15, Bordeaux, MUSEE DES BEAUX-ARTS, *La Peinture française, collections americaines*, foreword by Jacques Chabañ-Delmas, preface by Jean Cassou

456 March to September, Minneapolis, THE MINNEAPOLIS INSTITUTE OF ARTS, *Prints 1800-1945, A Loan Exhibition from Museums and Private Collections*, preface by Anthony M. Clark, foreword by Harold Joachim, introduction by Janet A. Flint and Edward A. Foster

457 September 16 to November 13, Brussels, PALAIS DES BEAUX-ARTS, *Art français contemporain, peintures*

458 November 21 to December 31, Luxembourg, MUSEE D'HISTOIRE ET D'ART 24 *peintres français 1946-1966*, introduction by Bernard Dorival, 1 painting

1967

459 April 15 to June 1, Rouen, MUSEE DES BEAUX-ARTS, *Les Duchamps, Jacques Villon, Raymond Duchamp-Villon, Marcel Duchamp, Suzanne Duchamp*, preface by Olga Popovitch, 46 paintings, 4 drawings and watercolors, 40 prints

460 May 19 to September 15, Bordeaux, MUSEE DE BORDEAUX, *La Peinture française en Suède*, 2 paintings

461 September 27 to October 22, Buffalo, New York, ALBRIGHT-KNOX ART GALLERY, *Painters of the Section D'Or — The Alternatives to Cubism*, catalogue by Richard V. West, 5 paintings

462 October 10 to 29, Raleigh, North Carolina, NORTH CAROLINA MUSEUM, *North Carolina Collects*, 1 print

463 October 10 to November 9, New York, KNOEDLER GALLERY, *Raymond Duchamp-Villon*, text by George Heard Hamilton and William C. Agee, 2 paintings, 1 print, 2 drawings

464 December to January, 1968, Basel, GALERIE BEYELER, *Petits formats*, 2 paintings

465 December 9 to February, 1968, Stuttgart, GALERIE VALENTIEN, *Gemälde Graphik Plastik*

1968

466 Stockholm, MUSEE D'ART MODERNE, *Collection Gerard Bonnier*

467 Washington, D.C., NATIONAL GALLERY OF ART, *Painting in France 1900-1967*, organized by the Ministry of Cultural Affairs and Le Musée National d'Art Moderne, Paris, foreword by Charles Lucet, preface by Pierre Moinot, 1 painting. Also New York, METROPOLITAN MUSEUM OF ART; Boston, MUSEUM OF FINE ARTS; Chicago, THE ART INSTITUTE OF CHICAGO; and San Francisco, M. H. DE YOUNG MEMORIAL MUSEUM

468 January 10 to February 7, New York, LUCIEN GOLDSCHMIDT, INC., *Landscape Drawings*, 2 drawings

469 May 8 to September 15, Strasbourg, MUSEE DE L'ANCIENNE DOUANE, *L'Art en Europe autour de 1918*, 1 painting

470 August, Oslo, THE FOUNDATIONS ART CENTER, *Sonja Henie-Niels Onstad Collection*, 10 paintings

471 October 22 to December 8, Baltimore, THE BALTIMORE MUSEUM OF ART, *From El Greco to Pollock: Early and Late Works by European and American Artists*, 2 paintings

471a October 25 to February 23, 1969, Milwaukee, MILWAUKEE ART CENTER, *The Collection of Mrs. Harry Lynde Bradley*

1969

472 New York, THE SOLOMON R. GUGGENHEIM MUSEUM, *Works from the Peggy Guggenheim Foundation*, introduction by Peggy Guggenheim, 1 painting

473 London, ROYAL ACADEMY OF ARTS, *French Paintings Since 1900*, 4 paintings

474 June 17 to September 1, Buffalo, New York, ALBRIGHT-KNOX ART GALLERY, *Contemporary Art — Acquisitions 1966-1969*

475 June 30 to August 1, Columbus, Ohio, BUCKEYE FEDERAL BUILDING AND LOAN CO., *Selections from the Gordion Knot Exhibition*

476 September 28 to November 2, Yonkers, New York, HUDSON RIVER MUSEUM, *Art in Westchester from Private Collections*, 1 painting

477 October 10 to December 31, Columbus, Ohio, THE COLUMBUS GALLERY OF FINE ARTS, *From the Collection of Ferdinand Howald*, introduction by Mahonri Sharp Young, 2 paintings

1970

478 January 11 to February 16, Dayton, Ohio, DAYTON ART INSTITUTE, *Paintings from the Howald Collection*

479 February 1 to March 1, Palm Beach, Florida, SOCIETY OF THE FOUR ARTS, *Paintings from the Phillips Collection*

480 June, Oshkosh, Wisconsin, PAINE ART CENTER, *Selections from the Collection of Mrs. Harry Lynde Bradley*

481 November to December, 1972, Washington, D.C., MERIDIAN HOUSE

482 December 15 to February 21, 1971, Los Angeles, LOS ANGELES COUNTY MUSEUM OF ART, *The Cubist Epoch*, foreword by Kenneth Donahue and Thomas P. F. Hoving, text by Douglas Cooper, 3 paintings, 6 prints. Also New York, METROPOLITAN MUSEUM OF ART, April 7 to June 7

1971

483 February 10 to March 21, Bloomington, INDIANA UNIVERSITY ART MUSEUM, *Reflection Through a Collector's Eye*, 2 prints. Also Milwaukee, UNIVERSITY OF WISCONSIN, March 30 to April 30

484 March 31 to May 9, Los Angeles, MUNICIPAL ART GALLERY, *Sonja Henie-Niels Onstad Collection*, 5 paintings

485 May 13 to June 13, Minneapolis, MINNEAPOLIS INSTITUTE OF ARTS, *Drawings and Watercolors from Minnesota Private Collections*, 1 drawing

486 October 10 to November 28, Omaha, Nebraska, JOSLYN ART MUSEUM, *The Thirties Decade: American Artists and their European Contemporaries*, 1 print

1972

487 Helsinki, ATENEUM, *Collection Gerard Bonnier*

488 February 5 to March 12, Madison, Wisconsin, UNIVERSITY OF WISCONSIN, ELVEHJEM ART CENTER, *Cubist Prints from the Collection of Dr. and Mrs. Abraham Melamed*, 7 prints

489 May to July, Geneva, GALERIE BONNIER, *Comparaisons: Oeuvres de Degas à Arman*

490 October 15 to December 17, Austin, THE UNIVERSITY OF TEXAS AT AUSTIN ART MUSEUM, *Not So Long Ago: Art in the 1920's in Europe and America*, preface by Donald B. Goodall, 1 painting

491 October 18 to January 7, 1973, New York, THE MUSEUM OF MODERN ART, *Philadelphia in New York*

1973

492 Belgrade, *De Bonnard à Soulages*

493 Chicago, THE ARTS CLUB, *Exhibition of Works Owned by the University of Iowa*, 1 painting

494 May 4 to September 1, Bordeaux, GALERIE DES BEAUX-ARTS, *Les Cubistes*, texts by Jacques Chaban-Delmas, Gilberte Martin-Mery, Jacques Lassaigne, and Jean Cassou, 4 paintings. Also Paris, MUSEE D'ART MODERNE DE LA VILLE DE PARIS, September 26 to November 10

495 May 16 to September 3, Paris, GRAND PALAIS DES CHAMPS-ELYSEES, *Hommage à Teriade*, 1 illustrated book

496 June 20 to July 21, London, WILDENSTEIN AND CO., LTD., *Ferdinand Howald Avant-garde Collector*, introduction by Mahonri Sharp Young, 2 paintings. Also Dublin, NATIONAL GALLERY OF IRELAND; and Cardiff, NATIONAL MUSEUM OF WALES

497 December 6 to January 13, 1974, Rome, GALERIA NAZIONALE D'ARTE MODERNA, *Il Cubismo*

1974

498 February to March, Palm Beach, Florida, THE SOCIETY OF THE FOUR ARTS, *Master Drawings from the Collection of Yale University*

1975

499 Milwaukee, BRADLEY FAMILY FOUNDATION, *Personal Selections from the Collection of Mrs. Harry Lynde Bradley*

WRITINGS BY JACQUES VILLON
(Chronological Listing)

1 "Sur la peinture abstraite." *Abstraction-Création, art non-figuratif* II (1933), 47-48 (see also bibl. 44).

2 "Couleurs et construction." In Diehl, Gaston, *Les Problèmes de la peinture,* pp. 256-258. Paris: Éditions Confluences, 1945.

3 "Sur le cubisme." *Art present* III (1947), 32 (see also bibl. 350). Reprinted in exhibition catalogue, *Dix peintres français autour de Jacques Villon,* 1961 (see exhibition no. 391).

4 "Thus is Cubism Cultivated." *Art News* XLVIII, 3 (May, 1949), 23-25, 51 (see also bibl. 263).

5 "Reflections on painting." In exhibition catalogue, *Jacques Villon — Lyonel Feininger,* 1949 (see exhibition no. 198), p. 7.

6 "Qu'est-ce que la peinture? Comment s'exprime la peinture?" In Lassaigne, Jacques, *Jacques Villon,* pp. 14-15. Paris: Les Éditions de Beaune, 1950 (see also bibl. 34). Reprinted in bibl. 40 and 263, and in exhibition catalogue, *Jacques Villon, Raymond Duchamp-Villon, Marcel Duchamp* (see exhibition no. 322).

7 "Comment on painting." In Mellquist, Jerome, "Jacques Villon, Maître de Puteaux." *Art-Documents* III (December, 1950), 4-5 (see also bibl. 236).

8 "Témoignages." *XXe Siècle.* N.S. II (January, 1952), 68.

9 "Villon om Konst." Translated by Yvon, Taillandier. *Konstrevy* XXVIII, 3 (1952), 139-140.

10 "Jacques Villon, graveur, par lui-même." Preface to Auberty, Jacqueline and Pérussaux, Charles, *Jacques Villon, Catalogue de son oeuvre gravé.* Paris: Paul Prouté, 1950 (see also bibl. 26). Reprinted as "Jacques Villon: Printmaker." *Art News* III, 6 (October, 1953), 38-40, 63.

11 "Peindre." *La Biennale di Venezia* (April, 1951), p. 25.

12 "Dufy." In exhibition catalogue, *Raoul Dufy.* Paris: Louis Carré et Cie, 1953, pp. 36-37.

13 "La Création artistique." *XXe Siècle.* N.S. IV (January, 1954), 29-31.

14 "Duchamp-Villon." In *Sept pionniers de la sculpture moderne,* Yverdon, July-September, 1954 and *Sculpteurs célèbres,* Paris: Mazenod, 1954, pp. 306-307.

15 "Gromaire." *Le Pont,* December, 1954, pp. 6-7.

16 "Le Peintre dans la société moderne." In *L'Artiste dans la société contemporaine,* pp. 107-115. UNESCO, 1954.

17 Statement on Brancusi. *Cahiers d'Art* XXX (1955), 226.

18 Letter to the editor. In Lassaigne, Jacques, *Éloge de Jacques Villon.* Paris: Manuel Bruker, 1955 (see also bibl. 35). Reprinted in bibl. 40 and exhibition catalogue, *Jacques Villon, Master Printmaker,* 1964 (see exhibition no. 59).

19 Preface to *Réalité de l'Art,* by Lucien Schwob. Lausanne: F. Rouge, 1955.

20 Introduction to *D'Espic, Gravures.* Paris: Galerie Marcel Guiot, December, 1955 (exhibition held February 1-24, 1956).

21 "J'attends le verdict d'octobre pour voir . . . mes cinq vitraux de Metz." *Les Lettres Françaises,* August 1, 1957.

22 "Le Grand Testament." In exhibition catalogue, *Jacques Villon, l'oeuvre gravé (1891-1958),* 1959 (see exhibition no. 43), p. 9.

23 "Un travail solitaire dans un chemin privé." *Arts, Lettres, Spectacles* 819 (April 26-May 2, 1961).

24 Preface to *Charpentes: la géométrie secrète des peintres,* by Charles Bouleau. Paris: Éditions du Seuil, 1963 (see also bibl. 384).

MONOGRAPHS

25 Adhémar, Jean. *Jacques Villon.* Paris: Louis Carré, 1954.

26 Auberty, Jacqueline and Pérussaux, Charles. *Jacques Villon, Catalogue de son oeuvre gravé.* Paris: Paul Prouté, 1950.

27 *Cent tableaux de Jacques Villon.* Paris: Louis Carré, 1961.

28 Cogniat, Raymond. *Villon-Peintures.* Paris: Fernand Hazan, 1963.

29 Crespelle, Jean-Paul. *Villon.* Paris: Fernand Hazan, 1958.

30 de Ginestet, Collette. *Jacques Villon. Oeuvre graphique.* Paris: Arts et Métiers graphiques (in preparation).

31 _____. "L'Oeuvre graphique de Villon." Unpublished thesis at the École du Louvre, 1959 (see also bibl. 42).

32 Dorival, Bernard. *Jacques Villon. Les Grands peintres* series. Photographs by Roger Hauert. Geneva: Éditions René Kister, 1956.

33 Eluard, Paul and René-Jean. *Jacques Villon ou L'Art glorieux.* Paris: Louis Carré, 1948.

34 Lassaigne, Jacques. *Jacques Villon.* Paris: Les Éditions de Beaune, 1950.

35 ———. *Éloge de Jacques Villon.* Paris: Manuel Bruker, 1955.

36 Mellquist, Jerome. *Les Caricatures de Jacques Villon.* Translated by Berthe Vulliemin. Geneva: Éditions Pierre Cailler, 1960.

37 Morel, Abbé Maurice; Picon, Gaetan; Daidel, Georges; and Cassou, Jean. *Souvenir de Jacques Villon.* Paris: Louis Carré, 1963.

38 Pach, Walter. *Villon.* New York: Société Anonyme, Inc., 1921.

39 René-Jean. *Jacques Villon.* Collection Initier. Paris: Braun, 1945.

40 Vallier, Dora. *Jacques Villon: Oeuvres de 1897 à 1956.* Paris: Éditions Cahiers d'Art, 1957.

41 Venturi, Lionello. *Jacques Villon.* Paris: Louis Carré, 1962.

42 *Jacques Villon: Cent croquis 1894-1904.* Paris: Pierre Berès, 1959.

ARTICLES

43 *Abstraction-Création, art non-figuratif* I (1932), 42.

44 *Abstraction-Création, art non-figuratif* II (1933), 47-48.

45 "Abstract of Villon." *Art Digest* XXVII, 7 (January 15, 1953), 14.

46 Adhémar, Jean. "Les Journaux amusants et les premiers peintres cubistes." *L'Oeil* IV (April 15, 1955), 40-43.

47 Advertisement for Galerie Louis Carré. *Cimaise* VIII, 52 (March-April, 1961), 97.

48 Alvard, Julien. "L'Espace cubiste." *Art d'Aujourd'hui* IV, 3-4 (Spring, 1953), 43-49.

49 Andrén, Gösta. "En mild och försynt Klassiker." *Konstperspektiv* II (1960), 4-6.

50 Apollinaire, Guillaume. "Quatre nouveaux artistes français." *Paris-Journal,* July 3, 1914.

51 Arbois, Simone. "Jacques Villon." *Volontés,* December 27, 1944.

52 Ashbery, John. "Paris Notes." *Art International,* June-August, 1961, pp. 42, 92-94.

53 Ashton, Dore. "The Duchamps Even." *Art Digest* XXVI, 12 (March 15, 1952), 16-17.

54 ———. "Jacques Villon, Master of Graphic Art." *Art International,* September 1964, pp. 31-33.

55 ———. "Jacques Villon 'Father of Modern Printmaking.' " *Art Digest,* XXVII, 20 (September 15, 1953), 8-9.

56 d'Aubarède, Gabriel. "Chez Jacques Villon." *Jardin des Arts,* April, 1963, pp. 2-13.

57 Auerbach, Edith. "Jacques Villon." *Die Weltkunst,* June, 1961, p. 14.

58 "Ausstellung, Kunsthalle, Bern." *Werk* XXXVIII, Sup. 104 (August, 1951).

59 Barotte, René. "La Côte délirante des tableaux." *Plaisir de France,* October, 1959.

60 ———. "Jacques Villon, Illustrateur." *Le Livre et Ses Amis* VIII (1946), 22-24.

61 ———. "Jacques Villon à la Galerie Charpentier." *Plaisir de France,* July, 1961, p. 63.

62 Bazaine, Jean. "Tour d'horizon." *Nouvelle Revue Française,* August, 1941, pp. 220-223.

63 ———. "Jacques Villon." *Poésie* XXI (November-December, 1944), 33-35.

64 Bazin, Germain. "Jacques Villon." In "Histoire de l'art contemporain." *L'Amour de l'Art* IX (November, 1933), 238.

65 Berger, René. "Jacques Villon." *XXe Siècle,* N.S. XXI, 13, Sup. 50-51 (December, 1959).

66 Bergmark, Torsten. "Biennalen 1950." *Paletten* I (1950), 91-93.

67 Besson, George. "Jacques Villon, doyen des jeunes peintres." *Ce Soir,* October 30, 1948.

68 Bill, Max. "Jacques Villon. Zum 75 Geburtstag." *Werk* XXXVII (August, 1950), 109.

69 Billedkronikk: Fra Jacques Villons utstilling i Kunstnernes Hus, Oslo." *Kunsten Idag* XLIX (1959), 50-53.

70 Bird, Paul. "First Post-War Carnegie International: An End and a Beginning." *The Art Digest* XXV, 3 (November 1, 1950), 7-8.

71 Bligne, Yvon. "Entretien avec Jacques Villon." *Le Peintre,* December, 1951, pp. 12-13.

72 Bonnefoy, Yves. "Jacques Villon." *Art de France* IV (1964), 259-260.

73 Bordier, Roger. "Jacques Villon." *Aujourd'hui art et architecture* I, 3 (May-June, 1955), 17.

74 Bouillier, Renée. "De Kupka à Villon." *Aux Ecoutes,* September 25, 1959.

75 ———. "Les Duchamp." *La Nouvelle Revue Française,* July, 1967, pp. 145-146.

76 Breuning, Margaret. "Jacques Villon." *The Art Digest* XXVIII, 15 (May 1, 1949), 17.

77 Brichot, Robert. "Les Vitraux modernes dan les monuments anciens: Jacques Villon à la cathédrale de Metz." *Construction Moderne* LXXIV (1958), 24-29.

78 "The Brothers." *Time* LXIX, 4 (April 8, 1957), 74-75.

79 Brown, Gordon. "Jacques Villon at Goldschmidt." *Arts Magazine* XLV, 1 (September-October, 1970), 62.

80 Brüschweiler, Jura. "L'Oeuvre gravé de Jacques Villon." *Musée de Genève,* July-August, 1955, p. 2.

81 Buffet, Gabrielle. "La Section d'Or." *Art d'Aujourd'hui* IV, 3-4 (Spring, 1953), 74-76.

82 *Bulletin of the Detroit Institute of Arts* LII, 1 (1972), 27.

83 Burrows, Carlyle. "Art in Review." *New York Herald Tribune,* May 1, 1949.

84 Busse, Jacques. "Le Salon à mai." *Journal de l'Amateur d'Art* XC-XCI (1952), 20.

85 Butler, Barbara. "Paris." *Arts* XXXI, 8 (May, 1957), 15.

86 R.F.C. "New York: La mostra di Jacques Villon, Raymond Duchamp-Villon e Marcel Duchamp." *Emporium* CXXV, 749 (May, 1957), 220-227.

87 Cabanne, Pierre. "Mes invités, mes peintres." *Connaissance des Arts* CLVIII (April, 1965), 88-99.

88 ———. "Une Tendre et pudique Jacques Villon." *Lecture pour Tous,* May, 1965.

89 ———. "Jacques Villon: j'ai decouvert dans la lumière le mystere du réel." *Arts, Lettres, Spectacles,* September 7, 1960, p. 16.

90 ———. "Villon: 60 ans de peinture, une longue histoire d'amour." *Arts, Lettres, Spectacles,* April 26-May 2, 1961.

91 Calas, Nicolas. "The brothers Duchamp all at once." *Art News* LV, 10 (February, 1957), 24-27, 56-57.

92 "California School of Fine Arts, Maintained by the San Francisco Art Association, Exhibition Surveys Cubism." *Architect and Engineer* CLXIV, 1 (January, 1946), 7.

93 Campbell, Lawrence. "The Father of Modern Print-Making." *Art News* LXVI, 8 (December, 1967), 38-39, 69-70.

94 ———. "Jacques Villon." *Art News* LII, 7, Part I (November, 1953), 43.

95 _____. "Jacques Villon." *Art News* LVIII, 4 (Summer, 1959), 14.

96 Canaday, John. "A Private Road: Sixty Years of Jacques Villon's Art Celebrated in Paris This Month." *The New York Times,* May 14, 1961, section 2, p. 11.

97 "Carnegie Contrasts." *Time* LVI, 18 (October 30, 1950), 67-70.

98 Carré, Louis. Letter to the editor in response to article by Lawrence Campbell of December, 1967. *Art News* LXVI, 10 (February, 1968), 6.

99 Cartier, Jean-Albert. "Lumière sur un chef d'oeuvre de Jacques Villon: le portrait de son frère." *Plaisir de France,* July, 1961, pp. 12-13.

100 Cassou, Jean. "Dessins des peintres et sculpteurs de l'École de Paris." *Art et Style* XLIII-XLIX (1958).

101 _____. "Réévocation du Cubisme." *XXe Siècle* XXXV, 41 (December, 1973), 17-26.

102 Chabanon, Jean. "Le Salon de Mai." *Le Peintre,* May 15, 1956.

103 Chastel, André. "Dix ans d'art français." *Médecine de France* C (1959), 52.

104 _____. "Une Semaine dans le monde." *Le Monde,* January 31, 1948.

105 _____. "Jacques Villon ou la conquête de l'espace." *Le Monde* XXXVIII, 5064 (April 29, 1961), 13.

106 Chebrun, Jean-François. "Jacques Villon." *L'Express,* May 4, 1961, pp. 50-52.

107 Chevalier, D. "Exposition de peintures à la galerie Louis Carré." *Beaux-Arts, Littérature, Spectacles,* January 30, 1948, p. 1.

108 "Chicago to See Villon Show." *Art Digest* XXVII, 5 (December 1, 1952), 13.

109 "La Chronique des arts." *Gazette des Beaux-Arts* No. 1213, Supplement (February, 1970), 92.

110 Coates, Robert M. "Three Brothers." *The New Yorker* XXXIII (March 2, 1957), 97-98.

111 *Combat,* VI, November, 1951.

112 Combe, Jacques. "Graveurs sur Cuivre." *L'Amour de l'Art* XVII (1936), 17-24.

113 "Coup d'oeil sur les ventes publiques." *L'Oeil* XXI (September, 1956), 42-46.

114 Courthion, Pierre. "Décomposition et recomposition de l'espace." *XXe Siècle,* N.S. II (January, 1952), 27-31.

115 _____. "Hier et aujourd'hui." *XXe Siècle,* N.S. I (February 15, 1951), 3-18.

116 _____. "Jacques Villon ou le don d'émouvoir." *Art-Documents,* May, 1951, p. 5.

117 Crespelle, J.-P. *Montmartre vivant.* Paris: Hachette, 1964.

118 Crook, Gordon. "Modern French Tapestries." *The Studio* CLX, 809 (September, 1960), 94-97.

119 "The Cube Root." *The Art Digest* XXIV, 7 (January 1, 1950), 9.

120 "Daubigny, Villon Retrospectives." *Art News* LXIII, 1 (March, 1964), 6.

121 Davis, F. "Talking about Sale-Rooms." *Country Life* CXLVIII (July 9, 1970), 108.

122 Degand, Léon. "La Peinture cubiste." *Art d'Aujourd'hui* IV, 3-4 (Spring, 1953), 9-31.

123 _____. "A propos de la rétrospective de Jacques Villon." *Art d'Aujourd'hui* II, 4 (March, 1951), 30.

124 "Delacroix et les peintres d'aujourd'hui." *Les Nouvelles Littéraires,* May 9, 1963.

125 Delorme, Hugues. " 'Jacques Villon' — portrait de l'artiste par Widhopff." *Le Courrier Français,* June 30, 1901.

126 De Man, Paul. "Jacques Villon." *Konstrevy* XXVIII, 3 (1952), 133-138.

127 Descargues, Pierre. "Jacques Villon, Prix Carnegie 1950." *Arts Paris,* October 27, 1950.

128 Devree, Howard. "Elder Modernist." *New York Times,* May 1, 1949.

129 "Documenta." *Das Kunstwerk* 2, IX (1955-56), 31.

130 Dorival, Bernard. "Musée National d'Art Moderne, un an d'activité." *La Revue des Arts* IV (1953).

131 _____. "Note sur quatre ouvrages français et anglais de 1913-14." *Zbornik Radova. Narodni Muzej* IV (1964), 444-452.

132 _____. "Jacques Villon." *La Table Ronde,* March, 1951, pp. 175-181.

133 "The Katherine S. Dreier Bequest." *The Museum of Modern Art Bulletin* XX, 3-4 (Summer, 1953), 8-9.

134 "Duchamp et al." *Art News* XLIV, 3 (March 15-31, 1945), 9.

135 Dumont, Pierre. "A propos d'un portrait du peintre Jacques Villon." *Rouen-Gazette,* June 18, 1910.

136 Eisendrath, William N., Jr. "Painting and Sculpture of the School of Paris in the Collection of Mr. and Mrs. Joseph Pulitzer, Jr. of St. Louis." *The Connoisseur* CLI, 607 (September, 1962), 26-35.

137 Elgar, Frank. "Jacques Villon." *Carrefour,* December 30, 1944.

138 _____. "Jacques Villon." *Dictionnaire de peinture moderne.* Pts. 1-4 edited by Joseph-Emile Muller, pt. 5 edited by Frank Elgar. Paris: Fernand Hazan (1954), pp. 316-317.

139 _____. "Jacques Villon." In *Dictionary of Modern Painting,* edited by Carlton Lake and Robert Maillard, translated by Lawrence Samuelson, et. al. New York: Tudor Publishing Co., 1963, pp. 395-398.

140 Estienne, Charles. "Jacques Villon." *Art d'Aujourd'hui* I, 5 (December, 1949), 14-17.

141 _____. "Jacques Villon eller ryrndens poesi." *Paletten* I (1950), 124-127.

142 "Exhibition of Paintings by Members of the Société Anonyme." *Bulletin of the Worcester Art Museum* XII, 4 (January, 1922), 72-78.

143 "Exposition à la Galerie Maurice Bridel et Nane Coiller, Lausanne." *Werk* XLIII, Sup. 150 (August, 1956).

144 Faunce, Sarah C. "Jacques Villon (Goldschmidt; to April 25)." *Art News* LXIII, 2 (April, 1964), 10.

145 _____. "Jacques Villon (Thaw; to April 18)." *Art News* LXIII, 2 (April, 1964), 10.

146 Feinstein, Sam. "Jacques Villon." *Arts Digest* XXIX, 13 (April 1, 1955), 18.

147 Fitzsimmons, James. "Art." *Arts and Architecture* LXX, 9 (September, 1953), 6-8, 33-34.

148 _____. "Art." *Arts and Architecture* LXXI, 5 (May, 1954), 9, 30.

149 Fosca, François. "Qu'est-ce que le cubisme?" *Jardin des Arts* XXXVIII (December, 1957), 135-143.

150 Frénaud, André. "Jacques Villon" (poem). *Horizon* XII (August, 1945).

151 Frigerio, Simone. "La Figure dans l'oeuvre graphique de Jacques Villon." *Aujourd'hui Art et Architecture* VII, 40 (January, 1963), 40.

152 _____. "Suisse. Réflexions sur quelques rétrospectives." *Aujourd'hui Art et Architecture* VII, 41 (May, 1963), 52.

153 _____. "Jacques Villon." *Aujourd'hui Art et Architecture* VI, 32 (July, 1961), 4-23.

154 Gallego, Julian. "Cronica de Paris. Dibujos de Jacques Villon." *Goya* XIII (May-June, 1956), 398-399.

155 _____. "Jacques Villon, Pintor Francés." *Goya* XIV (September-October, 1956), 89-96.

156 George, Waldemar. "Jacques Villon et le Cubisme français." *Le Peintre* XXI (February 15, 1951).

157 _____. "Jacques Villon, prix international de peinture de la Biennale de Venise." *Prisme des Arts* V (October, 1956), 13-14.

158 Gheerbrandt, Bernard. "L'incisione si rinnova." *Arti* V (1967), 34-39.

159 _____. "Villon, The Greatest of All." *Artist's Proof* III, 2 (Fall-Winter, 1963-1964), 8.

160 Gindertael, R. V. "Cent tableaux de Jacques Villon." *Les Beaux-Arts* (Brussels), May 5, 1961.

161 _____. "France." *Quadrum* X (1961), 174.

162 _____. "Pour aider à mieux comprendre 'le passage de la ligne.' " *Art d'Aujourd'hui* III, 6 (August, 1952), 18-22.

163 "Lucien Goldschmidt, New York." *Apollo*, N.S. XCII, 92 (December, 1970), 493.

164 Goodrich, Lloyd. "Villon." *The Arts* XVII, 2 (November, 1930), 119.

165 Göpel, (Dr.) Erhard. "Ein grosser norwgischer Sammler: Die Sammlung Ragnar Moltzau im Zürcher Kunsthaus ausgestellt." *Die Weltkunst* XXVII, 5 (March, 1957), 5-6.

166 Grafly, Dorothy. "The 1950 Pittsburgh International." *American Artist* XIV, 10 (December, 1950), 44-45, 76-77.

167 Gran, Henning. "Kubismens Hovedfremstöt Mot Norge til Jacques Villon's attiarsdag." *Kunst og Kultur* XXXVIII, 3 (1955), 173-190.

168 Grand, Paule-Marie. "Jacques Villon." *Art de France* I (1961), 390-391.

169 Gray, Cleve. "Jacques Villon." *Profils,* April, 1953, pp. 78-88.

170 _____. "Jacques Villon." *Perspectives U.S.A.* III (Spring, 1953), 68-78.

171 _____. "Jacques Villon, Print Review." *Art in America* LII, 5 (October, 1964), 98-101.

172 Grenier, Jean. "Jacques Villon." *Combat,* December 28, 1944.

173 Gross, John. "Current and Forthcoming Exhibitions." *The Burlington Magazine* XCVIII, 638 (May, 1956), 178-179.

174 Guiart, (Dr.) Jules. "Le Macabre dans l'Art." *Aesculape,* May, 1913, pp. 105-108.

175 Guichard-Meili, Jean. "Un Grand humaniste de la peinture." *Témoinage chrétien,* May 19, 1961.

176 _____. "Jacques Villon." *Esprit,* May, 1951.

177 Guinard, Paul. "Tendencias recientes de la pintura francesca." *Goya* I, 6 (May-June, 1955), 348-354.

178 Guth, Paul. "Jacques Villon, Fra Angelico normand." *Le Figaro Littéraire,* April 14, 1951, p. 4.

179 Haas, Irvin. "Jacques Villon's." *Art News* XLVIII, 3 (May, 1949), 42.

180 Hammer, Andrew. "Exhibitions." *The Architectural Review* CXI, 666 (June, 1952), 421-422.

181 Hamilton, George Heard. "The Dialectic of Later Cubism: Villon's Jockey." *Magazine of Art* XLI, 7 (November, 1948), 268-273.

182 _____. "Duchamp-Villon, Villon." *Bulletin of the Associates in Fine Arts at Yale University* XIII, 2 (March, 1945), 1-7.

183 _____. "The Exhibition of the Collection of the Société Anonyme — Museum of Modern Art: 1920." *Bulletin of the Associates in Fine Arts at Yale University* X, 3 (December, 1941), 1-5.

184 Hayter, Stanley William. "Atelier 17." *Graphis* X, 55 (1954), 392-397.

185 Henning, Edward B. "Two New Modern Paintings." *Cleveland Museum of Art Bulletin* LII (January, 1965), 7-18.

186 Hess, Thomas B. "Introduction to Abstract Art." *Art News Annual,* November, 1950, pp. 127-158.

187 _____. "Villon-Feininger: Refining Cubism." *Art News* XLVII, 7, Part I (November, 1949), 26, 60-61.

188 Hoffman, Edith. "New York." *The Burlington Magazine* XCIX, 649 (April, 1957), 132.

189 Hootin, Luce. "L'Art d'accomoder les cathédrales." *L'Oeil* XXXVIII (February, 1958), 10-17.

190 Howe, Russell Warren. "Jacques Villon." *Apollo* LVIII, 343 (September, 1953), 62-64.

191 "If Villon Were King!" *The Art Digest* VIII, 8 (January 15, 1934), 6.

192 Igé, Jean. "Parler de Jacques Villon." *Parler* 3, July, 1957, pp. 33-36.

193 Imbourg, Pierre. "Les Grands peintres chez eux: Jacques Villon." *Journal de l'Amateur d'Art* CXLII (December 25, 1954), 10-11.

194 "Les Intellectuels jouent-ils un rôle dans l'évolution de la peinture?" *Arts, Spectacles,* March 13, 1957, p. 16.

195 Jardot, Maurice. "Dessins de Jacques Villon." *Quadrum,* May, 1956, p. 204.

196 Jarlot, Gerard. "C'est moderne, mais est-ce de l'art?" *Elle,* June 25, 1956.

197 Jouffroy, Alain. "Portrait d'un artiste. (III) Jacques Villon." *Arts, Spectacles,* November 2-8, 1955, p. 9.

198 *Journal de l'Amateur d'Art,* II, November, 1951.

199 H. K. "Bemerkungen zu fünf Radierungen." *Werk* XXXVII (1950), 220-224.

200 Kahn, Gustave. "La Réalisation d'un ensemble d'architecture et de décoration." *L'Art décoratif,* February, 1913, pp. 89-102.

201 Kahnweiler, Daniel-Henry. "Cubism: the Creative Years." *Art News Annual* LIII, 7, Part II (November, 1954), 99-116.

202 _____. "Du Temps que les cubistes etaient jeunes." *L'Oeil* IV (January 15, 1955), 26-31.

203 Kimball, Fiske. "Cubism and the Arensbergs." *Art News Annual* LIII, 7, Part II (November, 1954), 117-122, 174-178.

204 Kuppers, P. E. "Die Sammlung Max Leon Flemming in Hamburg." *Der Cicerone* I (January, 1922), 3-15.

205 G. L. "Atelier Leblanc." *Artist's Proof* III, 2 (Fall-Winter, 1963-1964), 2-3.

206 La Farge, Henry A. "First Impressions." *Art News* LXIX, 6 (October, 1970), 79-80.

207 Landini, Lando. "Appunti: La Mostra di Jacques Villon alla Galeria Carré." *Paragone* LXVII (July, 1955), 58-62.

208 Langsner, Jules. "The Arensberg Riches of Cubism." *Art News* XLVIII, 7, Part I (November, 1949), 24-25, 61-62.

209 Lassaigne, Jacques. "Les Confrontations de Turin." *Revue de la pensée française,* December, 1953.

210 _____. "Développement de l'oeuvre de Jacques Villon." *Histoire de la Peinture Moderne* III (Geneva and Paris: Skira, 1950), 152-153.

211 _____. "Jacques Villon ou la constance." *Revue de la pensée française,* IX, 11 (November, 1950).

212 Legrand, Francine-Claire. "Expo 58 — Regards sur l'art moderne." *Quadrum* V (1958), 95-136.

213 Lenant, J. J. "L'Oeuvre de Jacques Villon au Musée des Beaux Arts de Lyon." *Bulletin des Musées et Monuments Lyonnais* IV (August, 1952).

214 Levin, Kim. "Jacques Villon's." *Art News* LXII, 10 (February, 1964), 15.

215 Lewis, Virginia. "Prints by Five French Contemporaries." *Carnegie Magazine* XXV, 2 (February, 1951), 57-59.

216 Lhote, André. "Cubisme." *Art d'Aujourd'hui* I, 7-8 (March, 1950), 11-15.

217 Lieberman, William S. "Jacques Villon: His Graphic Art." *The Museum of Modern Art Bulletin* XXI, 1 (Fall, 1953), 1-24.

218 Liberman, Alexander. "Villon." *Vogue,* February, 1955, pp. 78-83.

219 Lonngren, Lillian. "Matisse, Villon." *Art News* LVII, 9 (January, 1959), 15.

220 Lowengrund, Margaret. "Three Print Media." *The Art Digest* XXIII, 16 (May 15, 1949), 19.

221 Lundgren, Tyra. "Fransk-Modernt och Officiellt." *Konstrevy* XXVI, 1, (1950), 15-22.

222 McBride, Henry. "Duchamps du monde." *Art News* LI, 1 (March, 1952), 33-35, 61-62.

223 _____. "Modern Art." *The Dial* LXXIV, 2 (February, 1923), 217-219.

224 _____. "Style, c'est l'homme." *Art News* LI, 10 (February, 1953), 58.

225 "Les Maîtres répondent aux jeunes. Situation de la jeune peinture." *Arts, Spectacles,* October 3, 1956.

226 Marchand, André. "Le Village natal de Jacques Villon." *Catalogue du XXe Salon de Mai,* 1964.

227 Massat, René. "Jacques Villon." *Cahiers d'Art* XXVI (1951), 57-73.

228 Maublanc, Jean-Daniel. "Jacques Villon et le Cubisme." *Époque,* December 1, 1938.

229 Maugis, M. T. "Le Salon d'Automne 1955, salle par salle." *Arts, Spectacles,* November 9-15, 1955.

230 Mellquist, Jerome. "A la Bibliothèque Nationale: l'Oeuvre gravé de Jacques Villon." *XXe Siècle,* April, 1959, pp. 6-7.

231 _____. "La Carnegie International à Pittsburgh." *Art-Documents,* February, 1951.

232 _____. "La Compostezza di Jacques Villon." *Communità* XXVI (August, 1954), 56-59.

233 _____. "The Master of Puteaux and Others." *Apollo* LXXIV, 436 (June, 1961), 198-200.

234 _____. "Jacques Villon." *Art-Documents* XVI (August, 1955), 25.

235 _____. "Jacques Villon." *L'Oeil* II (February 15, 1955), 5-11.

236 _____. "Jacques Villon, Maître de Puteaux." *Art-Documents* III (December, 1950), 4-5.

237 _____. "Jacques Villon o il fuoco dello spirito." *La Biennale di Venezia* VII, 28-29 (June-September, 1957), 11-12.

238 _____. "Jacques Villon ou le feu de l'esprit." *Synthèses* XI, 119-120 (April-May, 1956), 133-137.

239 Melot, Michel. "The Cubists and Etching." Translated by Angus Malcolm. *Apollo,* N.S. XCVI, 126 (August, 1972), 138-143.

240 Menetrier, Jacques. "L'Oeuvre de Villon." *Planète,* October-November, 1961.

241 Mercier, Georges. "Le Renouveau de l'art sacré en France depuis 1945." *Médecine de France* XCII (1958), 21-36.

242 Michelson, Annette. "Paris: La Grande Saison." *Arts* XXXV, 8-9 (May-June, 1961), 44-51.

243 Mills, John F. "Portrait of the Artist as Printmaker." *Criticism* II, 4 (Fall, 1960), 342-350.

244 Mock, Jean Yves. "Jacques Villon at the Bibliothèque Nationale." *Apollo* LXX, 413 (July, 1959), 3.

245 Moholy, Lucia. "Switzerland." *The Burlington Magazine* CV, 721 (April, 1963), 184.

246 Morand, Kathleen. "Paris." *The Burlington Magazine* CIII, 699 (June, 1961), 292.

247 Morel, Abbé Maurice. "Hommage à Jacques Villon." *Journal de l'Amateur d'Art,* June 25, 1963.

248 Morsell, Mary. "Jacques Villon, Marie Harriman Galleries." *The Art News* XXXII, 16 (Januayr 20, 1934), 6.

249 Mortimer, Raymond. "Jacques Villon." *Horizon* XII (August, 1945).

250 Muller, Joseph-Emile. "Des Cubistes aux premiers abstraits." In *La Peinture Moderne* IV, published with the collaboration of Raymond Cogniat, et. al., and with the assistance of Robert Maillard. Paris: Fernand Hazan, 1965, 30-33.

251 Mundt, Alice. "Prints by Jacques Villon." *Worcester Art Museum Arts Bulletin* XXIV, 5 (February, 1959), 18-19.

252 Munro, Eleanor C. "Villon." *Art News* LV, 10 (February, 1957), 9.

253 Nacenta, Raymond. "École de Paris 1956." *Art et Style* XLI (1956), cover by Jacques Villon.

254 Neilson, Katharine B. "Prints and Drawings: Recent Acquisitions." *Bulletin of Rhode Island School of Design, Museum Notes* X, 1 (November, 1964), 1-3.

255 "News of Villon." *The Art Digest* XIX, 13 (April 1, 1945), p. 57.

256 Nicolson, Benedict. "Lucien Goldschmidt, Inc., New York." *The Burlington Magazine* CXII, 811 (October, 1970), 715.

257 "New York Season." *The Art Digest* V, 4 (November 15, 1930), 16-17.

258 Ozenfant, Amédée. "Les Arts." *France-Amérique,* May 1-8, 1949.

259 D. P. "Bianco e nero." *Graphis* XIII, 69 (January-February, 1957), 84-87.

260 D. P. "L'Exposition internationale de dessins et gravures de Lugano." *Alte und Neue Kunst* VI, 4 (1955), 10-11.

261 Pach, Walter. "Incarnation of Old Dutch." *The Saturday Review,* November 7, 1953.

262 _____. "The Outlook for Modern Art." *Parnassus* VIII, 4 (April, 1936), 5-8, 41.

263 _____ and Villon, Jacques. "Thus is Cubism Cultivated." *Art News* XLVIII, 3 (May, 1949), 23-25, 51.

264 "Petit dictionnaire des années héroiques (1907-1917)." *XXe Siècle,* N.S. XXVIII, 26 (May, 1966), 99-100.

265 Pia, Pascal. "Livres de peintres." *L'Oeil* XXXV (November, 1957), 63-71, 78.

266 Pichard, Joseph. "Modern Stained Glass in France." *Graphis* XVII, 96 (July-August, 1961), 276-283.

267 Picon, Gaëtan. "Discours sur Villon prononcé à ses funérailles." *Gazette des Beaux Arts* VI, 62 (October, 1963), 177-178.

268 Pincus-Witten, R. "New York." *Artforum* IX, 3 (November, 1970), 84.

269 Podestà, Attilio. "Le Sezioni Straniere." *Emporium* CXVI, 691-692 (July-August, 1952).

270 _____. "La XXVIII Biennale di Venezia. Gli stranieri." *Emporium* CXXIV, 741 (September, 1956), 116-123.

271 Ponente, Nello. "La Partecipazione Straniera alla Biennale." *Litteratura* IV, 23 (September-October, 1956), 20-26.

272 Popovitch, Olga. "Musée des Beaux-Arts de Rouen; l'Art contemporain." *La Revue du Louvre et des Musées de France* XVIII, 6 (1968), 431-434.

273 Poulain, Gaston. "De Valery à Villon." *La Dépêche du Midi,* June 2, 1955.

274 Pradel, Marie-Noëlle. "La Maison Cubiste en 1912." *Art de France* I (1961), 177-186.

275 Prinner, Anton. "La Gravure." *Art d'Aujourd'hui* I, 3 (October, 1949), 7-15.

276 "A propos de l'exposition: Le Mouvement dans l'art contemporain." *Pour l'art* XLIII (1955), 3-34.

277 "Propos de Jacques Villon." *Le Peintre,* October 15, 1963, p. 12.

278 "Propos sur les vitraux de la Cathédrale de Metz." *Art Chrétien* VII (1957), 25.

279 Prossor, John. "Jacques Villon at the Galerie Louis Carré." *Apollo* LXV, 386 (April, 1957), 153.

280 R. H. "Four judges 'go to town': the Pittsburgh International." *The Studio* CXLI, 695 (February, 1951), 58-59.

281 Ragghianti, Carlo L. "Jacques Villon." *Sele Arte* IV, 24 (May-June, 1956), 50-51.

282 Raymond, Marie. "Jacques Villon." *Kroniek van Kunst en Kultur,* July-August, 1956.

283 Raynor, Vivien. "Jacques Villon." *Arts Magazine* XXVIII, 9 (May-June, 1964), 35-36.

284 "Recent Acquisitions." *City Art Museum of Saint Louis Bulletin* II, 3 (September-October, 1966), 1-11.

285 "Recent Acquisitions." *Los Angeles County Museum Bulletin of the Art Division* VI, 2 (Spring, 1954), 23-30.

286 Refsum, Tor. "Jacques Villon." *Kunsten Idag* XXXI (1955), 16-25, 55-57.

287 Régamey, P.-R. "Ni Snobisme, ni démagogie." *Art Sacré* VII-VIII (March-April, 1952), 1-22.

288 René-Jean. "Devant les tableaux de Jacques Villon." *Arts de France,* February, 1948, pp. 31-36.

289 "Réponse à un questionnaire de Gaston Diehl et Yvon Taillander sur l'espace et le temps dans le peinture." *Amis de l'Art,* May, 1949.

290 "Réponse à une enquête de J. Villon sur l'art et le public." *Lettres Françaises,* March 29, 1946.

291 "Réponse de Jacques Villon à une enquête sur le réalisme socialiste." *Preuves,* April, 1952 (reprinted in *Preuves,* July, 1953, p. 19).

292 Revol, Jean. "Braque et Villon, message vivant du cubisme. I." *La Nouvelle Revue Française* IX, 104 (August 1, 1961), 321-325.

293 ———. "Braque et Villon (fin)." *La Nouvelle Revue Française* IX, 105 (September 1, 1961), 524-527.

294 ———. "La Figure dans l'oeuvre graphique de Villon." *La Nouvelle Revue Française,* March, 1963.

95 Rey, Jean Dominique. "La Figure dans l'oeuvre gravé de Jacques Villon." *Jardin des Arts,* February, 1963, pp. 72-73.

96 Ribemont-Dessaignes, Georges. "Avant Dada." *Les Lettres Nouvelles,* November, 1955, pp. 534-548; continued in December, 1955, pp. 733-753.

97 Robbins, Daniel. "Recent Acquisitions." *Bulletin of Rhode Island School of Design, Museum Notes* LV, 2 (December, 1968), 67.

98 Roberts, Keith. "Current and Forthcoming Exhibitions." *The Burlington Magazine* CVI, 730 (January, 1964), 49.

99 Rolfsen, Alf. "Painting and Sculpture at Freia and Marabou." *Oslo-Stockholm,* 1955.

300 Rosenblum, Robert. "The Duchamp Family." *Arts* XXXI, 7 (April, 1957), 20-23.

301 Rostrup, Haavard. "Jacques Villon." *Konstrevy* XXIV, 3 (1948), 116-120.

302 Rouir, Eugène. "Essai de classement des estampes de Jacques Villon." *Le Livre et L'Estampe* LV-LVI (1968), 213-222.

303 ———. "Une Lithographie non décrite de Jacques Villon." *Le Livre et L'Estampe* XXIX-XL (1964), 276-277.

304 Russoli, Franco. "La Collezione Thompson alla Galleria d'Arte Moderna a Torino." *Arti,* 1961, pp. 111-115.

305 Rydbeck-Zuhn, Ingrid. "Fauvister, Kubister, Blaue Reiter, utländska paviljonger-franska separatut ställningar." *Konstrevy* XXVI, 4-5 (1950), 219.

306 B. S. "Il Premio Carnegie a Jacques Villon." *Emporium* CXIII, 675 (April, 1951).

307 Sargeant, Winthrop. "Dada's Daddy." *Life* XXXII, 17 (April 28, 1952), 101-111.

308 Sayre, Ann. "Exhibitions." *International Studio* XCVII, 403 (December, 1930), 100-101.

309 Schiff, Gert. "The VI Sao Paulo Bienal." *Art International* V, 10 (Christmas, 1961), 55-64.

310 Schneider, Pierre. "The indefatigable." *Art News* LVIII, 6 (September, 1959), 47.

311 ———. "Paris." *Art News* LXII, 1 (March, 1963), 47.

312 Schulze, Franz. "Degas, Villon graphics." *Art News* LXIII, 4 (Summer, 1964), 48.

313 Scialoja, Toti. "Jacques Villon." *L'Immagine,* January-February, 1948, pp. 406-411.

314 Seligmann, Kurt. "Simplicity in Art." *Magazine of Art* XLIV, 3 (March, 1951), 102-106.

315 Selvig, F. "Recent Accessions." *The Minneapolis Institute of Arts Bulletin* LI (September, 1962), 102-103.

316 Senez, Monique. "Interview avec Jacques Villon, Prix Carnegie." *Point de vue,* November 2, 1950, pp. 15-17.

317 "Sens de l'art moderne. Enquête menée par l'Atelier avec les réponses inédites de quelques-uns des grands artistes de notre temps." *Zodiaque* I & II, 18 & 19 (1954), 5-52, 57-123.

318 Serullaz, Maurice. "A travers les expositions." *France Illustration* No. 426 (September, 1955), 72.

319 Seuphor, Michel. "Klee et Villon." *Preuves* LV (July, 1955), 69-70.

320 ———. "Paris." *Arts Digest* XXIX, 18 (July 1, 1955), 24.

321 Sibert, C.-H. "Souvenirs de Jacques Villon sur une époque héroïque." *Arts, Spectacles,* October 29, 1953.

322 Silvagni. "Chez Jacques Villon." *Gazette de Lausanne (La Gazette Littéraire),* December 10, 1955.

323 Smith, Lawrence. "Jacques Villon." *Arts* XXXV, 3 (December, 1960), 53-54.

324 "The Solid Gold Muse." *Time* LXXVIII, 21 (November 24, 1961), 58.

325 Souriau, Etienne. "Note sur le cheval dans l'art." *Revue d'esthétique,* 1955, pp. 398-408.

326 Spencer, Charles S. "Documenta III, Creative individuality in contemporary art surveyed at Kassel." *Studio International* CLXVIII, 857 (September, 1964), 110-117.

327 Staber, Margit. "Austellungen in Zurich." *Art International* VII, 5 (May 25, 1963), 66-68.

328 Stahly, Francois. "Jacques Villon et son oeuvre graphique." *Graphis* X, 53 (1954), 236-237, 257-258.

329 ———. "Pariser Kunstchronik." *Werk,* July, 1955.

330 Steegmuller, Francis. "A Master of 'Volupté.' " *Apollo,* N.S. LXXIX (March, 1964), 229-231.

331 ———. "Jacques Villon: an Appreciation." *Artist's Proof* IV, 1 (1964), 11-22.

332 Sthyr, Jorgen. "Kobberstiksamlingens nyerhvervelser." *Kunstmuseets Asskrift* XXXVII (1950), 138-152.

333 Taillandier, Yvon. "De la pyramide au Carré: Causerie avec Jacques Villon." *XXe Siècle,* N.S. XXI, 12 (May-June, 1959), 17-24.

334 ———. "Jacques Villon et la peinture contemporaine." *Catalogue du Salon de Mai,* 1952.

335 ———. "Propos de Jacques Villon." *Amis de l'Art,* March, 1952.

336 ———. "Propos de Jacques Villon." *Catalogue du Salon de mai,* 1955.

337 Tériade, E. "Documentaire sur la jeune peinture, III. Conséquences du cubisme." *Cahiers d'Art* V (1930), 17-27.

338 Thormé, J.-R. "Jacques Villon graveur et illustrateur." *Le Courrier Graphique* XXIV, 104 (May-June, 1959), 3-10.

339 "Torino: Mostra di pittori d'oggi, Italiani e Francesi." *Emporium* CXV, 685 (January, 1952), pp. 31-33.

340 Tyler, Parker. "Jacques Villon." *Art News* LIV, 2 (April, 1955), 44-45.

341 Valancay, Robert. "Visite à Jacques Villon." *Sang Nouveau* (Charleroi), 1929.

342 Vallier, Dora. "Intelligence de Jacques Villon." *Cahiers d'Art* XXX (1955), 33-136.

343 "La XXVIa Biennale de Venezia." *Sele Arte* I (July-August, 1952), pp. 25-29.

344 Veronesi, Giulia. "Cento Quadri di Jacques Villon." *Emporium* CXXIV, 800 (August, 1961), 51-54.

345 _____. "Disegni di Villon." *Emporium* CXXIII, 737 (May, 1956), 228-229.

346 _____. "L'Opera intera di Jacques Villon." *Emporium* CXIII, 677 (May, 1951), 233-234.

347 _____. "Parigi: une mostra di Jacques Villon." *Emporium* CXXII, 727 (July, 1955), 38-41.

348 Vieillard, Roger. "Les Gravures de Jacques Villon." *Jardin des Arts* LV (May, 1959), 446-450.

349 Vieira, Jose Feraldo. "VI Bienal de Arti de São Paolo." *Habitat* XII, 65 (1961), 43.

350 "Jacques Villon." *Art Présent* III (1947), 32.

351 "Jacques Villon." *Das Kunstwerk* XVII, 1 (July, 1963).

352 "Jacques Villon." *Vancouver Art Gallery Bulletin* XXIII, 6 (1956), 2.

353 "Jacques Villon." *XXe Siècle* XXV 22, Sup. 8-9 (December, 1963).

354 "Jacques Villon, Brummer Galleries." *The Art News* XXVI, 26 (March 31, 1928), 11.

355 "Jacques Villon, Brummer Galleries." *The Art News* XXIX, 4 (October 25, 1930), 10.

356 "Jacques Villon. L'Exposition, Galerie Guiot." *Beaux-Arts*, June 10, 1938, p. 4.

357 "Jacques Villon, Jean Bazaine, Hans Hartung; ausstellung im Kunsthaus, Zürich." *Werk* L, Sup. 103 (May, 1963).

358 "Virgil by Villon." *Time*, May 6, 1955, pp. 42-43.

359 Volboudt, Pierre. "L'Esprit de la ligne." *XXe Siècle*, March, 1958.

360 _____. "Gravures de Villon." *XXe Siècle*, June, 1957.

361 Vox, Maximilien. "Jacques Villon, peinture d'aviation." *Air-France Revue* (Autumn, 1954), 23-30.

362 Warnod, André. "L'Assiette au Beurre." *Prisme des Arts* X (March, 1957), 16-17.

363 Watson, Forbes. "The Month in the Galleries." *The Arts* XIII, 5 (May, 1928), 313, 320.

364 Watt, Alexander. "Art as the Inspiration for Art." *The Studio* CLXVI, 845 (September, 1963), 122.

365 _____. "Paris Commentary." *The Studio* CLXII, 821 (September, 1961), 99-101.

366 _____. "Jacques Villon doyen of the School of Paris." *The Studio* CLXIV, 831 (July, 1962), 10-11, 35.

367 _____. "Villon." *Art in America* L, 3 (Fall, 1962), 114-116.

368 Weller, Arthur S. "Chicago." *Art Digest* XXVII, 7 (January 1, 1953), 11.

369 Wellman, Rita. "Pioneers and Contemporaries." *Parnassus* VI, 1 (January, 1934), 20.

370 Wheelock, Warren. "Understanding Modern Art: A Discussion of Jacques Villon's 'The Philosopher.'" *Art Instruction* II, 5 (May, 1938), 26-27.

371 Wojciechowski, Aleksander. "XXVIII Biennale w Wenecji." *Przeglad Artystyczny* III (1956), 6-30.

372 "Worcester Museum Has 'Ultra' Show." *American Art News* XX, 5 (November 12, 1921), 1, 7.

373 Young, Mahonri-Sharp. "The Man from Ohio: Ferdinand Howald and his Painters." *The Arts in Ireland* II, 3 (1973), 13.

374 Young, Vernon. "Villon: Prints and Drawings." *Arts* XXXI, 5 (February, 1957), 55.

375 "Zwei schweizer Sammler." *Schweizer Kunst*, 1959, p. 81.

BOOKS AND GENERAL WORKS

376 Angoulvent, P.-J., *La Chalcographie du Louvre, Histoire et description des collections.* Paris: Musées Nationaux, Palais du Louvre, 1926.

377 *Annual Report 1967-1968.* Chicago: The Art Institute of Chicago, 1968.

378 Apollinaire, Guillaume. *Les Peintres cubistes; méditations esthétiques.* Paris: Figuiere, 1913.

379 *The Louise and Walter Arensberg Collection: 20th Century Section.* Introduction by Henry Clifford. Philadelphia: Philadelphia Museum of Art, 1954.

380 Arland, Marcel. *Chroniques de la peinture moderne.* Paris: Corréa, 1949.

381 Arnason, H. Harvard. *History of Modern Art: Painting, Sculpture, Architecture.* New York: Harry N. Abrams, Inc., 1968.

382 Barr, Alfred H., Jr. *Cubism and Abstract Art.* New York: The Museum of Modern Art, 1936.

383 _____. *Masters of Modern Art.* New York: The Museum of Modern Art, 1954.

384 *La Bibliothèque de Fr. Sabatier D'Espeyran.* Montpellier: Causse and Castelnau, 1966.

385 Bouleau, Charles. *Charpentes; la géométrie secrète des peintres.* Preface by Jacques Villon, Paris: Editions du Seuil, 1963. (See also the translation by Jonathan Griffin: *The Painters' Secret Geometry: a Study of Composition in Art.* New York: Harcourt, Brace, and World, 1963).

386 Brown, Milton W. *The Story of the Armory Show.* New York: The Joseph H. Hirshhorn Foundation, 1963.

387 Brun, H. J. *Sonja Henie-Niels Onstad Collection.* Oslo, 1968.

388 Canaday, John. *Mainstreams of Modern Art.* New York: Simon and Schuster, 1959.

389 *Catalogue de la Chalcographie du Louvre.* Paris: Musées Nationaux, Palais du Louvre, 1954.

390 Charbonnier, Georges. *Le Monologue du peintre.* Paris: Julliard, 1959.

391 Charensol, Georges. *Les Grands maîtres de la peinture moderne. (Histoire générale de la peinture, V. 22.)* Lausanne: Editions Recontre, 1967.

392 Cooper, Douglas. *The Cubist Epoch.* London: Phaidon Press, 1971.

393 Dauberville, Henry. *La Bataille de l'Impressionnisme.* Paris: Bernheim-Jeune, 1967).

394 Delevoy, Robert L. *Dimensions of the 20th Century 1900-1945.* Translated by Stuart Gilbert. Geneva: Skira, 1965.

395 *Le Dessin francais au XXe Siècle.* Preface by Jean Cassou. Lausanne: Editions Mermod, 1951.

396 *Dictionnaire universel d l'art et des artistes.* V. 3. Paris: Fernand Hazan, 1967.

397 Dorazio, Piero. *La fantasia dell'arte nella vita moderna.* Rome: Polverone e Quinti, 1955.

398 Dorival, Bernard. *Les Etapes de la peinture française contemporaine.* Vol. II: *Le Fauvisme et le Cubisme.* Paris: Gallimard, 1944.

399 _____. *Histoire de l'art.* Paris: Gallimard, La Pléiade, 1969.

400 _____. *Les Peintres du XXe siècle: Nabis, Fauves, Cubistes.* Paris: Editions Pierre Tisne, 1957.

01 _____. *The School of Paris in the Musée d'Art Moderne*. New York: Harry N. Abrams, Inc., 1962.

02 Dreier, Katherine S. *Western Art and the New Era*. New York: Brentano's, 1923.

03 _____. *Modern Art*. New York: Société Anonyme, Inc., 1926.

04 _____; Sweeney, James Johnson; and Gabo, Naum. *Three Lectures on Modern Art*. New York: Philosophical Library, 1949.

05 Eddy, Arthur Jerome. *Cubists and Post-Impressionism*. Chicago: A. C. McClurg and Co., 1914.

06 Fels, Florent. *L'Art vivant de nos jours: de 1900 à nos jours, 1914-1955*. Geneva: Pierre Cailleur, 1950-1956.

07 Forster-Hahn, Francoise. *French and School of Paris Paintings in the Yale University Art Gallery*. New Haven: Yale University Press, 1968.

08 Francastel, Pierre. *Histoire de la peinture française*. Paris and Brussels: Elsevier, 1955.

09 *French Drawing of the XXth Century*. Introduction by Jean Cassou. London: Thames and Hudson, 1955.

10 Fry, Edward F. *Cubism*. London: Thames and Hudson, 1966.

11 Gleizes, Albert. *Du Cubisme et des moyens de la comprendre*. Paris: La Cible, Povolozky, 1920.

12 _____, and Metzinger, Jean. *Du Cubisme*. Paris: Compagnie Française des Arts graphiques, 1947.

13 Golding, John. *Cubism: A History and an Analysis, 1907-1914*. London: Faber and Faber, Ltd., 1968.

14 Gonse, Henriette. *La Composition*. Paris: Publications filmées d'art et d'histoire, 1965.

15 Guggenheim, Peggy. *Art of This Century 1910-1942*. New York: Art of This Century Gallery, 1942.

16 Gyllensten, Lars. *Sonja Henie-Niels Onstad Collection 1960-1962*. Olso: Kirstes Boktrykkheri, 1962.

17 Habasque, Guy. *Le Cubisme*. Geneva: Skira, 1959.

18 Haftmann, Werner. *Malerei im 20. Jahrhundert*. Munich: Prestel Verlag, 1965.

19 Hamilton, George Heard. *Collection of the Société Anonyme: Museum of Modern Art 1920*. New Haven: Yale University Art Gallery, 1950.

20 _____. *Painting and Sculpture in Europe, 1880 to 1940*. Harmondsworth, Middlesex: Penguin Books, 1967.

421 _____, and Agee, William C. *Raymond Duchamp-Villon*. New York: Walker and Co., 1967.

422 *A Handbook to the Solomon R. Guggenheim Museum Collection*. New York: The Solomon R. Guggenheim Foundation, 1959.

423 *Illustrated Books from the Renaissance to the Present*. Catalogue No. 40. New York: Lucien Goldschmidt, Inc., 1972.

424 *Important Original Prints for Museums and Collectors*. Catalogue No. 10. New York: Peter H. Deitsch Gallery, 1961.

425 Johnson, Una E. *Twentieth Century Drawings Part I: 1900-1940*. "Drawings of the Masters" series. New York: Shorewood Publishers, Inc., 1964.

426 Lambert, Jean-Clarence. *La Peinture abstraite. (Histoire générale de la peinture, V. 23.)* Lausanne: Editions Recontre, 1966.

427 Lebel, Robert. *Marcel Duchamp*. Translated by George Heard Hamilton. New York: Grove Press, 1959.

428 Lhote, André. *Traité du paysage*. Paris: Floury, 1948.

429 Liberman, Alexander. *The Artist in His Studio*. New York: Viking Press, 1960.

430 Maywald, Wilhelm. *Portrait + Atelier*. Zurich: Verlags AG "Die Arche," 1958.

431 Miguel, Jean. *Cours de philosophie: exposés et documents*. Paris: H. Roudil, 1961.

432 Muller, Joseph-Emile. *La Peinture moderne de Manet à Mondrian*. Paris: Fernand Hazan, 1960.

433 Pach, Walter. *The Masters of Modern Art*. New York: B. W. Huebsch, Inc., 1924.

434 _____. *Queer Thing, Painting*. New York and London: Harper and Brothers, 1938.

435 _____. *Raymond Duchamp-Villon, sculpteur (1876-1918)*. Paris: J. Povolozky, 1924.

436 *Les Peintres et le livre*. No. 6. Geneva: Nicolas Rausch, 1957.

437 Pierre, Jose. *Le Cubisme. (Histoire Générale de la peinture, V. 19.)* Lausanne: Editions Recontre, 1966.

438 *The John Quinn Collection of Paintings, Water Colors, Drawings and Sculpture*. Huntington, New York: Pidgeon Hill Press, 1926.

439 Raynal, Maurice. *A History of Modern Painting from Picasso to Surrealism*. Geneva: Skira, 1950.

440 _____. *Peinture moderne*. Geneva: Skira, 1953.

441 Reid, B. L. *The Man from New York: John Quinn and his Friends*. New York: Oxford University Press, 1968.

442 *Report, 1920-1921*. New York: Société Anonyme, Inc., 1920-1921.

443 Rheims, Maurice. *Catalogue Bolaffi d'Art Moderne: Le Marché de Paris*. Turin: Giulio Bolaffi, 1966.

444 Robbins, Daniel. *Painting Between the Wars, 1918-1940*. New York, Toronto, London: McGraw Hill Book Co., 1966.

445 Rosenbloom, Robert. *Cubism and Twentieth Century Art*. New York: Harry N. Abrams, Inc., 1960.

446 *Sculptures de Duchamp-Villon*. Paris: Louis Carré, 1963.

447 Serullaz, Maurice. *Le Cubisme*. Paris: Presses Universitaires Francaises, 1963.

448 Seuphor, Michel. *L'Art abstrait, 2. 1918/1938*. Paris: Maeght, 1972.

449 _____. *Dictionnaire de la peinture abstraite*, Paris: Fernand Hazan, 1957.

450 _____. *La Peinture abstraite: sa genèse, son expansion*. Paris: Flammarion, 1962.

451 Sima, Michel. *21 visages d'artistes*. Paris: Nathan, 1959.

452 *Société Anonyme (The First Museum of Modern Art 1920-1944). Volume I: Documents*. New York: Arno Press, 1972.

453 *Société Anonyme (The First Museum of Modern Art 1920-1944). Volume II: Pamphlets*. New York: Arno Press, 1972.

454 Tardieu, Jean. *De la Peinture abstraite*. Lausanne: H.-L. Mermod, 1960.

455 *Twentieth Century Graphic Art: the Ernest Steefel Collection*. New Haven: Yale University Art Gallery, 1959.

456 Vallier, Dora. *L'Art abstrait*. Paris: Livre de Poche, 1967.

457 _____. *Histoire de la peinture 1870-1940: les mouvements d'avant-garde*. Brussels: La Connaissance, 1963.

458 _____. *Kunst und Zeugnis*. Zurich: Peter Schifferli Verlags AG "Die Arche," 1961. (Conversations with G. Braque, J. Miró, F. Léger, Brancusi, J. Villon.)

459 Walden, Nell. *Der Sturm*. Baden-Baden: W. Klein, 1954.

460 Warnod, André. *Ceux de la Butte*. Paris: René Julliard, 1947.

461 *Works from the Peggy Guggenheim Foundation*. New York: The Solomon R. Guggenheim Foundation, 1969.

For full information, see Bibliography. Numbers in parentheses refer to Bibliography.

MONOGRAPHS

1921
(38) Pach, Walter. *Villon.*

1945
(39) René-Jean. *Jacques Villon.*

1948
(33) Eluard, Paul and René-Jean. *Jacques Villon ou L'Art glorieux.*

1950
(26) Auberty, Jacqueline and Pérussaux, Charles. *Jacques Villon, Catalogue de son oeuvre gravé.*

(34) Lassaigne, Jacques. *Jacques Villon.*

1954
(25) Adhémar, Jean. *Jacques Villon.*

1955
(35) Lassaigne, Jacques. *Eloge de Jacques Villon.*

1956
(32) Dorival, Bernard. *Jacques Villon.*

1957
(40) Vallier, Dora. *Jacques Villon: Oeuvres de 1897 à 1956.*

1958
(29) Crespelle, Jean-Paul. *Villon.*

1959
(30) de Ginestet, Colette. "L'Oeuvre graphique de Villon." Unpublished thesis at the École de Louvre.

(42) *Jacques Villon: Cent croquis 1894-1904.*

1960
(36) Mellquist, Jerome. *Les Caricatures de Jacques Villon.*

1961
(27) *Cent tableaux de Jacques Villon.*

1962
(41) Venturi, Lionello. *Jacques Villon.*

1963
(28) Cogniat, Raymond. *Villon-Peintures.*

(37) Morel, Abbé Maurice; Picon, Gaëtan; Daidel, Georges; and Cassou, Jean. *Souvenir de Jacques Villon.*

In preparation
(30) de Ginestet, Colette. *Jacques Villon. Oeuvre graphique.*

ARTICLES

1901
(125) Delorme, Hugues. " 'Jacques Villon'—portrait de l'artiste par Widhopff." *Le Courrier Français.*

1910
(135) Dumont, Pierre. "A propos d'un portrait du peintre Jacques Villon." *Rouen-Gazette.*

1913
(200) Kahn, Gustave. "La Réalisation d'un ensemble d'architecture et de décoration." *L'Art décoratif.*

(174) Guiart, (Dr.) Jules. "Le Macabre dans l'Art." *Aesculape.*

1914
(50) Apollinaire, Guillaume. "Quatre nouveaux artistes français." *Paris-Journal.*

1921
(372) "Worcester Museum Has 'Ultra' Show." *American Art News.*

1922
(142) "Exhibition of Paintings by Members of the Société Anonyme." *Bulletin of the Worcester Art Museum.*

(204) Kuppers, P. E. "Die Sammlung Max Leon Flemming in Hamburg." *Der Cicerone.*

1923
(222) McBride, Henry. "Modern Art." *The Dial.*

1928
(354) "Jacques Villon, Brummer Galleries." *The Art News.*

(363) Watson, Forbes. "The Month in the Galleries." *The Arts.*

1929
(341) Valancay, Robert. "Visite à Jacques Villon." *Sang Nouveau.*

1930
(355) "Jacques Villon, Brummer Galleries." *The Art News.*

(257) "New York Season." *The Art Digest.*

(164) Goodrich, Lloyd. "Villon." *The Arts.*

(308) Sayre, Ann. "Exhibitions." *International Studio.*

(337) Tériade, E. "Documentaire sur la jeune peinture. III. Conséquences du cubisme." *Cahiers d'Art.*

1932
(43) *Abstraction-Création, art non-figuratif, I.*

1933

(44) *Abstraction-Création, art non-figuratif, II.*

(64) Bazin, Germain. "Jacques Villon" in "Histoire de l'art contemporaine," *L'Amour de l'Art.*

1934

(191) "If Villon Were King!" *The Art Digest.*

(248) Morsell, Mary. "Jacques Villon, Marie Harriman Galleries." *The Art News.*

(369) Wellman, Rita. "Pioneers and Contemporaries." *Parnassus.*

1936

(262) Pach, Walter. "The Outlook for Modern Art." *Parnassus.*

(112) Combe, Jacques. "Graveurs sur Cuivre." *L'Amour de l'Art.*

1938

(370) Wheelock, Warren. "Understanding Modern Art, A Discussion of Jacques Villon's 'The Philosopher.'" *Art Instruction.*

(356) "Jacques Villon. L'Exposition, Galerie Guiot." *Beaux-Arts.*

(228) Maublanc, Jean-Daniel. "Jacques Villon et le Cubisme." *Epoque.*

1941

(62) Bazaine, Jean. "Tour d'Horizon." *Nouvelle Revue Française.*

(183) Hamilton, George Heard. "The Exhibition of the Collection of the Société Anonyme—Museum of Modern Art: 1920." *Bulletin of the Associates in Fine Arts at Yale University.*

1944

(63) Bazaine, Jean. "Jacques Villon." *Poésie.*

(51) Arbois, Simone. "Jacques Villon." *Volontés.*

(172) Grenier, Jean. "Jacques Villon." *Combat.*

(137) Elgar, Frank. "Jacques Villon." *Carrefour.*

1945

(182) Hamilton, George Heard. "Duchamp-Villon, Villon." *Bulletin of the Associates in Fine Arts at Yale University.*

(134) "Duchamp et al." *Art News.*

(255) "News of Villon." *The Art Digest.*

(150) Frénaud, André. "Jacques Villon." (poem). *Horizon.*

(249) Mortimer, Raymond. "Jacques Villon." *Horizon.*

1946

(92) "California School of Fine Arts, Maintained by the San Francisco Art Association, Exhibition Surveys Cubism." *Architect and Engineer.*

(290) "Réponse à une enquête de J. Villon sur l'art et le public." *Lettres Françaises.*

(60) Barotte, René. "Jacques Villon, illustrateur." *Le Livre et Ses Amis.*

1947

(350) "Jacques Villon." *Art Présent.*

1948

(107) Chevalier, D. "Exposition de peintures a la galerie Louis Carré." *Beaux-Arts, Littérature, Spectacles.*

(104) Chastel, André. "Une Semaine dans le monde." *Le Monde.*

(313) Scialoja, Toti. "Jacques Villon." *L'Immagine.*

(288) René-Jean. "Devant les tableaux de Jacques Villon." *Arts de France.*

(67) Beeson, George. "Jacques Villon, doyen des jeunes peintres." *Ce Soir.*

(181) Hamilton, George Heard. "The Dialectic of Later Cubism: Villon's Jockey." *Magazine of Art.*

(301) Rostrup, Haavard. "Jacques Villon." *Konstrevy.*

1949

(76) Breuning, Margaret. "Jacques Villon." *The Art Digest.*

(84) Burrows, Carlyle. "Art in Review." *New York Herald Tribune.*

(128) Deveree, Howard. "Elder Modernist." *New York Times.*

(258) Ozenfant, Amédée. *Les Arts, France-Amerique.*

(220) Lowengrund, Margaret. "Three Print Media." *The Art Digest.*

(289) "Réponse à un questionnaire de Gaston Diehl et Yvon Taillandier sur l'espace et le temps dans le peinture." *Amis de l'Art.*

(263) Pach, Walter and Villon, Jacques. "Thus is Cubism Cultivated." *Art News.*

(179) Haas, Irvin. "Jacques Villon's." *Art News.*

(275) Prinner, Anton. "La Gravure." *Art d'Aujourd'hui.*

(208) Langsner, Jules. "The Arensberg Riches of Cubism." *Art News.*

(187) Hess, Thomas B. "Villon-Feininger: Refining Cubism." *Art News.*

(104) Estienne, Charles. "Jacques Villon." *Art d'Aujourd'hui.*

1950

(119) "The Cube Root." *The Art Digest.*

(216) Lhote, André. "Cubisme." *Art d'Aujourd'hui.*

(68) Bill, Max. "Jacques Villon. Zum 75 Geburtstag." *Werk.*

(127) Descargues, Pierre. "Jacques Villon, Prix Carnegie 1950." *Arts Paris.*

(97) "Carnegie Contrasts." *Time.*

(186) Hess, Thomas B. "Introduction to Abstract Art." *Art News Annual.*

(316) Senez, Monique. "Interview avec Jacques Villon, Prix Carnegie." *Point de vue.*

(70) Bird, Paul. "First Post-War Carnegie International: An End and a Beginning." *The Art Digest.*

(211) Lassaigne, Jacques. "Jacques Villon ou la constance." *Revue de la Pensée Française.*

(166) Grafly, Dorothy. "The 1950 Pittsburgh International." *American Artist.*

(236) Mellquist, Jerome. "Jacques Villon, Maître de Puteaux." *Art-Documents.*

(210) Lassaigne, Jacques. "Développement de l'oeuvre de Jacques Villon." *Histoire de la Peinture Moderne.*

(221) Lundgren, Tyra. "Fransk-Modernt och Officiellt." *Konstrevy.*

(305) Rydbeck-Zuhn, Ingrid. "Fauvister, Kubister, Blaue Reiter, utländska paviljonger-franska separatut ställningar." *Konstrevy.*

(332) Sthyr, Jorgen. "Kobberstiksamlingens nyerhvervelser." *Kunstmuseets Asskrift.*

(66) Bergmark, Torsten. "Biennalen 1950." *Paletten.*

(141) Estienne, Charles. "Jacques Villon eller ryrdens poesi." *Paletten.*

(199) H. K. "Bemerkungen zu fünf Radierungen." *Werk.*

1951

(231) Mellquist, Jerome. "La Carnegie International à Pittsburgh." *Art-Documents.*

(215) Lewis, Virginia. "Prints by Five French Contemporaries." *Carnegie Magazine.*

(280) R. H. "Four judges 'go to town': The Pittsburgh International." *The Studio.*

(156) George, Waldemar. "Jacques Villon et le Cubisme français." *Le Peintre.*

(115) Courthion, Pierre. "Hier et aujourd'hui." *XXᵉ Siècle.*

(123) Degand, Léon. "A propos de la rétrospective de Jacques Villon." *Art d'Aujourd'hui.*

(314) Seligmann, Kurt. "Simplicity in Art." *Magazine of Art.*

(132) Dorival, Bernard. "Jacques Villon." *La Table Ronde.*

(178) Guth, Paul. "Jacques Villon, Fra Angelico normand." *Le Figaro Littéraire.*

(306) B. S. "Il Premio Carnegie à Jacques Villon." *Emporium.*

(116) Courthion, Pierre. "Jacques Villon ou le don d'émouvoir." *Art-Documents.*

(346) Veronesi, Giulia. "L'Opera intera di Jacques Villon." *Emporium.*

(176) Guichard-Meili, Jean. "Jacques Villon." *Esprit.*

(58) "Ausstellung, Kunsthalle, Bern." *Werk.*

(111) *Combat.*

(198) *Journal de l'Amateur d'Art.*

(71) Bligne, Yvon. "Entretien avec Jacques Villon." *Le Peintre.*

(227) Massat, René. "Jacques Villon." *Cahiers d'Art.*

1952
(339) "Torino: Mostra di pittori d'oggi, Italiani e Francesi." *Emporium.*

(114) Courthion, Pierre. "Décomposition et recomposition de l'Espace." *XXᵉ Siècle.*

(335) Taillandier, Yvon. "Propos de Jacques Villon." *Amis de l'Art.*

(222) McBride, Henry. "Duchamps du monde." *Art News.*

(53) Ashton, Dore. "The Duchamps Even." *Art Digest.*

(287) Régamey, P.-R. "Ni Snobisme, ni démagogie." *Art Sacré.*

(291) "Réponse de Jacques Villon à une enquête sur le réalisme socialiste." *Preuves.*

(307) Sargeant, Winthrop. "Dada's Daddy." *Life.*

(334) Taillandier, Yvon. "Jacques Villon et la peinture contemporaine." *Catalogue du Salon de Mai.*

(83) Busse, Jacques. "Le Salon à mai." *Journal de l'Amateur d'Art.*

(81) Hammer, Andrew. "Exhibitions." *The Architectural Review.*

(269) Podestà, Attilio. "Le Sezioni Straniere." *Emporium.*

(343) "La XXVIᵃ Biennale di Venezia." *Sele Arte.*

(162) Gindertael, R. V. "Pour aider à mieux comprendre 'le passage de la ligne.' " *Art d'Aujourd'hui.*

(213) Lenant, J. J. "L'Oeuvre de Jacques Villon au Musée des Beaux Arts de Lyon." *Bulletin des Musées et Monuments Lyonnais.*

(108) "Chicago to See Villon Show." *Art Digest.*

(126) De Man, Paul. "Jacques Villon." *Konstrevy.*

1953
(368) Weller, Arthur S. "Chicago." *Art Digest.*

(45) "Abstract of Villon." *Art Digest.*

(224) McBride, Henry. "Style, c'est l'homme." *Art News.*

(169) Gray, Cleve. "Jacques Villon." *Profils.*

(170)_____. "Jacques Villon." *Perspectives U.S.A.*

(122) Degand, Léon. "La Peinture cubiste." *Art d'Aujourd'hui.*

(48) Alvard, Julien. "L'Espace cubiste." *Art d'Aujourd'hui.*

(81) Buffet, Gabrielle. "La Section d'Or." *Art d'Aujourd'hui.*

(133) "The Katherine S. Dreier Bequest." *The Museum of Modern Art Bulletin.*

(217) Lieberman, William S. "Jacques Villon: His Graphic Art." *The Museum of Modern Art Bulletin.*

(190) Howe, Russell Warren. "Jacques Villon." *Apollo.*

(55) Ashton, Dore. "Jacques Villon 'Father of Modern Printmaking.' " *Art Digest.*

(147) Fitzsimmons, James. "Art." *Arts and Architecture.*

(321) Sibert, C.-H. "Souvenirs de Jacques Villon sur une époque héroïque." *Arts, Spectacles.*

(94) Campbell, Lawrence. "Jacques Villon." *Art News.*

(261) Pach, Walter. "Incarnation of Old Dutch." *The Saturday Review.*

(209) Lassaigne, Jacques. "Les Confrontations de Turin." *Revue de la Pensée Française.*

(130) Dorival, Bernard. "Musée National d'Art Moderne, un an d'activité." *La Revue des Arts.*

1954
(148) Fitzsimmons, James. "Art." *Arts and Architecture.*

(285) "Recent Acquisitions." *Los Angeles County Museum Bulletin of the Art Division.*

(232) Mellquist, Jerome. "La Compostezza di Jacques Villon." *Communità.*

(361) Vox, Maximilien. "Jacques Villon, peinture d'aviation." *Air-France Revue.*

(201) Kahnweiler, Daniel-Henry. "Cubism: the Creative Years." *Art News Annual.*

(203) Kimball, Fiske. "Cubism and the Arensbergs." *Art News Annual.*

(193) Imbourg, Pierre. "Les Grands peintres chez eux, Jacques Villon." *Journal de l'Amateur d'Art.*

(138) Elgar, Frank. "Jacques Villon." *Dictionnaire de Peinture Moderne.*

(328) Stahly, Francois. "Jacques Villon et son oeuvre graphique." *Graphis.*

(184) Hayter, Stanley William. "Atelier 17." *Graphis.*

(317) "Sens de l'art moderne. Enquête menée par l'Atelier avec les réponses inédites de quelques-uns des grands artistes de notre temps." *Zodiaque.*

1955
(202) Kahnweiler, Daniel-Henry. "Du Temps que les cubistes etaient jeunes." *L'Oeil.*

(235) Mellquist, Jerome. "Jacques Villon." *L'Oeil.*

(218) Liberman, Alexander. "Villon." *Vogue.*

(146) Feinstein, Sam. "Jacques Villon." *Arts Digest.*

(340) Tyler, Parker. "Jacques Villon." *Art News.*

(46) Adhémar, Jean. "Les Journaux amusants et les premiers peintres cubistes." *L'Oeil.*

(358) "Virgil by Villon." *Time.*

(336) Taillandier, Yvon. "Propos de Jacques Villon." *Catalogue du Salon de Mai.*

(73) Bordier, Roger. "Jacques Villon." *Aujourd'hui art et architecture.*

(177) Guinard, Paul. "Tendencias recientes de la pintura francesca." *Goya.*

(273) Poulain, Gaston. "De Valery à Villon." *La Dépêche du Midi.*

(320) Seuphor, Michel. "Paris." *Art Digest.*

(347) Veronesi, Giulia. "Parigi: une mostra di Jacques Villon." *Emporium.*

(207) Landini, Lando. "Appunti: La Mostra di Jacques Villon alla Galeria Carré." *Paragone.*

(319) Seuphor, Michel. "Klee et Villon." *Preuves*.

(329) Stahly, Francois. "Pariser Kunst-chronik." *Werk*.

(80) Brüschweiler, Jura. "L'Oeuvre gravé de Jacques Villon." *Musée de Genève*.

(234) Mellquist, Jerome. "Jacques Villon." *Art-Documents*.

(318) Serullaz, Maurice. "A travers les ex-positions." *France Illustration*.

(197) Jouffroy, Alain. "Portrait d'un artiste. (III) Jacques Villon." *Arts, Spectacles*.

(229) Maugis, M. T. "Le Salon d'Automne 1955, salle par salle." *Arts, Spectacles*.

(296) Ribemont-Dessaignes, Georges. "Avant Dada." *Les Lettres Nouvelles*.

(322) Silvagni. "Chez Jacques Villon." *Gazette de Lausanne (La Gazette Littéraire)*.

(260) D. P. "L'Exposition internationale de dessins et gravures de Lugano." *Alte und Neue Kunst*.

(342) Vallier, Dora. "Intelligence de Jacques Villon." *Cahiers d'Art*.

(167) Gran, Henning. "Kubismens Hovedfremstöt Mot Norge til Jacques Villon's attiarsdag." *Kunst og Kultur*.

(286) Refsum, Tor. "Jacques Villon." *Kunsten Idag*.

(299) Rolfsen, Alf. "Painting and Sculpture at Freia and Marabou." *Oslo-Stockholm*.

(214) "A propos de l'exposition: Le Mouvement dans l'art contemporain." *Pour l'art*.

(325) Souriau, Etienne. "Note sur le cheval dans l'art." *Revue d'esthétique*.

(129) "Documenta." *Das Kunstwerk*.

1956
(238) Mellquist, Jerome. "Jacques Villon ou le feu de l'esprit." *Synthèses*.

(173) Gross, John. "Current and Forthcoming Exhibitions." *The Burlington Magazine*.

(345) Veronesi, Giulia. "Disegni di Villon." *Emporium*.

(220) Chabanon, Jean. "Le Salon de Mai." *Le Peintre*.

(195) Jardot, Maurice. "Dessins de Jacques Villon." *Quadrum*.

(154) Gallego, Julian. "Cronica de Paris. Dibujos de Jacques Villon." *Goya*.

(281) Ragghianti, Carlo L. "Jacques Villon." *Sele Arte*.

(196) Jarlot, Gerard. "C'est moderne, mais est-ce de l'art?" *Elle*.

(282) Raymond, Marie. "Jacques Villon." *Kroniek van Kunst en Kultur*.

(143) "Exposition à la Galerie Maurice Bridel et Nane Coiller, Lausanne." *Werk*.

(270) Podestà, Attilio. "La XXVIII Biennale di Venezia. Gli stranieri." *Emporium*.

(113) "Coup d'oeil sur les ventes publiques." *L'Oeil*.

(155) Gallego, Julian. "Jacques Villon, Pintor Francés." *Goya*.

(271) Ponente, Nello. "La Partecipazione Straniera alla Biennale." *Letteratura*.

(225) "Les Maîtres répondent aux jeunes. Situation de la jeune peinture." *Arts, Spectacles*.

(157) George, Waldemar. "Jacques Villon, Prix international de peinture de la Biennale de Venise." *Prisme des Arts*.

(253) Nacenta, Raymond. "École de Paris 1956." *Art et Style*. (Cover by Jacques Villon.)

(371) Wojciechowski, Aleksander. "XXVIII Biennale w Wenecji." *Przegląd Artystyczny*.

(352) "Jacques Villon." *Vancouver Art Gallery Bulletin*.

1957
(259) D. P. "Bianco e nero." *Graphis*.

(252) Munro, Eleanor C. "Villon." *Art News*.

(91) Calas, Nicolas. "The brothers Duchamp all at once." *Art News*.

(374) Young, Vernon. "Villon: Prints and Drawings." *Arts*.

(110) Coates, Robert M. "Three Brothers." *The New Yorker*.

(194) "Les Intellectuals jouent-ils un rôle dans l'évolution de la peinture?" *Arts, Spectacles*.

(362) Warnod, André. "L'Assiette au beurre." *Prisme des Arts*.

(165) Göpel, (Dr.) Erhard. "Ein grosser norwgischer Sammler: Die Sammlung Ragnar Moltzau im Zürcher Kunsthaus ausguestellt." *Die Weltkunst*.

(239) Prossor, John. "Jacques Villon at the Galerie Louis Carré." *Apollo*.

(78) "The Brothers." *Time*.

(300) Rosenblum, Robert. "The Duchamp Family." *Arts*.

(188) Hoffmann, Edith. "New York." *The Burlington Magazine*.

(85) Butler, Barbara. "Paris." *Arts*.

(86) R. F. C. "New York: La mostra di Jacques Villon, Raymond Duchamp-Villon e Marcel Duchamp." *Emporium*.

(360) Volboudt, Pierre. "Gravures de Villon." *XXe Siècle*.

(237) Mellquist, Jerome. "Jacques Villon o il fuoco dello spirito." *La Biennale di Venezia*.

(192) Igé, Jean. "Parler de Jacques Villon." *Parler 3*.

(265) Pia, Pascal. "Livres de peintres." *L'Oeil*.

(149) Fosca, François. "Qu'est-ce que le cubisme?" *Jardin des Arts*.

(278) "Propos sur les vitraux de la Cathédrale de Metz." *Art Chrétien*.

1958
(256) Hootin, Luce. "L'Art d'accomoder les cathédrales." *L'Oeil*.

(359) Volboudt, Pierre. "L'Esprit de la ligne." *XXe Siècle*.

(100) Cassou, Jean. "Dessins des peintres et sculpteurs de l'École de Paris." *Art et Style*.

(77) Brichot, Robert. "Les Vitraux modernes dans les monuments anciens: Jacques Villon a la cathédrale de Metz." *Construction Moderne*.

(241) Mercier, Georges. "Le Renouveau de l'art sacré en France depuis 1945." *Médecine de France*.

(212) Legrand, Francine-Claire. "Expo 58 — Regards sur l'art moderne." *Quadrum*.

1959
(219) Lonngren, Lillian. "Matisse, Villon." *Art News*.

(251) Mundt, Alice. "Prints by Jacques Villon." *Worcester Art Museum News Bulletin*.

(230) Mellquist, Jerome. "A la Bibliothèque Nationale. L'Oeuvre gravé de Jacques Villon." *XXe Siècle*.

(348) Vieillard, Roger. "Les Gravures de Jacques Villon." *Jardin des Arts*.

(338) Thormé, J.-R. "Jacques Villon graveur et illustrateur." *Le Courrier Graphique*.

(333) Taillandier, Yvon. "De la pyramide au Carré: Causerie avec Jacques Villon." *XXe Siècle*.

(95) Campbell, Lawrence. "Jacques Villon." *Art News*.

(244) Mock, Jean Yves. "Jacques Villon at the Bibliothèque Nationale." *Apollo*.

(310) Schneider, Pierre. "The indefatigable." *Art News*.

(74) Boullier, Renée. "De Kupka à Villon." *Aux Écoutes.*

(59) Barotte, René. "La Côte déliarante des tableaux." *Plaisir de France.*

(65) Berger, René. "Jacques Villon." *XXe Siècle.*

(69) "Billedkranikk: Fra Jacques Villons utstelling i Kunstnernes Hus, Olso." *Kunsten Idag.*

(103) Chastel, André. "Dix ans d'art français." *Médecine de France.*

(375) "Zwei schweizer Sammler." *Schweizer Kunst.*

1960
(89) Cabanne, Pierre, "Jacques Villon, j'ai découvert dans la lumière le mystère du réel." *Arts, Lettres, Spectacles.*

(118) Crook, Gordon. "Modern French Tapestries." *The Studio.*

(243) Mills, John F. "Portrait of the Artist as Printmaker." *Criticism.*

(323) Smith, Lawrence. "Jacques Villon." *Arts.*

(49) Andrén, Gösta. "En mild och försynt Klassiker." *Konstperspektiv.*

1961
(47) Advertisement for Galerie Louis Carré. *Cimaise.*

(90) Cabanne, Pierre. "Villon: 60 ans de peinture une longue histoire d'amour." *Arts, Lettres, Spectacles.*

(105) Chastel, André. "Jacques Villon ou la conquête de l'espace." *Le Monde.*

(106) Chebrun, Jean-François. "Jacques Villon." *L'Express.*

(160) Gindertael, R. V. "Cent tableaux de Jacques Villon." *Les Beaux-Arts.*

(96) Canaday, John. "A Private Road: Sixty Years of Jacques Villon's Art Celebrated in Paris This Month." *The New York Times.*

(175) Guichard-Meili, Jean. "Un Grand humaniste de la peinture." *Témoinage chrétien.*

(242) Michelson, Annette. "Paris: La Grand saison." *Arts.*

(233) Mellquist, Jerome. "The Master of Puteaux and Others." *Apollo.*

(246) Morand, Kathleen. "Paris." *The Burlington Magazine.*

(57) Auerbach, Edith. "Jacques Villon." *Die Weltkunst.*

(52) Ashbery, John. "Paris Notes." *Art International.*

(153) Frigerio, Simone. "Jacques Villon." *Aujourd'hui Art et Architecture.*

(99) Cartier, Jean-Albert. "Lumière sur un chef d'oeuvre de Jacques Villon: le portrait de son frère." *Plaisir de France.*

(61) Barotte, René. "Jacques Villon à la Galerie Charpentier." *Plaisir de France.*

(266) Pichard, Joseph. "Modern Stained Glass in France." *Graphis.*

(298) Veronesi, Giulia. "Cento Quadri di Jacques Villon." *Emporium.*

(292) Revol, Jean. "Braque et Villon, message vivant du cubisme. I." *La Nouvelle Revue Française.*

(293) _____. "Braque et Villon (fin)." *La Nouvelle Revue Française.*

(365) Watt, Alexander. "Paris Commentary." *The Studio.*

(240) Menetrier, Jacques. "L'Oeuvre de Villon." *Planète.*

(324) "The Solid Gold Muse." *Time.*

(309) Schiff, Gert. "The VI Sâo Paolo Bienal." *Art International.*

(274) Pradel, Marie-Noëlle. "La Maison Cubiste en 1912." *Art de France.*

(168) Grand, Paule-Marie. "Jacques Villon." *Art de France.*

(304) Russoli, Franco. "La Collezione Thompson alla Galleria d'Arte Moderna a Torino." *Arti.*

(349) Vieira, Jose Geraldo. "VI Bienal de Arti de Sâo Paolo." *Habitat.*

(161) Gindertael, R. V. "France." *Quadrum.*

1962
(366) Watt, Alexander. "Jacques Villon doyen of the School of Paris." *The Studio.*

(367) _____. "Villon." *Art in America.*

(136) Eisendrath, William N., Jr. "Painting and Sculpture of the School of Paris in the Collection of Mr. and Mrs. Joseph Pulitzer, Jr. of St. Louis." *The Connoisseur.*

(315) Selvig, F. "Recent Accessions." *The Minneapolis Institute of Arts Bulletin.*

1963
(151) Frigerio, Simone. "La Figure dans l'oeuvre graphique de Jacques Villon." *Aujourd'hui Art et Architecture.*

(295) Rey, Jean Dominique. "La Figure dans l'oeuvre gravé de Jacques Villon." *Jardin des Arts.*

(311) Schneider, Pierre. "Paris." *Art News.*

(294) Revol, Jean. "La Figure dans l'oeuvre graphique de Villon." *La Nouvelle Revue Française.*

(245) Moholy, Lucia. "Switzerland." *The Burlington Magazine.*

(56) d'Aubarède, Gabriel. "Chez Jacques Villon." *Jardin des Arts.*

(152) Frigerio, Simone. "Suisse. Réflexions sur quelques rétrospectives." *Aujourd'hui Art et Architecture.*

(357) "Jacques Villon, Jean Bazaine, Hans Hartung: ausstellung im Kunsthaus, Zürich." *Werk.*

(124) "Delacroix et les peintres d'aujourd'hui." *Les Nouvelles Littéraires.*

(327) Staber, Margit. "Austellungen in Zurich." *Art International.*

(247) Morel, Abbé Maurice. "Hommage à Jacques Villon." *Journal de l'Amateur d'Art.*

(351) "Jacques Villon." *Das Kunstwerk.*

(364) Watt, Alexander. "Art as the Inspiration for Art." *The Studio.*

(267) Picon, Gaëtan. "Discours sur Villon prononcé à ses funérailles." *Gazette des Beaux Arts.*

(277) "Propos de Jacques Villon." *Le Peintre.*

(353) "Jacques Villon." *XXe Siècle.*

(139) Elgar, Frank. "Jacques Villon." *Dictionary of Modern Painting.*

(159) Gheerbrandt, Bernard. "Villon, The Greatest of All." *Artist's Proof.*

(205) G. L. "Atelier Leblanc." *Artist's Proof*

1964
(298) Roberts, Keith. "Current and Forthcoming Exhibitions." *The Burlington Magazine.*

(214) Levin, Kim. "Jacques Villon's." *Art News.*

(330) Steegmuller, Francis. "A Master of 'Volupté.' " *Apollo.*

(120) "Daubigny, Villon retrospectives." *Art News.*

(144) Faunce, Sarah C. "Jacques Villon (Goldschmidt; to April 25)." *Art News.*

(145) _____. "Jacques Villon (Thaw; to April 18)." *Art News.*

(283) Raynor, Vivien. "Jacques Villon." *Arts Magazine.*

(312) Schulze, Franz. "Degas, Villon graphics." *Art News.*

(54) Ashton, Dore. "Jacques Villon, Master of Graphic Art." *Art International.*

(326) Spencer, Charles S. "Documenta III, Creative individuality in contemporary art surveyed at Kassel." *Studio International.*

(171) Gray, Cleve. "Jacques Villon, Print Review." *Art in America.*

(254) Neilson, Katharine B. "Prints and Drawings: Recent Acquisitions." *Museum Notes* (Museum of Art, Rhode Island School of Design).

(72) Bonnefoy, Yves. "Jacques Villon." *Art de France.*

(331) Steegmuller, Francis. "Jacques Villon: an Appreciation." *Artists's Proof.*

(226) Marchand, André. "Le Village natal de Jacques Villon." *Catalogue du XXe Salon de Mai.*

(303) Rouir, Eugène. "Une Lithographie non décrite de Jacques Villon." *Le Livre et L'Estampe.*

(131) Dorival, Bernard. "Note sur quatre ouvrages français et anglais de 1913-14. *Zbornik Radova. Narodni Muzej.*

1965
(185) Henning, Edward B. "Two New Modern Paintings." *Cleveland Museum of Art Bulletin.*

(87) Cabanne, Pierre. "Mes invités, mes peintres." *Connaissance des Arts.*

(88)_____ . "Une Tendre et pudique Jacques Villon." *Lecture pour Tous.*

(250) Muller, Joseph-Emile. "Des Cubistes aux premiers abstraits." *La Peinture Moderne.*

1966
(264) "Petit dictionnaire des années héroiques (1907-1917)." *XXe Siècle.*

(284) "Recent Acquisitions." *City Art Museum of Saint Louis Bulletin.*

1967
(75) Boullier, Renée. "Les Duchamp." *La Nouvelle Revue Française.*

(93) Campbell, Lawrence. "The Father of Modern Print-making." *Art News.*

(158) Gheerbrandt, Bernard. "L'incisione si rinnova." *Arti.*

(98) Carré, Louis. Letter to the editor. *Art News.*

1968
(297) Robbins, Daniel. "Recent Acquisitions." *Bulletin of Rhode Island School of Design Museum Notes.*

(302) Rouir, Eugène. "Essai de classement des estampes de Jacques Villon." *Le Livre et L'Estampe.*

(272) Popovitch, Olga. "Musée des Beaux-Arts de Rouen; l'Art contemporain." *La Revue du Louvre et des Musées de France.*

1970
(109) "La Chronique des arts." *Gazette des Beaux-Arts.*

(121) Davis, F. "Talking about Sale-Rooms." *Country Life.*

(79) Brown, Gordon. "Jacques Villon at Goldschmidt." *Arts Magazine.*

(206) La Farge, Henry A. "First Impressions." *Art News.*

(256) Nicolson, Benedict. "Lucien Goldschmidt, Inc., New York." *The Burlington Magazine.*

(268) Pincus-Witten, R. "New York." *Artforum.*

(163) "Lucien Goldschmidt, New York." *Apollo.*

1972
(239) Melot, Michel. "The Cubists and Etching." *Apollo.*

(82) *Bulletin of the Detroit Institute of Arts.*

1973
(101) Cassou, Jean. "Reévocation du Cubisme." *XXe Siècle.*

(373) Young, Mahonri-Sharp. "The Man from Ohio. Ferdinand Howald and his Painters." *The Arts in Ireland.*

BOOKS AND GENERAL WORKS

1913
(378) Apollinaire, Guillaume. *Les Peintres cubistes; méditations esthétiques.*

1914
(405) Eddy, Arthur Jerome. *Cubists and Post-Impressionism.*

1920
(411) Gleizes, Albert. *Du Cubisme et des moyens de la comprendre.*

1920-21
(442) *Report, 1920-1921.*

1923
(402) Dreier, Katherine S. *Western Art and the New Era.*

1924
(433) Pach, Walter. *The Masters of Modern Art.*

(435)_____. *Raymond Duchamp-Villon, sculpteur (1876-1918).*

1926
(376) Angoulvent, P.-J. *La Chalcographie du Louvre: Histoire et description des collections.*

(403) Dreier, Katherine S. *Modern Art.*

(438) *The John Quinn Collection of Paintings, Water Colors, Drawings and Sculpture.*

1936
(382) Barr, Alfred H., Jr., *Cubism and Abstract Art.*

1938
(434) Pach, Walter. *Queer Thing, Painting.*

1942
(415) Guggenheim, Peggy. *Art of This Century 1910-1942.*

1944
(398) Dorival, Bernard. *Les Étapes de la peinture française contemporaine, Vol. II: Le Fauvisme et le Cubisme.*

1947
(412) Gleizes, Albert and Metzinger, Jean. *Du Cubisme.*

(460) Warnod, André. *Ceux de la Butte.*

1948
(428) Lhote, André. *Traité du paysage.*

1949
(380) Arland, Marcel. *Chroniques de la peinture moderne.*

(404) Dreier, Katherine S.; Sweeney, James Johnson; and Gabo, Naum. *Three Lectures on Modern Art.*

1950
(406) Fels, Florent. *L'Art vivant de nos jours: 1914-1955.*

(419) Hamilton, George Heard. *Collection of the Société Anonyme: Museum of Modern Art 1920.*

(439) Raymal, Maurice. *A History of Modern Painting from Picasso to Surrealism.*

1951
(395) *Le Dessin français au XXe Siècle.* Preface by Jean Cassou.

1953
(440) Raynal, Maurice. *Peinture moderne.*

1954
(383) Barr, Alfred H., Jr. *Masters of Modern Art.*

(389) *Catalogue de la Chalcographie du Louvre.*

(379) *The Louise and Walter Arensberg Collection, 20th Century Section.* Introduction by Henry Clifford.

(459) Walden, Nell. *Der Sturm.*

1955
(397) Dorazio, Piero. *La fantasia dell'arte nella vita moderna.*

(408) Francastel, Pierre. *Histoire de la peinture française.*

(409) *French Drawing of the XXth Century.* Introduction by Jean Cassou.

1957
(400) Dorival, Bernard. *Les Peintures du XXe siècle: Nabis, Fauves, Cubistes.*

(436) *Les Peintres et le livre.* No. 6.

(449) Seuphor, Michel. *Dictionnaire de la peinture abstraite.*

1958
(430) Maywald, Wilhelm. *Portrait + Atelier.*

1959
(388) Canaday, John. *Mainstreams of Modern Art.*

(390) Charbonnier, Georges. *Le Monologue du peintre.*

(417) Habasque, Guy. *Le Cubisme.*

(422) *A Handbook to the Solomon R. Guggenheim Museum Collection.*

(427) Lebel, Robert. *Marcel Duchamp.*

(451) Sima, Michel. *21 visages d'artistes.*

(455) *Twentieth Century Graphic Art: The Ernest Steefel Collection.*

1960
(429) Liberman, Alexander. *The Artist in his Studio.*

(432) Muller, Joseph-Emile. *La Peinture moderne de Manet à Mondrian.*

(445) Rosenbloom, Robert. *Cubism and Twentieth Century Art.*

(454) Tardieu, Jean. *De la Peinture abstraite.*

1961
(424) *Important Original Prints for Museums and Collectors.* Catalogue No. 10.

(431) Miguel, Jean. *Cours de philosophie, exposés et documents.*

(458) Vallier, Dora. *Kunst und Zeugnis.*

1962
(401) Dorival, Bernard. *The School of Paris in the Musée d'Art Moderne.*

(416) Gyllensten, Lars. *Sonja Henie-Niels Onstad Collection 1960-1962.*

(450) Seuphor, Michel. *La Peinture Abstraite, sa genèse, son expansion.*

1963
(385) Bouleau, Charles. *Charpentes; la géométrie secrète des peintres.* Preface by Jacques Villon.

(386) Brown, Milton W. *The Story of the Armory Show.*

(446) *Sculptures de Duchamp-Villon.*

(447) Serullaz, Maurice. *Le Cubisme.*

(457) Vallier, Dora. *Histoire de la peinture 1870-1940. Les Mouvements d'avant-garde.*

1964
(117) Crespelle, J.-P. *Montmartre vivant.*

(425) Johnson, Una E. *Twentieth Century Drawings Part I: 1900-1940.*

1965
(394) Delevoy, Robert L. *Dimensions of the 20th Century 1900-1945.*

(414) Gonse, Henriette. *La Composition.*

(418) Haftmann, Werner. *Malerei im 20. Jahrhundert.*

1966
(384) *La Bibliothèque de Fr. Sabatier D'Espeyran.*

(410) Fry, Edward F. *Cubism.*

(426) Lambert, Jean-Clarence. *La Peinture abstraite.*

(437) Pierre, Jose. *Le Cubisme.*

(443) Rheims, Maurice. *Catalogue Bolaffi d'Art Moderne: Le Marché de Paris.*

(444) Robbins, Daniel. *Painting Between the Wars 1918-1940.*

1967
(391) Charensol, Georges. *Les Grands maîtres de la peinture moderne.*

(393) Dauberville, Henry. *La Bataille de l'Impressionnisme.*

(396) *Dictionnaire universel d l'art et des Artistes.* Vol. 3.

(420) Hamilton, George Heard. *Painting and Sculpture in Europe, 1880 to 1940.*

(421) Hamilton, George Heard, and Agee, William C. *Raymond Duchamp-Villon.*

(456) Vallier, Dora. *L'Art abstrait.*

1968
(377) The Art Institute of Chicago. *Annual Report 1967-1968.*

(381) Arnason, H. Harvard. *History of Modern Art: Painting, Sculpture, Architecture.*

(387) Brun, H. J. *Sonja Henie-Niels Onstad Collection.*

(407) Forster-Hahn, Françoise. *French and School of Paris Paintings in the Yale University Art Gallery.*

(413) Golding, John. *Cubism: A History and an Analysis, 1907-1914.*

(441) Reid, B. L. *The Man from New York: John Quinn and his Friends.*

1969
(399) Dorival, Bernard. *Histoire de l'art.*

(461) *Works from the Peggy Guggenheim Foundation.*

1971
(392) Cooper, Douglas. *The Cubist Epoch.*

1972
(423) *Illustrated Books from the Renaissance to the Present.* Catalogue No. 40.

(448) Seuphor, Michel. *L'Art abstrait, 2. 1918/1938.*

(452) *Société Anonyme (The First Museum of Modern Art 1920-1944).* Volume I: Documents.

(453) *Société Anonyme (The First Museum of Modern Art 1920-1944).* Volume II: Pamphlets.

Albright-Knox Art Gallery, Buffalo

The Art Institute of Chicago

Bacci Fotografo, Milan

Freddy Bertrand, Geneva

Bibliothèque Nationale, Paris

The Brooklyn Museum

Bulloz, Paris

Barney Burstein, Boston

Geoffrey Clements, Staten Island

The Cleveland Museum of Art

Cliché des Musées Nationaux, Paris

The Columbus Gallery of Fine Arts

A. C. Cooper, Ltd., London

Galerie Louis Carré, Paris

The Hirshhorn Museum and Sculpture Garden, Smithsonian Institution

R. S. Johnson-International Gallery, Chicago

Bruce C. Jones, New York

Paulus Leeser, New York

Los Angeles County Museum of Art

Robert E. Mates, New York

Claude Mercier, Geneva

The Metropolitan Museum of Art, New York

Milwaukee Art Center

The Minneapolis Institute of Arts

Musée de Rouen

Museum of Fine Arts, Boston

The Museum of Modern Art, New York

Narodni Gallery, Prague

Michael Nedzweski, Fogg Art Museum, Cambridge, Massachusetts

Lennart Olson, Enskede

Perls Galleries, New York

Andre Philippon, New York

Nathan Rabin, New York

The St. Louis Art Museum

J. H. Schaefer and Son, Baltimore

John D. Schiff, New York

The Solomon R. Guggenheim Museum, New York

Soichi Sunami, New York

E .V. Thaw and Co., New York

James Ufford, Fogg Art Museum, Cambridge, Massachusetts

O. Vaering, Oslo

A. J. Wyatt, Philadelphia Museum of Art

Yale University Art Gallery, New Haven